THE FATHERS
OF THE CHURCH

A NEW TRANSLATION

VOLUME 23

THE FATHERS OF THE CHURCH

A NEW TRANSLATION

Founded by
LUDWIG SCHOPP

EDITORIAL BOARD

ROY JOSEPH DEFERRARI
The Catholic University of America
Editorial Director

RUDOLPH ARBESMANN, O.S.A.
Fordham University

BERNARD M. PEEBLES
The Catholic University of America

STEPHAN KUTTNER
The Catholic University of America

ROBERT P. RUSSELL, O.S.A.
Villanova University

MARTIN R. P. MCGUIRE
The Catholic University of America

ANSELM STRITTMATTER, O.S.B.
St. Anselm's Priory

WILFRID PARSONS, S.J.
The Catholic University of America

JAMES EDWARD TOBIN
Queens College

GERALD G. WALSH, S.J.
Fordham University

CLEMENT OF ALEXANDRIA

CHRIST THE EDUCATOR

Translated by

SIMON P. WOOD, C.P.

THE CATHOLIC UNIVERSITY OF AMERICA PRESS
Washington, D. C. 20017

PRINTED WITH ECCLESIASTICAL PERMISSION
November 15, 1953

Library of Congress Catalog Card No.: 64-20313
ISBN-13: 978-0-8132-1562-4 (pbk)

Copyright © 1954 by
THE CATHOLIC UNIVERSITY OF AMERICA PRESS, INC.
All rights reserved

First paperback reprint 2008

INTRODUCTION

IN THE PAST CENTURY, much interest has been shown in Clement of Alexandria, and many studies made of his place in the history of Christian thought. Non-Catholics and rationalists have been extravagant in their praise. They see in him, in the words of J. Patrick, 'the first systematic teacher of Christian doctrine, the formal champion of liberal culture in the Church.'[1] The same writer joins A. Harnack in endorsing the tribute of Overbeck that Clement's work is perhaps the most daring undertaking in the history of the Church.[2] C. Bigg, speaking of the school whose teachings found their way into Clement's writings, remarks that 'it may be doubted whether any nobler scheme of Christian education has ever been projected than this which we find in actual working at Alexandria at the end of the second century A.D.'[3] Swete adds words that would be hard to surpass: 'Perhaps nothing in the whole range of early

---
1 J. Patrick, *Clement of Alexandria* (London 1914) 13.
2 *Ibid.* 30; A. Harnack, *History of Dogma,* trans. N. Buchanan (London 1896) II 324.
3 C. Bigg, *Christian Platonists of Alexandria* (Oxford 1913) 70.

patristic literature is more stimulating to the modern reader than [Clement's] great trilogy of graduated instruction in the Christian life . . . Clement's conception of Christianity, in its relation to the whole field of human thought, is one which has an especial value for our own times . . . and promises to be increasingly useful in the present century.'[4]

The Catholic attitude, which expects not only intellectual vigor and richness of culture, but also exact adherence to the truth, is more hesitant. While admiring his humanism and appreciating his richness of thought, it regrets some of the Gnostic developments of that thought. The Catholic opinion is well represented by F. Cayré's appraisal: 'Clement must be read prudently. Nevertheless these flaws do not destroy his work, nor should they be allowed to conceal much that is precious within it, both from a moral and a theological point of view.'[5]

We can, then, expect from Clement a stimulating and rich study of Christian thought, not always entirely orthodox, yet always sincere and loyal, original in its approach to truth if sometimes out of step with tradition.

Titus Flavius Clemens was born c. 150, most probably in Athens.[6] The tone of his writings, his intimate familiarity with Greek literature and customs, even the orientation of his thought, suggest that he was a Greek of the Greeks, steeped from infancy in the glory that was Greece. The more common opinion is that he was born a pagan, was introduced to the pagan mysteries in his youth, and became a Christian only during the travels he undertook, like all the youths of well-to-do Greek families, in search of a broader education.

---
4 H. B. Swete, *Patristic Study* (London 1902) 48.
5 F. Cayré, *Manual of Patrology*, Trans. H. Howitt (Paris 1936).
6 Cf. Eusebius, *Hist. Eccles.* I. p. 188, 5.11.

Mondésert, however, raises doubt about this assumption, on the ground that Clement's evident profound familiarity with the Scriptures suggests an early acquaintance with Christianity.[7]

If Clement became a Christian only after a youth spent in paganism, the tone of his writings indicates that conversion came to him 'as untroubled as to any of the educated heathen who found their way within the Church's doors. He does not seem to have had gross sins to surrender. Great renunciations were not apparently involved. And the things he had found most precious in paganism he took over with him in a new allegiance. There is no sort of parallel between Clement's conversion and the stress and pain of the transition as Saint Augustine knew it.'[8]

Be that as it may, Clement settled in Alexandria, around 180, as a Christian, there to cultivate the friendship and benefit from the instruction of the Christian Stoic, St. Pantaenus, in charge of the catechetical school in that city. Gradually he took over many of the duties of the catechetical school, and it is indicative of his peaceful nature and of the humility of Pantaenus that there is no evidence of any opposition or rivalry between the two men. When Pantaenus died at the close of the century, Clement became the head of the school, continuing the policies and methods practised under Pantaenus. Origen was his most famous pupil, and became his successor. Pantaenus is remembered largely because of Clement, but there is no such close continuity be-

---

[7] 'The Bible . . . became for him almost a language and a mentality; and what is strange, one can say the same about Greek philosophy and above all, Platonism. This raises a problem which the complete absence of biographical information makes insoluble: was he truly raised a Greek pagan? Or how did he become, in manhood, so profoundly Christian?' C. Modésert, *Clément d'Alexandrie* (Paris 1944) 265.

[8] R. B. Tollinton, *Clement of Alexandria* (London 1914) 13.

tween Clement and Origen. The more famous successor shows only a vague, unacknowledged dependence upon his predecessor, for he retained the broad humanism of Clement, but differed in many points of doctrine and of method. In 202 or 203, only a few years after the death of Pantaenus, Clement felt constrained to flee the persecution set in motion by Sulpicius Severus, traveling first to Cappadocia, then to Antioch, which seems to be the place of his death, before 215. History reveres Clement principally as a man of thought, for these few facts, most of them uncertain, are all that it records of a life so rich in intellectual and spiritual adventure, but uneventful to the eyes of the biographer. He was regarded as a saint in many localities, but was excluded from the Roman Martyrology by Popes Clement VIII and Benedict XIV.

The writings of Clement, and particularly the work here translated, are largely the literary account of the instruction and investigation conducted at the catechetical school. For a long while, Alexandria had been the center of a vigorous intellectual and literary achievement. Its famous libraries, the Serapeion and the Museum, were both the witness and sustainer of that spirit. The famous Neo-Platonic Alexandrian, Philo the Jew, a century and a half before, had left a deep Hellenistic imprint upon the culture of the city. He had sought particularly to enrich Scriptural studies by reference to Greek thought and by the use of allegory, a method which, handled intelligently, demanded quickness of mind and a well-disciplined imagination. It was only natural, then, that the Christian community in Alexandria should turn to a deeper study of the faith than prevailed in ruder missionary regions. Such was the origin of the catechetical school which Clement found under the leadership of Pantaenus. Its liberal culture and humanism must have been completely congenial to

Clement's temperament and convictions, for he never sought any other instructor.

The school was conducted privately, neither begun nor directed by ecclesiastical authority, at least in Clement's time. We might compare it to a modern study club, meeting in a private home without formal class or public pretensions, vigorous in its search for truth. The pupils, if we may call them that, were not Jews but almost entirely Alexandrian Greeks, whether pagan or Christian, drawn from the more well-to-do members of society. Much of the advice given in the *Paidagōgos,* for example, or in the *Quis dives salvetur,* would have been of little use to workmen or to the poor. Evidently, women as well as men attended his classes, for Clement makes a special point of their equality before the *Logos.*[9]

The subject matter of the program was varied. It stressed not so much the elementary lessons of Christianity, although, naturally, that must have had its place, as a deeper study of the Scriptures. To counteract the false Gnosticism of Marcion, Valentinus, and Theodotus, Clement evolved a more orthodox system which has been called a 'Christian Gnosticism.' He did not rid himself entirely of the esotericism of the heretical *Gnōsis,* nor of its exaggerations of the role of knowledge in salvation, but he did succeed in saving his followers from the fascination of a more harmful false mysticism. *Gnōsis* was for Clement 'Christian doctrine, in its entirety and in all its richness, that is to say, not only elementary truths which are the object of the faith of the "simple" and which, according to Clement, all can attain, but also and above all the more spiritual and mysterious truths which should be desired, sought after and both merited by a more perfect life and obtained by divine grace, and which are

---
9 Cf. below, pp. 11-12.

revealed only to the Gnostic.'[10] This deeper and richer meaning of the faith was to be gained by interpreting the Scriptures allegorically, a method employed so deftly by Philo and adopted by many of the early Fathers, called by Rand 'the higher criticism of the day.'[11]

Clement also shared Philo's Hellenism, his humanism. More than any previous Christian writer, Clement recognized the integral relationship between all that was worth while in pagan literature and the new Christian faith. Like Philo, he calls on Homer and Plato, the dramatists and the Stoics and all the best writers of Greece to substantiate his arguments. There are those even today who can learn from the integrity of his humanism, but when we remember that Clement wrote before the Edict of Milan, while Christianity was still maturing, we are all the more impressed by the daring of his project. It argues well for the peace and literary atmosphere of Alexandria, as well as for the non-controversial, gentle nature of Clement, that he could even attempt such a project. His writings prove how steeped his thought was in the Greek classics. His works contain over 700 quotations from some 300 pagan authors, an achievement which well justifies Cayré's remark that his prodigious erudition was unsurpassed even by that of Origen.[12] In fact, Tollinton can say that 'whoever invites interest in Clement of Alexandria pleads, directly or indirectly, the cause of Hellenism in Christianity.'[13]

However, Clement is not another Minucius Felix or Boethius, whose writings give more evidence of pagan than Christian humanism. Commentators may call him Platonist

---

10 Mondésert, *op. cit.* 109.
11 Cf. E. K. Rand, *Founders of the Middle Ages* (Cambridge, Mass. 1941) 87. For those interested in Clement's use of allegory, cf. Mondésert, *op. cit.*
12 F. Cayré, *op. cit.* 179.
13 Tollinton, *op. cit.* ix.

or Neo-Platonic, Stoic or Aristotelian,[14] but they must also call him an exegete of the Scriptures. Mondésert does not hesitate to say that his style is above all else Scriptural.[15] There are copious quotations from Old and New Testaments, constant allusions and turns of thought too numerous to be noted. And for Clement, Scripture is the final appeal; when he says, as he often does: *graphetai* ('it is written'), he is invoking an authority from which he feels there is no appeal. The Alexandrian school may have stressed Christian philosophy, but it is a philosophy drawn from the pages of the Scriptures.

Faithful reflection of the instruction imparted at the school is the trilogy made up of the *Protreptikos,* commonly called *An Exhortation to the Greeks,* the *Paidagōgos* and the *Strōmateis.* Clement himself showed that these three works are but a continuation of the same subject, for he says: 'The all-loving Word, anxious to perfect us in a way that leads to salvation by progressive degrees, makes effective use of an order excellently adapted to our education: first He persuades us, then He educates, and, after all this, He teaches.'[16] The *Protreptikos,* written possibly around 189, is a glowing appeal to the Greeks to recognize all the truth and beauty praised by their poets and philosophers in the New Song that is Christ. It is not so much an apologetic—an approach alien to Clement's peaceful mentality—as a rhetorical plea for Christianity. The *Paidagōgos* was written shortly after, possibly the next year. In this work, Clement pictures Christ as

---
14 'According to Merk, he is an adherent of the Stoics; according to Reinkens, of Aristotle; Ritter regards him as fundamentally a Platonist; Dahne as a Neo-Platonist. The truth is, if we accept his own statement, that he refused to be considered a narrow partisan of any school' (Patrick, *op. cit.* 141).
15 Modésert, *op. cit.* 71.
16 Cf. below, p. 5.

an educator who molds the character of those entrusted to His care, cautioning them what to avoid and turning them toward a truly Christian way of life. Finally, the *Strōmateis* sets out to develop the *Gnōsis* that will initiate the Christian into the higher perfection of Christian knowledge. It is a patchwork treatment rather than a consistent systematic explanation, proceeding at random and with much retracing of ground already covered. Some authors think that Clement had actually intended to write another work, and that the *Strōmateis* was not even meant to be a unified treatise. We are not concerned with this problem here, except to suggest the very likely possibility that the first four books of the *Strōmateis* were written before the *Paidagōgos* while Clement was still at Alexandria; possibly they represent the work on marriage referred to in several places in the present work. The remaining books were probably composed after his flight from Alexandria in 202. This trilogy comprises Clement's major writings. The *Quis dives salvetur* is a delightful little work, possibly the last from his pen, presenting a sane, balanced treatment of the Christian virtue of detachment. There are fragments extant of the lost *Hypotypseis*, which purported to be a commentary on the Scriptures; of the *Excerpta ex Theodoto*; and of the *Eclogae propheticae*; and there is a doctored Latin translation made by Cassiodorus of the *Adumbrationes*. Besides these, there are other works too minor to be mentioned, especially when they have survived only in a few fragments.

Clement's style is not always easy or polished. He writes from a full heart and rich culture, but his mind never seems completely disciplined, or at home with logic. He writes in keeping with his character: peaceful, non-controversial, gentle. Clement was far from the apologist who aggressively hammers away at possible antagonists, boldly defending the truth against all objections. He was a contemplative who preferred to speak of the beauties of truth rather than to argue to its existence, who preferred to win the heart rather than to crush all opposition. This trait accounts for many of his weaknesses: Clement often piles up impressive quotations that do not clearly apply to the point under discussion; he sometimes does not make one point fully before passing on to another point whose connection it is not easy to grasp; occasionally he contradicts himself, not violently, but as a man who sees now one, now the opposite, side of a problem. These traits evidently exasperated E. Molland, for he claims that Clement is one of the most difficult authors in the whole Christian literature, and that he had no theological system at all.[17] In fact, Molland quotes Jülicher approvingly as saying that the reason Clement was not repudiated as a heretic in the fifth and sixth centuries is the fact that he was unintelligible.[18] These are too harsh words, for anyone who takes Clement as he finds him will appreciate the witness he gives to the faith, the richness he adds to Christian culture, and, while he regrets, will respect the gentleness that made him hesitate to become rigorously logical. Another authority has words much more indulgent: Clement's was 'a singularly lovable personality. He gives the impression of a certain intellectual naivete, combined with a moral austerity . . . . "I do not know," says Maurice, "where we shall look for a purer or truer man than this Clement of Alexandria . . . . He seems to me that one of the old fathers whom we should all have reverenced most as a teacher, and loved most as a friend." '[19]

---

17 E. Molland, *The Conception of the Gospel in the Alexandrian Theology* (Oslo 1938) 5.
18 *Ibid.*
19 Patrick, *op. cit.* 9-10.

The *Paidagōgos* holds the central place in Clement's trilogy, not only in position, but also, I believe, in content. It is longer than the *Protreptikos* but less unwieldy than the *Strōmateis;* it contains more doctrine than the first, yet does not evidence the exaggerations of doctrine, at least to the same degree, as the third; it does not have the unity and the beauty of the earlier work, yet avoids the random, scattered style of the later one. For all these reasons, it is the most practical work for our purposes. It represents the thought of Clement and of the whole Alexandrian Church very well and so will give the reader an adequate introduction to Clement's teachings.

It is difficult to translate the word *Paidagōgos* into English, for there is no one word that conveys all that the Greek expresses. Etymologically, *Paidagōgos* means 'leader of children,' and this is the sense Clement sometimes confines himself to. However, in its ordinary usage, it meant first the slave who conducted the children of the household back and forth from school, and later, the slave, usually an educated one, who supervised their training and the formation of their characters. Clement makes use of all these senses of the word, but is careful to confine it to one who supervises only moral training, for he reserved the treatment of Christ the Teacher to a later work. I have settled upon 'Educator' as the best English equivalent, but the reader must keep in mind that it refers only to an education of character.

In Book 1, Clement lays down the general principles of his thesis, often in beautiful rhetoric: Christ is our Educator, and we are little ones in God's eyes. Sometimes He treats us with severity, sometimes with kind indulgence, but always as the loving Father of mankind. Books 2-3 descend to details that become tiring and even overly blunt and crude: how a Christian should eat and drink, sleep and dress; what companions he should associate with; what attitude he should take toward the wild, effeminate practices found in a city as prosperous and commercial as Alexandria was. The picture that emerges, with all its defects and excessive details, is a clear outline of what Clement thought the Christian life should be. That is why the *Paidagōgos* is the source book for Alexandrian spirituality to the historian and to the student of the spiritual life.

In it Clement quotes from the Old Testament, with heavy reliance on Ecclesiasticus and Proverbs, and also from the New, particularly from the Epistles of St. Paul. He also draws arguments from the Epistle of Pseudo-Barnabas and, among pagan authors, from Plato and the Stoics, Homer and the dramatists, and occasionally Pindar, Herodotus, and the poets. Add to this the many excerpts from and allusions to Philo the Jew, and the extent of Clement's erudition becomes impressive. Although the quotations from the Greek classics may have come at second-hand from the *florilegia* and anthologies common in his day, the general development of his thought proves him a man who was directly acquainted with his sources.

The influence of Stoicism upon Clement deserves special attention, for it explains much that otherwise would seem excessive or offensive. The *Strōmateis,* treating more fully of Christian Gnosticism, is strongly Platonic, but even a casual reader of the *Paidagōgos* will be struck by the evidences there of Clement's Stoicism. The very first chapter begins with a reference to the divisions of discourse as taught by the Stoic school. The treatment of his subject in such detail is obviously following the pattern of the works of Stoic writers. Even the general character of the work shows a marked resemblance to the writings of such Stoics as the Roman Seneca: the determinedly practical orientation, the care to avoid excessive speculation, the easy superficiality and attention to details, the moderation that comes close, at times, to compromise.

But the influence is much deeper. Clement actually adopts much of the Stoic moral doctrine. For him, virtue is living according to the *logos,* a term lending itself naturally to a play on words: either in the strict Stoic sense of living according to reason or in the Christian sense of living according to the Word. It often is difficult to be sure which he intends in a given passage.

There are three virtues which Clement could have learned only from the Stoa: self-sufficiency, frugality, and apathy. The first, *autarkeia,* strange to the Christian ear, is stressed by Clement as by the Stoics. It means self-reliance, and even a self-determination which will keep the individual from being a burden to others, and will always prefer to wait on oneself rather than expect service from others, even slaves.[20] Closely allied is the virtue of frugality. The reader will often be reminded of Seneca's treatment of this subject, or that of other Stoic philosophers. It implies a restriction of conveniences and of luxuries that will enable a person to be independent of material things, and free for service to others. Finally, Clement's inclusion of apathy is frankly embarrassing. Apathy is a doctrine peculiar to the Stoics, and rejected by Christianity. Yet Clement states plainly that Christ was *apathēs,* without passion or emotion, and the Christian must

---

20 It will be well to keep in mind the observation of Patrick (*op. cit.* 146) that 'the prominence given by Clement to the self-determination of man seems to leave little scope for the action of divine grace in the specifically Christian sense of the word.' This is true evidence of Clement's Stoicism.

try to be like him.[21] The Christian must instead cultivate reason, the god within him. At times, however, Clement, like Seneca, mitigates the severity of this concept, and recognizes the function of the emotions and of moderate comforts in life.

Even more damaging to Clement's reputation is the accusation made by Wendland[22] and seconded by Parker,[23] that Books 2-3 of the *Paidagōgos* are nothing but a worked-over copy of a treatise by Musonius, the Stoic teacher of Epictetus. It is a charge that would surely undermine both Clement's integrity and the value of the work. However, while there are clear proofs that Clement did use Musonius, both in general arrangement and in many details, such an arbitrary method of higher criticism cannot be taken seriously. The words of R. Casey hold out a common-sense judgment: 'It must be remembered that an author is not explained, or even fairly represented, by showing how much he may have derived from others, for in the last analysis, his finished thought is his own, however extensive the foreign material employed in its construction.'[24] And Tollinton warns that the theory of Clement's indebtedness to Musonius cannot be pressed beyond the limits of probability, because 'the *Paidagōgos* was most likely, in substance first delivered in the lecture-room ... And it is quite improbable that Clement would have set before his hearers a description of luxury which was wholly out of keeping with the facts.'[25]

The more famous editions of Clement's works are those

---
21 Cf. below, p. 5.
22 P. Wendland, *Quaestiones Musoniae* (Berlin 1886).
23 C. P. Parker, 'Musonius in Clement,' *Harvard Studies in Classical Philology* 12 (1901) 191-200.
24 R. Casey, 'Clement of Alexandria and the Beginnings of Christian Platonism,' *Harvard Theological Review* 18 (1925) 39.
25 Tollinton, *op. cit.* 245.

by J. Potter (Oxford 1715); by Le Nourry, in the Migne *Patrologiae Graecae Cursus* (1891); by Dindorf (1869), although his edition is defective in many ways; and by O. Stählin (1905), whose edition is definitive and has made all others obsolete. The only English translation of the *Paidagōgos* is that made by W. Wilson in 1884 in the Ante-Nicene Christian Library, which leaves much to be desired.

The translator wishes to acknowledge his indebtedness to all those who have assisted him in any way. He is particularly grateful to those of his confreres of the staff of Holy Cross Seminary who patiently read his manuscript and made many helpful suggestions. He is also grateful to Rev. Iraeneus Herscher, O.F.M., Librarian of St. Bonaventure University, and to Miss Ida Briggs of the Dunkirk Public Library for their kind assistance. The members of the staffs of the Mullen Library at the Catholic University of America, the Library of Congress, and the New York Public Library were also most helpful and courteous.

SELECT BIBLIOGRAPHY

Text:

Clemens Alexandrinus, ed. O. Stählin, in Die Grieshischen Christichen Schriftsteller der Ersten Drei Jahrhunderte I (Leipzig 1905).

Secondary Sources:

Bigg, Ch., *The Christian Platonists of Alexandria* (Oxford 1913).
Casey, R., 'Clement of Alexandria and the Beginnings of Christian Platonism,' *Harvard Theological Review* 18 (1925) 39-101.
Comicorum Atticorum Fragmenta, ed. T. Kock, 3 vols. (Leipzig 1880-1888).
Echle, H. A., *Terminology of the Sacrament of Regeneration according to Clement of Alexandria* (Washington, D. C. 1949).
Faye, E. de, *Clément d'Alexandrie. Etude sur les rapports du Christianisme et de philosophie grecque au IIe siècle* (Paris 1898).
Kaye, J., *Some Account of the Writings and Opinions of Clement of Alexandria* (London 1898).
La Barre, A. de, 'Clément d'Alexandrie,' *Dictionnaire de Théologie Catholique*, tome iii, cols. 137-199 (Paris 1939).
Molland, E., *The Conception of the Gospel in the Alexandrian Theology* (Oslo 1938).
Mondésert, C., *Clément d'Alexandrie. Introduction a l'étude de sa pensée religieuse a partir de l'écriture* (Paris 1944).
Parker, C. P., 'Musonius in Clement,' *Harvard Studies in Classical Philology* 12 (1901) 191-200.
Patrick, J., *Clement of Alexandria* (London 1914).
Tollinton, R. B., *Clement of Alexandria. A Study in Christian Liberalism*, 2 vols. (London 1914).
Tragicorum Graecorum Fragmenta, ed. A. Nauck, 2nd ed. (1889).
Wendland, R., *Quaestiones Musoniae* (Berlin 1886).

CONTENTS

BOOK ONE

Chapter   *Page*

1. What the Educator of little ones professes to accomplish 3
2. That it is because of our sinfulness that He has taken charge of us as Educator 5
3. The Educator's love for men 9
4. That the Word is the Educator of both men and women alike 11
5. That all who seek the truth are children in God's eyes 12
6. An answer to those who consider that the designation 'child' and 'little one' implies the teaching of purely elementary lessons 24
7. Who the Educator of little ones is, and what sort of training He imparts 49
8. An answer to those who refuse to consider justice good 56
9. That it is the same faculty which performs acts of kindness and administers just punishment 67
10. That it is through the same Word that God restrains mankind from sin by the use of threats and saves it by the use of encouragement 79
11. That it is through the Law and the Prophets that the Word once educated 84

Chapter	Page

12 That our Educator, in keeping with His paternal character, makes use of both severity and kindness . . 86
13 That just as living virtuously is living according to right reason, so sin is contrary to reason 89

BOOK TWO

1 How we should conduct ourselves in eating 93
2 How we should act in drinking 110
3 That we should not be overeager for precious vessels . 124
4 How we should enjoy ourselves at banquets 129
5 On laughter 134
6 On obscene talk 137
7 What those who live peacefully together should avoid 140
8 Whether ornaments and crowns should be used . . . 146
9 How we should regard sleep 159
10 What is to be discussed in the matter of procreation of children 164
11 Of footwear 189
12 That we should not be dazzled by stones and gold . . 190

BOOK THREE

1 On true beauty 199
2 That we ought not to cultivate artificial beauty . . . 202
3 Against men who cultivate artificial beauty 211
4 On the companions we should associate with 220
5 How we should act at the baths 225
6 That only the Christian is rich 227

Chapter	Page
7 That frugality is an adequate means of sustenance for the Christian	230
8 That images and examples are the most important part of good instruction	233
9 On the motive permitting us to indulge in the baths	237
10 That even bodily exercise is allowed those who live according to reason	239
11 A general summary of the more excellent way of life	242
12 Continuation of the same, with many passages from Scripture describing the life of Christians	263

CLEMENT OF ALEXANDRIA

CHRIST, THE EDUCATOR OF LITTLE ONES

Translated by

SIMON P. WOOD, C.P., M.A.

Holy Cross Seminary

Dunkirk, N. Y.

BOOK ONE

Chapter 1

O YOU WHO ARE CHILDREN! An indestructible corner stone of knowledge, holy temple of the great God, has been hewn out especially for us as a foundation for the truth. This corner stone is noble persuasion, or the desire for eternal life aroused by an intelligent response to it, laid in the ground of our minds.

For, be it noted, there are these three things in man: habits, deeds, and passions. Of these, habits come under the influence of the word of persuasion, the guide to godliness. This is the word that underlies and supports, like the keel of a ship, the whole structure of the faith. Under its spell, we surrender, even cheerfully, our old ideas, become young again to gain salvation, and sing in the inspired words of the psalm: 'How good is God to Israel, to those who are upright of heart.'[1] As for deeds, they are affected by the word of counsel, and passions are healed by that of consolation.[2]

---
1 Ps. 72.1.
2 This seemingly strained division of rhetoric is typical both of the age and of the Stoic school. Cf. the division made by Posidonius as quoted by Seneca, *Ep.* 95.65.

These three words, however, are but one: the self-same Word who forcibly draws men from their natural, worldly way of life and educates them to the only true salvation: faith in God. That is to say, the heavenly Guide, the Word, once He begins to call men to salvation, takes to Himself the name of persuasion (this sort of appeal, although only one type, is properly given the name of the whole, that is, word, since the whole service of God has a persuasive appeal, instilling in a receptive mind the desire for life now and for the life to come); but the Word also heals and counsels, all at the same time. In fact, He follows up His own activity by encouraging the one He has already persuaded, and particularly by offering a cure for his passions.

Let us call Him, then, by the one title: Educator of little ones, an Educator who does not simply follow behind, but who leads the way, for His aim is to improve the soul, not just to instruct it; to guide to a life of virtue, not merely to one of knowledge. (2) Yet, that same Word does teach. It is simply that in this work we are not considering Him in that light. As Teacher, He explains and reveals through instruction, but as Educator He is practical. First He persuades men to form habits of life, then He encourages them to fulfill their duties by laying down clear-cut counsels and by holding up, for us who follow, examples of those who have erred in the past. Both are most useful: the advice, that it may be obeyed; the other, given in the form of example, has a twofold object—either that we may choose the good and imitate it or condemn and avoid the bad.

(3) Healing of the passions follows as a consequence. The Educator strengthens souls with the persuasion implied in these examples, and then He gives the nourishing, mild medicine, so to speak, of His loving counsels to the sick

man that he may come to a full knowledge of the truth. Health and knowledge are not the same; one is a result of study, the other of healing. In fact, if a person is sick, he cannot master any of the things taught him until he is first completely cured. We give instructions to someone who is sick for an entirely different reason than we do to someone who is learning; the latter, we instruct that he may acquire knowledge, the first, that he may regain health. Just as our body needs a physician when it is sick, so, too, when we are weak, our soul needs the Educator to cure its ills. Only then does it need the Teacher to guide it and develop its capacity to know, once it is made pure and capable of retaining the revelation of the Word.

Therefore, the all-loving Word, anxious to perfect us in a way that leads progressively to salvation, makes effective use of an order well adapted to our development; at first, He persuades, then He educates, and after all this He teaches.

Chapter 2

(4) Our Educator, O children, resembles His Father, God, whose Son He is. He is without sin, without blame, without passion of soul,[1] God immaculate in form of man, accomplishing His Father's will. He is God the Word, who is in the bosom of the Father, and also at the right hand of the Father, with even the nature of God.

He it is who is the spotless image.[2] We must try, then, to resemble Him in spirit as far as we are able. It is true that He Himself is entirely free from human passion; that is why

---

1 *Apathēs*. For this typical Stoic term, cf. Introduction, p. xvi.
2 Cf. 2 Cor. 4.4; Col. 1.15.

He alone is sinless. Yet we must strive, to the best of our ability, to be as sinless as we can. There is nothing more important for us than first to be rid of sin and weakness, and then to uproot any habitual sinful inclination. The highest perfection, of course, is never to sin in any least way; but this can be said of God alone. The next highest is never deliberately to commit wrong; this is the state proper to the man who possesses wisdom. In the third place comes not sinning except on rare occasions; this marks a man who is well educated. Finally, in the lowest degree, we must place delaying in sin for a brief moment; but even this, for those who are called to recover their loss and repent, is a step on the path to salvation.

(5) It seems to me that the Educator expresses it aptly through Moses when He says: 'If anyone die suddenly before him [the priest], the head of his consecration shall be defiled; and he shall immediately shave it.'[3] By 'sudden death' He means an indeliberate sin, and says that it 'defiles' because it pollutes the soul. For the cure He prescribes that the head be shaved on the spot as soon as possible, meaning that the locks of ignorance that darken the reason should be shorn so that the reason (which has its seat in the head), stripped of hair, that is, wickedness, may the better retrace its course to repentance.

A few words afterwards He adds: 'The former days were without reason,'[4] by which He surely means that deliberate sin is an act done contrary to reason. Involuntary sin He calls 'sudden,' but deliberate sin 'without reason.' It is precisely for this purpose that the Word, Reason Itself,[5] has

---

3 Num. 6.9.
4 Num. 6.12.
5 *Logos*, which Clement uses here for Word, with a play on the secondary meaning of reason. Cf. Introduction, p. xvi.

taken upon Himself, as the Educator of little ones, the task of preventing sins against reason. Understand in this light that expression in the Scriptures: 'For this reason, thus speaks the Lord . . . .'[6] The words that follow describe and condemn some sin that has been committed. The judgment contained in these words is just, for it is as if He were giving notice in the words of the Prophet that, if you had not sinned, He would not have made these threats. The same is true of those other words: 'For this reason, the Lord says these things . . . ,'[7] and 'Because you have not heard these words, the Lord says these things . . . ,'[8] and 'Behold, for this reason, the Lord says . . .'[9] In fact, the inspired Word exists because of both obedience and disobedience: that we may be saved by obeying it, and educated because we have disobeyed.

(6) Therefore, the Word is our Educator who heals the unnatural passions of our soul with His counsel. The art of healing, strictly speaking, is the relief of the ills of the body, an art learned by man's wisdom. Yet, the only true divine Healer of human sickness, the holy Comforter of the soul when it is ill, is the Word of the Father. Scripture says: 'Save Thy servant, O my God, who puts his trust in Thee. Have mercy on me, O Lord, because I have cried to Thee the whole day through.'[10] In the words of Democritus, 'The healer, by his art, cures the body of its diseases, but it is wisdom that rids the spirit of its ills.'[11] The good Educator of little ones, however, Wisdom Himself, the Word of the Father, who created

---
6 Ezech. 13.13,20. Here, Clement is obviously influenced by the fuller account of these Scriptural expressions in *Ep. of Barnabas* 9.1-5.
7 Isa. 30.12; Ezech. 13.18.
8 Cf. Num. 14.22; Jer. 35.14; 42.21; 44.23.
9 Cf. Jer. 7.20.
10 Ps. 85.2,3.
11 *Fragment 50*, N. 31. H. Diels, *Die Fragmente der Vorsakratiker griechisch und deutsch* (Berlin 1903).

man, concerns Himself with the whole creature, and as the Physician of the whole man heals both body and soul.

'Arise,' the Saviour said to the paralytic, 'take up the bed on which you are lying and go home.'[12] And immediately the sick man regained his health. To the man who was dead He said: 'Lazarus, come forth.' And the dead man came forth from his tomb,[13] the same as he had been before he underwent [death], except for having tasted resurrection.

But the soul He heals in a way suitable to the nature of the soul: by His commandments and by His gifts. We would perhaps expect Him to heal with His counsels, but, generous with His gifts, He also says to us sinners: 'Thy sins are forgiven thee.'[14] With these words we have become little ones in spirit, for by them we share in the magnificent and unvarying order established by His providence. That providence begins by ordering the world and the heavens, the course of the sun's orbit and the movements of the other heavenly bodies, all for the sake of man. Then, it concerns itself with man himself, for whom it had undertaken all these other labors. And because it considers this as its most important work, it guides man's soul on the right path by the virtues of prudence and temperance, and equips his body with beauty and harmony. Finally, into the actions of mankind it infuses uprightness and some of its own good order.

---

12 Cf. Matt. 9.6,7.
13 Cf. John 11.43.
14 Luke 5.20; 7.48.

Chapter 3

(7) Both as God and as man, the Lord renders us every kind of service and assistance. As God, He forgives sin; as man, He educates us to avoid sin completely.

But, since man is the creation of God, he is naturally dear to Him. Other things God made by a simple word of command, but man He fashioned by His own direct action and breathed into him something proper to Himself. Now, a being which God Himself has fashioned, and in such a way that it resembles Himself closely, must have been created either because it is desirable to God in itself, or because it is useful for some other creature. If man has been created as desirable in himself, then God loves him as good, since He Himself is good, and there is a certain lovableness in man, which is the very quality breathed into him by God.[1]

But, if God made man only because He considered him useful for some other creature, even then He had no other reason for actually creating him than that with him He could become a good Creator, and man could come to a knowledge of God[2] (remember, in this case, unless man had been created, God would not have made the other creature for whose sake man was being created). So, the power which God already possessed, hidden deep within Himself, the power of willing, He was actualizing by this display of the external power of creating, drawing from man a motive for creating him. Thus, He saw what He possessed all

---
1 Cf. *Gen.* 2.7.
2 This difficult passage seems to mean, in the words of J. Patrick: 'The creation of man, of something capable of knowledge of God, seems to be represented in a sense as essential to the complete goodness of the Creator' (*Clement of Alexandria* 93).

along, and the creature whom God had willed to be, actually came into existence. For there is nothing that God cannot do.

(8) Therefore, man, the creation of God, is desirable in himself. But being desirable in oneself means being connatural to the person to whom one is desirable, and being acceptable and pleasing. But what does being pleasing to someone mean, if not being loved by him? Man is, then, an object of love; yes, man is loved by God.

It must be so, for it was on man's account that the Only-begotten was sent from the bosom of the Father, as the Word evoking trust. Evoking trust, indeed, trust in abundance, the Lord clearly professes to do when He says: 'The Father Himself loves you, because you have loved Me.'[3] And again: 'And thou hast loved them, just as thou hast loved Me.'[4]

I believe it is already evident what the Educator desires and what He professes to accomplish, what He has in mind in His words and in His deeds when He commands what we are to do and what we are to avoid. It is clear, too, that the other kind of discourse, that of the Teacher, is at once direct and spiritual, in unmistakable language, but meant only for those initiated into the mysteries. But, for the present, let that be.

(9) As for Him who lovingly guides us along the way to the better life, we ought to return Him love and live according to the dictate of His principles. This we should do not only by fulfilling His commandments and obeying His prohibitions, but also by turning away from the evil examples we just mentioned and imitating the good. In this way, we shall make our own actions, as far as we are able, like those

---
3 John 16.27.
4 John 17.23.

of our Educator, that the ancient saying, 'according to His own image and likeness,'[5] may be accomplished.

But we wander in thick darkness; we need an unerring guide in life who will keep us from stumbling. The best guide is not that blind one who, in the words of Scripture, 'leads the blind into a ditch,'[6] but the Word, keen of sight, penetrating into the secret places of the heart. Just as there cannot be a light that does not give light, nor a cause unless it produces some effect, nor a lover unless he loves, just so He can not be good unless He rendered us service and led us to salvation.

Let us, then, express our love for the commandments of the Lord by our actions. (Indeed, the Word Himself, when He became flesh in visible form, unceasingly showed not only the theory but also the practise of virtue.) Further, considering the Word as our law, let us see in His commandments and counsels direct and sure paths to eternity. For His precepts are filled with the spirit, not of fear, but of persuasion.

Chapter 4

(10) Let us welcome more and more gladly this holy subjection, and let us surrender ourselves more and more completely to the Lord, holding to the steadfast cable of His persuasion. Let us recognize, too, that both men and women practise the same sort of virtue. Surely, if there is but one God for both, then there is but one Educator for both.

One Church, one virtue, one modesty, a common food, wedlock in common, breath, sight, hearing, knowledge, hope,

---
5 Cf. Gen. 1.26.
6 Matt. 15.14.

obedience, love, all are alike [in man and woman]. They who possess life in common, grace in common, and salvation in common have also virtue in common and, therefore, education too. The Scripture says: 'For in this world, they marry and are given in marriage,' for this world is the only place in which the female is distinguished from the male, 'but in that other world, no longer.'¹ There, the rewards of this life, lived in the holy union of wedlock, await not man or woman as such, but the human person, freed from the lust that in this life had made it either male or female.

(11) The very name 'mankind' is a name common to both men and women. Similarly, the Attic Greeks called, I believe, not only the boy but also the girl by the one name of 'child,' if Menander, the comic poet, is to be believed in a passage of his play *Rapizomene*: 'My little daughter, . . . indeed, she is by nature an exceedingly loving child.'²

Notice, too, that 'sheep' is the general name used for the male and female. Yet, 'the Lord is our shepherd'³ for ever, Amen. 'Now, neither sheep nor any other animal should live without a shepherd, nor should children, without an educator, nor servants without a master.'⁴

Chapter 5

(12) That education is the training given children is evident from the very name.¹ It remains for us to consider who

---
1 Cf. Luke 20.34.
2 *Fragment 428*, T. Kock, *CAF* III 124.
3 Cf. Ps. 22.1.
4 Plato, *Laws* VII 808D.

1 The Greek word for education, *paidagōgía*, etymologically means the guidance or training of children.

the children are as explained by the Scriptures and, from the same Scriptural passages, to understand the Educator.

We are the children. Scripture mentions us very often and in many different ways, and refers to us under different titles, thereby introducing variety in the simple language of the faith. For example, in the Gospel, it says: 'And the Lord, standing on the shore, said to His disciples (they were fishing): Children, do you have no fish?'[2] Those who already had the position of disciples He now calls 'children.'

Again, we read: 'And they brought the children to Him, that He might lay hands on them and bless them, and when the disciples tried to prevent it, Jesus said: Let the little children be and do not hinder them from coming to Me, for of such is the kingdom of heaven.'[3] What such a remark means the Lord Himself explains plainly later on: 'Unless you turn and become like little children, you shall not enter into the kingdom of heaven.'[4] Those words are not a figure of speech for some kind of rebirth, but recommend the simplicity of childhood for our imitation.

The Spirit, in prophetic strain, also describes us as children: 'Plucking branches of olives,' He says, 'or of palm, the children came out to meet the Lord, and they cried out, saying: Hosanna to the Son of David, blessed is He who comes in the name of the Lord.'[5] The word 'Hosanna,' translated into Greek, means 'light, glory, praise, supplication to the Lord.' (13) Incidentally, it seems to me that the Scripture, in this inspired passage, intends to accuse and condemn the luke-

---
2 Cf. John 21.4,5.
3 Cf. Matt. 19.14.
4 Matt. 18.3.
5 Cf. Matt. 21.8,9; John 12.13.

warm: 'Have you never read that out of the mouths of babes and sucklings, Thou hast brought forth praise?'⁶

Notice the same name again in the Gospel, when the Lord shocked His disciples, attempting to arouse their attention when He was about to go to His Father. To dispose them to listen more intently, He tells them in advance that in a little while He will go away; it is as if He would make them understand that while the Word has not yet ascended into heaven, they must gather in the fruits of truth with greater care. So it is that once more He calls them children: 'Children,' He says, 'yet a little while and I am with you.'⁷

Another time He likened the kingdom of heaven to 'children seated in the market-place and saying: We have piped for you and you have not danced; we have wept and you have not mourned.'⁸ He uses this same expression many other times.

But it is not only the Gospel that speaks in this way. The prophetic books also adopt the same attitude. David, for example, says: 'Praise the Lord, O children, praise the name of the Lord.'⁹ And Isaias: 'Behold, I and my children whom God has given me.'¹⁰

(14) Does it surprise you to hear that full-grown men of all nations are children in God's eyes? Then you do not know much about the Greek language, I think, where we

---
6 Matt. 21.16.
7 John 13.33.
8 Matt. 11.16,17. The Scholion calls attention to the fact that Clement here applies Christ's words to the 'kingdom of heaven,' although they were originally applied to 'this generation.' Cf., also, E. L. Titus, *The Motivation of Change Made in the New Testament Text by Justin Martyr and Clement of Alexandria* (Chicago 1942) 27, for a discussion of the change.
9 Ps. 112.1.
10 Isa. 8.18.

can see that a beautiful and attractive young woman who is moreover also free-born, is to this day called 'child,' and slaves are called 'little children,'[11] although both are young women. They are complimented by such pet names because of the flower of their youth.

Whenever He says: 'Let My lambs stand on My right,'[12] He means the simple: children, not men, for they are in the category of sheep. He considers the lambs as deserving to be mentioned first, thereby praising, before all other qualities men can possess, gentleness and simplicity of mind and guilelessness.

Again, whenever He speaks of 'young suckling calves,'[13] and of 'the guileless and meek dove,'[14] He means us. Through Moses He orders that two young birds, a pair of pigeons or of turtle doves, be offered for any sin; this means that the sinlessness of such gentle birds and their guilelessness and forgetfulness of injury is very acceptable to God. So He is instructing us to offer a sacrifice bearing the character of that which we have offended against. The plight of the poor doves, moreover, will instil into us a beginning of abhorrence for sin.

There is a passage in Scripture which shows that He refers to us also as young birds: 'As the hen gathers her chicks under her wings . . .'[15] In that sense we are young birds, a name which graphically and mystically describes the simplicity of soul belonging to childhood. At times, He calls us children, at other times, chicks, sometimes, little ones, here

---

11 That is, *paidiskē*, a diminutive for *pais* ('child'), and *paidiskárion*, an intensified diminutive.
12 Cf. Matt. 25.33.
13 Cf. Amos 6.4; 2 Kings 17.29.
14 Lev. 5.11; 12.8; cf. Luke. 2.24; Matt. 10.16.
15 Matt. 23.37.

and there sons, and very often offspring, a new people, a young people. 'A new name,' He says, 'will be given My servants' (by new name He means one that is different and everlasting, pure and simple, suggestive of childhood and of candor), 'which will be blessed upon the earth.'[16]

(15) At another time, He speaks of us under the figure of a colt. He means by that that we are unyoked to evil, unsubdued by wickedness, unaffected, high-spirited only with Him our Father. We are colts, not stallions 'who whinny lustfully for their neighbor's wife, beasts of burden unrestrained in their lust.'[17] Rather, we are free and newly born, joyous in our faith, holding fast to the course of truth, swift in seeking salvation, spurning and trampling upon worldliness. 'Rejoice greatly, O daughter of Sion. Shout for joy, O daughter of Jerusalem. Behold, thy King comes to thee, the just and saviour, and He is poor and riding upon an ass and upon a young colt.'[18] He is not satisfied to say 'colt'; He adds 'young,' to emphasize mankind's rejuvenation in Christ and its unending, eternal youth and simplicity. Such young colts as we little ones are our divine Tamer trains. Although the passage means a young ass, it, too, is a colt.

Again, it is said: 'He tethers his colt to the vine.'[19] This means He united the simple, new people to the Word, whom the vine signifies. For, the product of the vine is wine; of the Word, blood. Both are saving potions:[20] wine, for the health of the body; the other, blood, for the salvation of the soul.

---
16 Isa. 65.15,16 (Septuagint).
17 Cf. Jer. 5.8.
18 Zach. 9.9.
19 Cf. Gen. 49.11.
20 *Potòn eis sōterian*. J. Patrick (*op. cit.* 123) has called attention to the sense in which Clement uses this word, *sōteria*: 'The fundamental conception of salvation in Clement is that of spiritual health.'

But that He calls us lambs, too, the Spirit gives unmistakeable evidence. He says through Isaias: 'He shall feed His flock like a shepherd; He shall gather together the lambs with His arm.'[21] Once again, He uses the more innocent class of sheep, lambs, as a figure for simplicity.

(16) There can be no doubt that we also call the most excellent and perfect possessions in life by names derived from the word 'child,' that is, education and culture.[22] We define education as a sound training from childhood in the path of virtue. Be that as it may, the Lord once very clearly revealed what He means by the name 'little child': A dispute having arisen among the Apostles as to which of them was greater, Jesus made a little child stand among them, saying: 'If anyone will humble himself as this little child, he is greater in the kingdom of heaven.'[23] Therefore, He does not mean by 'little child' one who has not yet reached the use of reason because of his immaturity,[24] as some have thought. When He says: 'Unless you become as these children, you shall not enter the kingdom of heaven,' we must not foolishly mistake His meaning. We are not little ones in the sense that we roll on the floor or crawl on the ground as snakes do. That is to grovel in unreasoning desires with our whole body prostrate. We strain upward with our minds, we have given up sin and the world, we tread the earth, although with light foot, only to the degree that appearances demand, that we may be in this world. We, indeed, cultivate holy wisdom, which seems foolishness to those bent on evil.

(17) Really, then, children are those who look upon

---

21 Isa. 40.11.
22 *Paideia* and *paidagōgia*, words derived from *pais* ('child').
23 Cf. Matt. 18.1-4.
24 Cf. 1 Cor. 14.20.

God alone as their father, who are simple, little ones, uncontaminated, who are lovers of the horn of the unicorn.[25] To these, surely, who have matured in the Word, He has proclaimed His message, bidding them not to be concerned with the affairs of this life and encouraging them to imitate children and devote themselves to the Father alone. So it is that He says to those who have some possessions: 'Do not be anxious about the morrow; for tomorrow will have anxieties of its own.'[26] Here He commands us to lay aside the cares of life and give our whole mind and heart to the Father alone. Whoever fulfills this command is a little one, indeed, and a child, both before God and the world: to the world, in the sense of one who has lost his wits; to God, in the sense of one dearly beloved.

Now, if there is, as the Scripture says, but 'one teacher, in heaven,'[27] then, surely all who are on earth can with good reason be called disciples. The plain truth is that what is perfect belongs to the Lord, who is ever teaching, while the role of child and little one belongs to us, who are ever learning. (18) In fact, the inspired word reserves the name 'man' to what is complete and consummate; David, for example, says of the Devil: 'The Lord abominates the man of blood,'[28] man in the sense that he is consummate in wickedness. Scripture calls the Lord man, too, in the sense that He is consummate in goodness. The Apostle, for example, writing to the Corinthians, says: 'For I have betrothed you to one man, that I might present you a chaste virgin to Christ,'[29] or as little

---

25 Cf. Deut. 33.17; Ps. 91.11. This difficult figure suggests those who rely upon the strength of God and of Christ.
26 Matt. 6.8.
27 Matt. 23.9,10.
28 Ps. 5.7.
29 2 Cor. 11.2.

ones and saints, but, at any rate, only to the Lord. And in writing to the Ephesians he expresses clearly just what we are saying: 'Until we all attain to the unity of the faith and of the deep knowledge of God, to perfect manhood, to the mature measure of the fullness of Christ. And this He has done that we may be no longer children, tossed to and fro and carried about by every wind of doctrine devised in the wickedness of man, in craftiness, according to the wiles of error. Rather are we to practise the truth in love, and to grow up in all things in Him.'[30] He says these things to build up the body of Christ,[31] 'who is the Head,'[32] and man because He alone is perfect in goodness. If we, the children, protect ourselves from the winds that blow us off our course into the pride of heresy and refuse to listen to those who set up other fathers for us, we are made perfect by accepting Christ as our Head and becoming ourselves the Church.

(19) We ought now to be in a position to understand that the name 'little one' is not used in the sense of lacking intelligence. Childishness means that, but 'little one' really means 'one newly become gentle,'[33] just as the word 'gentle' means being mild-mannered. So, a 'little one' means one just recently become gentle and meek of disposition. St. Paul obviously suggests this when he says: 'Although as the Apostle of Christ we could have claimed a position of honor among you, still while in your midst we were children,[34] as if a nurse were cherishing her own children.'[35] A little one is

---

30 Eph. 4.13-15.
31 Eph. 4.12.
32 Eph. 4.15.
33 Clement falsely derives the word for 'little one' (*népios*) from *nē-* ('new') and *épios* ('gentle').
34 *Népios*.
35 1 Thess. 2.7.

gentle and for that reason decidedly amenable, mild and simple, without deceit or pretense,[36] direct and upright of mind. Childlikeness is the foundation for simplicity and truthfulness. 'For upon whom shall I look,' it is said in Scripture, 'if not the meek and the peaceful?'[37] Of such sort is the virginal Word, gentle and unaffected. This is why, too, we speak of a virgin as a tender maid, and of a child as tender-minded. We are tender, too, in the sense that we have become amenable to persuasion, and we are ever ready to practise virtue, with anger under control and unhampered by ill-will or dishonesty.

The old people were perverse and hard of heart, but we, the new people, the assembly of little ones, are amenable as a child. In the Epistle to the Romans, the Apostle declares that he rejoices in 'the hearts of the innocent,'[38] but notice that he goes on to set limits, so to speak, to this childlikeness: 'I would have you wise as to what is good, and guileless as to what is evil.'[39] (20) That is well put, because we should not understand the Greek word *népios,* little one, in a negative sense, even though the grammarians have decided that the prefix *nē-* is a privative.[40]

Indeed, if they who decry childlikeness call us simple-minded, you see they are really speaking evil of the Lord. They imply that those who seek the protection of God are lacking in intelligence. But, if even they will accept the term 'little one' in the sense of the innocent—and it must be taken in this sense—then we glory in the name. Little ones

---

36 There is an interesting parechesis here: *atalós,* (h) *apalós,* (h) *aploús, ádolos.*
37 Isa. 66.2.
38 Cf. Rom. 16.18.
39 Rom. 16.19.
40 Cf. above, note 33.

are indeed the new spirits, they who have newly become wise despite their former folly, who have risen up according to the new Covenant. Only recently, in fact, has God become known, because of the coming of Christ. 'For no one has known God, but the Son, and him to whom the Son has revealed Him.'[41]

Then the new people, in contrast to the older people, are young, because they have heard the new good things. The fertile time of life is this unaging youth of ours in which we are ever at the prime of intelligence, ever young, ever childlike, ever new. For, those who have partaken of the new Word must themselves be new. But whatever partakes of eternity assumes, by that very fact, the qualities of the incorruptible; therefore, the name 'childhood' is for us a life-long springtime, because the truth abiding in us is ageless and our being, made to overflow with that truth, is ageless, too. (21) Surely, wisdom is ever fruitful, ever fixed unchangeably on the same truths, never varying.

'The children,' Scripture says, 'shall be put upon the shoulders, and they shall be comforted on the knees, as one whom the mother comforts, so will I comfort you.'[42] A mother draws her children near her; we seek our mother, the Church. Whatever is weak and young has an appeal and sweetness and lovableness of its own, just because in its weakness it does stand in need of assistance. But God does not withhold assistance from such an age of life. Just as the male and female parent regard their young tenderly—whether it be horses their colts, or cows their calves, or lions their cubs, or deer their fawn, or men their children—so, too, does the Father of all draw near to those who seek His aid, giving them a new

---
41 Matt. 11.27.
42 Isa. 66.12,13.

birth and making them His own adopted sons. He recognizes them as His little ones, He loves only them, and He comes to the aid of such as these and defends them. That is why He calls them His children.

I appeal to Isaac as an illustration of this sort of childhood. Isaac means 'rejoicing.' The inquisitive king saw him playing with his wife and help-mate, Rebecca.[43] The king (his name was Abimelec) represents, I believe, a wisdom above this world, looking down upon the mystery signified by such child-like playing. Rebecca means 'submission.' Oh, what prudent playing! Rejoicing joined to submission, with the king as audience.[44] The Spirit exults in such merry-making in Christ, attended with submissiveness. This is in truth godly child-likeness.

(22)   Heraclitus tells us that his Zeus, too, indulges in such a pastime.[45] Indeed, what occupation is more becoming a wise and perfect man than to play and rejoice at the celebration of a solemn religious festival, with submissive reception and the performance of what is holy?

It is possible to interpret the meaning of the inspired word in still another sense: that it refers to our rejoicing and making merry because of our salvation, like Isaac's. He rejoiced because he had been saved from death; that is why he played and rejoiced with his spouse, as we with our helpmate in salvation, the Church. The Church, too, has been given the reassuring name 'submissive endurance,' either because her enduring continues for all eternity in unending joy, or because she is formed of the submission of those who

---

43 Cf. Gen. 26.8. For Clement's interpretation of this passage, cf. Philo, *De plant.* 3 (p. 301) 169,170.
44 Cf. Philo, *loc. cit.*
45 *Fragment 52* (H. Diels, *op. cit.*).

believe: of us who are the members of Christ. The testimony given by those who have submissively endured until the end, and their gratitude, as well, is a mystical playing; the helpmate of this holy gladness of heart is salvation. The king is Christ, looking down from above on our rejoicing, and 'peering through the door,'[46] as Scripture says, on our gratitude and benediction that works in us joy and cheerfulness with submission. He gazes upon the assembly of such as these, His own Church; all He does is to manifest His own absent person to the Church, thus become complete with its kingly Head. (23) What is the door by which the Lord makes Himself manifest? It is His flesh by which He becomes visible.

Isaac is another type, too (he can easily be taken in this other sense), this time of the Lord. He was a son, just as is the Son (he is the son of Abraham; Christ, of God); he was a victim, as was the Lord, but his sacrifice was not consummated, while the Lord's was. All he did was to carry the wood of his sacrifice, just as the Lord bore the wood of the Cross. Isaac rejoiced for a mystical reason, to prefigure the joy with which the Lord has filled us, in saving us from destruction through His blood. Isaac did not actually suffer, not only to concede the primacy of suffering to the Word, but also to suggest, by not being slain, the divinity of the Lord; Jesus rose again after His burial,[47] as if He had not suffered, like Isaac delivered from the altar of sacrifice.

(24) But there is another and even greater support for this argument of ours, which I shall now explain. The Spirit inspired Isaias to call the Lord a child: 'Behold, a child is born to us, and a son is given us, and the government is upon

---

46 Cf. Gen. 26.8.
47 The sense is somewhat obscured here by damaged text.

His shoulders: and His name shall be called Angel of the great council.'[48] What is this child, this little one, after whose image we also are little ones? Through the same Prophet He goes on to describe His greatness: 'Wonderful, Counsellor, God the mighty, eternal Father, Prince of peace; because He maintains His childhood, of His peace there shall be no end.'[49] O, the great God; O, the perfect Child! Son, while He is Father; Father, while He is Son. Is not the childhood of this child perfect, embracing as it does all of us children, educating us little ones as His children? This is He who stretches out His hands to us,[50] hands so clearly to be trusted.

Again, St. John, 'the prophet greatest among those born of woman,'[51] also testifies to His childhood: 'Behold the Lamb of God.'[52] Scripture speaks of children and little ones as 'lambs'; then in this passage, in calling God the Word, become man for us, 'the Lamb of God,' because of His desire to be like us in all things, he is speaking of Him as the Son of God, the little one of the Father.

Chapter 6

(25) It is possible, too, for us to make a completely adequate answer to any carping critics.[1] We are children and little ones, but certainly not because the learning we acquire is puerile or rudimentary, as those puffed up in their own knowledge falsely charge. On the contrary, when we

---
48 Isa. 9.6,7 (Septuagint).
49 *Idem.* Cf. reading of Symmachus.
50 Cf. Isa. 65.2; Rom. 10.21. Possibly a reference to the Cross.
51 Luke 7.28.
52 John 1.29,36.

---
1 The Gnostics.

were reborn, we straightway received the perfection for which we strive. For we were enlightened,[2] that is, we came to the knowledge of God. Certainly, he who possesses knowledge of the Perfect Being is not imperfect.

But do not find fault with me for claiming that I have such knowledge of God. This claim was rightfully made by the Word, and He is outspoken. When the Lord was baptized, a voice loudly sounded from heaven, as a witness to Him who was beloved: 'Thou art My beloved Son; this day have I begotten Thee.'[3]

Now let us ask the wise: on that day when Christ was reborn, was He already perfect, or—a very foolish question— was He defective? If this last, then He needed to add to His knowledge. But, since He is God, it is not likely that He learned even one thing more. No one can be greater than the Word, nor can anyone teach Him who is the one only Teacher. Are they unwilling, then, to admit that the Word, perfect Son born of a perfect Father, was perfectly reborn, as a prefigurement of the divine plan? But, if He is perfect, then why was one already perfect baptized?

It was necessary, they tell us, that the commandment given to men might be fulfilled.

Very good, I reply. But was He, by that baptism conferred through John, made perfect?

It is clear that He was.

But not by learning anything more?

No, indeed.

---
2 *phōtizō*, taken from pagan mysteries, but applied by Clement to baptism. Cf. H. A. Echle, *Terminology of the Sacrament of Regeneration according to Clement of Alexandria* (Washington, D. C. 1949) 208-209.
3 Cf. Matt. 3.17; Ps. 2.7. This is the reading of Codex D and a few Latin manuscripts and of other early Christian writings. Cf. Titus, *op. cit.* 14.

Is it, then, that He was made perfect only in the sense of being washed, and that He was consecrated by the descent of the Holy Spirit?

Yes, that is the true explanation.

(26) This is what happens with us, whose model the Lord made Himself. When we are baptized, we are enlightened; being enlightened, we become adopted sons;[4] becoming adopted sons, we are made perfect; and becoming perfect, we are made divine. 'I have said,' it is written, 'you are gods and all of you the sons of the most High.'[5]

This ceremony is often called 'free gift,'[6] 'enlightenment,'[7] 'perfection,'[8] and 'cleansing'[9]—'cleansing,' because through it we are completely purified of our sins; 'free gift,' because by it the punishments due to our sins are remitted; 'enlightenment,' since by it we behold the wonderful holy light of salvation, that is, it enables us to see God clearly; finally, we call it 'perfection' as needing nothing further,[10] for what more does he need who possesses the knowledge of God? It would indeed be out of place to call something that was not fully perfect a gift of God. He is perfect; therefore, the gifts He bestows are also perfect. Just as at His command all things came into existence, so, on His mere desire to give, there immediately arises an overflowing measure of His gifts. What is yet to come, His will alone has already anticipated.

Moreover, release from evil is only the beginning of salvation. (27) Only those who have first reached the end of life, therefore, are those we can call already perfect. But we

---

4 Cf. Gal. 4.5.
5 Ps. 81.6.
6 Cf. Rom. 5.2; 5.15; 7.24.
7 Cf. Heb. 6.4; 10.32.
8 Cf. James 1.17; Heb. 7.11.
9 Cf. Titus 3.5;.Eph. 5.26.
10 *aprosdeēs*, a Stoic term applied to the wise man who is perfect.

live, we who have even now been freed from commerce with death. Salvation is the following of Christ. 'What was made in Him is life.'[11] 'Amen, amen,' He tells us, 'I say to you, he who hears My word and believes Him who sent Me has life everlasting and does not come to judgment, but has passed from death to life.'[12] The very fact that we believe in Him and are reborn is perfection of life. For God is by no means powerless. As His will is creation, and is called the universe, so His desire is the salvation of men,[13] and is called the Church. He knows whom He has called; and whom He has called He has saved; He has called and at the same time saved.[14] 'Now you yourselves,' the Apostle says, 'are taught of God.'[15] It is not right, then, for us to consider imperfect the teaching that is given by Him. That teaching is the immortal salvation that comes through the immortal Saviour, to whom be thanksgiving for ever. Amen.

Even though a man receive nothing more than this rebirth, still, because he is by that fact enlightened, he is straightway rid of darkness, as the name itself suggests, and automatically receives light. (28) It is just like men who shake off sleep and then are wide-awake interiorly; or, better, like those suffering from some blinding eye-disease who meanwhile receive no light from the outside and have none themselves, but must first remove the impediment from their eyes before they can have clear vision. In the same way, those who are baptized are cleansed of the sins which like a mist overcloud their divine spirit and then acquire a spiritual sight which is clear and unimpeded and lightsome, the sort of sight which alone enables

---

11 Cf. John 1.3. This is the reading of some of the manuscripts.
12 John 5.24.
13 Cf. 1 Thess. 4.3.
14 Cf. Rom. 8.30.
15 1 Thess. 4.9.

us to behold divinity, with the help of the Holy Spirit who is poured forth from heaven upon us. This is an admixture of eternal sunlight, giving us the power to see the eternal light. Like indeed attracts like; so it is that what is holy attracts Him who is the source of holiness, who properly speaking is called Light. 'For you once were darkness, but now light in the Lord.'[16] That is why, I believe, the ancients once called man by a name that means light.[17]

But, they object, man has not yet received the gift of perfection. I agree with them, except that I insist he is already in the light and that darkness does not overtake him.[18] There is nothing at all in between light and darkness. Perfection lies ahead, in the resurrection of the faithful, but it consists in obtaining the promise which has already been given to us. We say emphatically that both of these things cannot co-exist at the same time: arrival at the goal and the anticipation of that arrival by the mind. Eternity and time are not the same thing, nor are the beginning and the completion. They cannot be. But both are concerned about the same thing, and there is only one person involved in both. Faith, for example, begotten in time, is the starting point, if we may use the term, while the completion is the possession of the promise, made enduring for all eternity.

The Lord has Himself revealed clearly that salvation will be bestowed impartially, when He said: 'This is the will of My Father . . . , that whoever beholds the Son, and believes in Him, has life everlasting, and I will raise Him up on the last day.'[19] (29) Certainly, as far as is possible in this world (which

---

16 Eph. 5.8.
17 *phōs*, which, however, is not related etymologically to the word for light (*phôs*).
18 Cf. John 1.5.
19 John 6.40.

is the significance of the expression 'last day'), we believe that, while we wait for the time it will come to an end, we have already been made perfect. For, the perfection of knowledge is faith. That is why He says: 'He who believes in the Son has life everlasting.'[20] Assuredly, if we who believe already have life everlasting, what more remains but the enjoyment of that life everlasting? Nothing is lacking to faith, for of its nature it is perfect and entirely complete. If there is anything lacking to it, it is not wholly perfect, nor is it truly faith, if defective in any way. After our departure from this life, there is not a different sort of thing awaiting us who have believed in this life, and who have already received a pledge and foretaste of the same nature [as the fulfillment]. In believing, we already anticipate in advance what we will receive as an actuality after the resurrection, that the words may be accomplished: 'Be it done unto thee according to thy faith.'[21] In this world, we have the promise of what we believe; the enjoyment of that promise will be perfection. Therefore, while our knowledge consists in enlightenment, the goal of knowledge is enjoyment, which is the last thing to be obtained.

In the same way that inexperience yields to experience, and impossibility to possibility, so darkness is completely dispelled by light. Darkness is ignorance, for it makes us fall into sin and lose the ability to see the truth clearly. But knowledge is light, for it dispels the darkness of ignorance and endows us with keenness of vision. The very act of expelling things that are bad reveals what is good. To be sure, the things that ignorance restricts, to our harm, knowledge sets free, for our good. The quickest way to loose those bonds is to make use

---
20 John 3.36.
21 Matt. 9.29.

of man's faith, and God's grace, for sins are forgiven through the one divine remedy,[22] baptism in the Word. (30) All our sins, in fact, are washed away; instantaneously we are no longer bad. This is one grace of enlightenment, that we no longer are in the same state as before we were cleansed. Even before this teaching was given us, we who were uninstructed, but were learning, heard that knowledge is engendered together with enlightenment, bathing the mind in light. Yet, no one could say just when. Instruction[23] is given to engender faith, but faith comes by the Holy Spirit and by baptism.

The Apostle states very clearly that faith is salvation reaching the whole of mankind, and that it is an impartial share of union with the just and loving God, given to all. He says: 'But before the faith came, we were kept imprisoned under the Law, shut up for the faith that was to be revealed. Therefore, the Law has been our educator in Christ, that we might be justified by faith. But now that faith has come, we are no longer under an educator.'[24]

(31) Do you not hear those words: 'that we are no longer under the Law' which was accompanied by fear, but under the Word, the Educator of our free wills? Then, he adds these words, without making any distinction of persons: 'For you are all the children of God through faith in Christ Jesus. For all you who have been baptized into Christ have put on Christ. There is neither Jew nor Greek; there is neither slave nor freeman; there is neither male nor female.

---

22 *phármakòn paiónion*. This term refers literally to Paean, the healer, or the physician of the gods. It also suggests Clement's interest in medical terms, so prevalent in the Alexandria of Galen. Cf. Echle, *op. cit.* 240 n. 45.
23 *katéchēsis*, the term used to designate elementary instruction of catechumens.
24 Cf. Gal. 3.23-25.

CHRIST THE EDUCATOR 31

You are all one in Christ Jesus.'[25] It is not, then, that some are enlightened Gnostics and others are only less perfect Spirituals[26] in the same Word, but all, putting aside their carnal desires, are equal and spiritual before the Lord. He writes again, in another passage: 'For in one Spirit we were all baptized into one body, whether Jews or Greeks, whether slaves or free; and we were all given one drink to drink.'[27]

(32) It will not be improper to adopt the words of those[28] who teach that the remembrance of higher things is a dematerializing of the spirit and who hold that the process of dematerialization is a withdrawal from inferior things by recalling higher things. Recalling higher things necessarily leads to repentance for the lower. That is to say, these [philosophers] maintain that the spirit retraces its steps when it repents. In the same way, after we have repented of our sins, renounced our wickedness and been purified by baptism, we turn back to the eternal light, as children to their Father. 'Rejoicing in the spirit, Jesus said: I praise Thee, Father, God of heaven and earth, that Thou didst hide these things from the wise and prudent, and didst reveal them to little ones.'[29] The Educator and Teacher is there naming us little ones, meaning that we are more ready for salvation than the worldly wise who, believing themselves wise, have blinded their own eyes. And He cries out in joy and in great delight, as

---

25 Gal. 3.26-28.
26 According to the Gnostics, they themselves were the perfect, possessors of perfect knowledge; the less prefect, but still partially enlightened were the *Psychikoi*, or Spirituals, while the unenlightened were *Hylikoi*, or Materialists. They base their terminology on 1 Cor. 15.44. Cf. E. de Faye, *Clément d'Alexandrie* (Paris 1898) 188-190.
27 1 Cor. 12.13.
28 Clement tells us in *Strōmateis* V.11, that he is referring to Pythagoras and his followers. The Gnostics had adopted this teaching.
29 Luke 10.21.

if attuning Himself to the spirit of the little ones: 'Yes, Father, for such was Thy good pleasure.' That is why He has revealed to little ones what has been hid from the wise and prudent of this world.

It is with good reason, then, that we consider ourselves, the little ones, as the children of God, who, having put off the old man and the cloak of wickedness,[30] have put on the incorruption of Christ, so that, being renewed, a holy people, reborn, we might keep the [new] man unstained, and might be little ones in the sense of new-born children of God, purified of uncleaness and vice. (33) St. Paul, at any rate, settles the matter for us in unmistakable words, when he writes in the First Epistle to the Corinthians: 'Brethren, do not become children in mind, but in malice be children and in mind mature.'[31]

That other passage of his: 'When I was a child, I thought as a child, I spoke as a child,'[32] is a figure of speech for his manner of living under the Law, when he persecuted the Word, not as one become simple, but as one still senseless, because he thought childish things, and spoke childish things, blaspheming Him. (The word 'childish' can signify these two different things, one good and one bad.)

'Now that I have become a man,' Paul continues, 'I have put away the things of a child.' He is not referring to the growing stature that comes with age, nor yet to any definite period of time, nor even to any secret teaching reserved only for men and the more mature when he claims that he left and put away all childishness. Rather, he means to say that those who live by the Law are childish in the sense that

---
30 This is most probably a reference to a rite in the baptismal ceremony at which the clothes were put off, as symbol of the former way of life. Cf. Echle, *op. cit.* 101.
31 1 Cor.14.20.
32 1 Cor. 13.11.

they are subject to fear, like children afraid of ghosts, while those who are obedient to the Word and are completely free are, in his opinion, men: we who have believed, who are saved by our own voluntary choice and who are not subject to fear, save for an urgent cause. We will find proof of this in the Apostle himself, for he says that the Jews were heirs according to the Old Testament, but according to the promise, we are: 'Now I say, as long as the heir is a child, he differs in no way from a slave, though he is the master of all; but he is under guardians and stewards until the time set by his father. So we, too, when we were children, were enslaved under the elements of the world. But when the fullness of time came, God sent His Son, born of a woman, born under the Law, that He might redeem those who were under the Law, that we might receive the adoption of sons,' through Him.[33] (34) Notice that he claims that those who are subject to fear and to sin are little ones, but considers those who are subject to faith mature, and calls them sons, in contrast with those little ones who live by the Law. 'For you are no longer a slave,' he says, 'but a son; and if a son, an heir also through God.'[34] But what is lacking to the son after he has obtained the inheritance?

But it is well to expound that first passage. 'When I was a child,' that is, when I was a Jew (he was a Hebrew from the first), 'I thought as a child,' since I followed the Law; 'Now that I have become a man,' no longer thinking the things of a child—that is, of the Law—but those of a man—that is, of Christ who is, as I remarked before, the only one Scripture considers a man—'I put away the things of a

---
33 Gal. 4.1-5.
34 Gal. 4.7.

child.' Yet there is a childhood in Christ, which is perfection, in contrast to that of the Law.

Now that we have reached this point, let us defend this childlikeness of ours by interpreting the passage from the Apostle in which he says: 'I fed you with milk, as little ones in Christ, not solid food, for you were not yet ready for it. Nor are you now ready for it.'[35] Now, it does not seem to me that these words should be taken as the Jews took them. I will set beside it another passage from Scripture: 'I will bring you forth to a good land that flows with milk and honey.'[36] (35) A considerable difficulty arises from the figure used in these passages; what do they mean to convey? If the childhood implied by the reference to milk is only the beginning of faith in Christ, and is minimized as puerile and imperfect, then how can the repose enjoyed by the perfect and the enlightened, implied by the expression 'strong meat,' be spoken of in any favorable way as the milk of children? Can it not be that the particle 'as,' which shows that a metaphor is being used, really indicates some such thing as this (in fact, do we not have to read the whole sentence in this way?): 'I have fed you milk in Christ,' and then, after a short pause, adding 'as little ones'? If we break up the reading in this way, we shall convey this meaning: 'I have instructed you in Christ, who is the simple and true and real spiritual nourishment.' That is what life-giving milk really is by nature, flowing from breasts of tender love. Therefore, understand the whole passage in this way: 'Just as nurses nourish new-born children with milk, so also I have nourished you with Christ the Word who is milk, feeding you, bit by bit, a spiritual nourishment.'

---

35 1 Cor. 3.2.
36 Exod. 3.8,17.

(36) Therefore, milk is perfection because it is the perfect food, and leads those who are without rest to perfection. So it is that even for their place of rest this same milk, with honey, is promised them. With reason, then, is milk promised the just in the other passage, that the Word may be revealed unmistakably as both Alpha and Omega, the beginning and the end:[37] the Word, symbolized by milk. Even Homer unwittingly foreshadowed some such thing when he called the just among men 'milk-fed.'[38]

We can also interpret the Scripture in another sense: 'And I, brethren, could not speak to you as to spiritual men, but only as carnal, as to little ones in Christ.'[39] So, it is possible to consider those who are just recently instructed in the faith and are still little ones in Christ as carnal, for he calls those who have already believed by the Holy Spirit, spiritual, and those newly taught and not yet purified, carnal. He speaks of these last as carnal with good reason, for, like the pagans, they still 'mind the things of the flesh.'[40] 'For since there are jealousy and strife among you, are you not carnal and walking as mere men?'[41] For the same reason he says: 'I gave you milk to drink': I have poured out upon you knowledge in instruction as nourishment for life everlasting. Even the word 'drink' is a figurative sign for perfection, since it is only the completely mature who are said to drink, while infants suck.

The Lord says: 'My blood is true drink.'[42] Do not, then, the words 'I gave you milk to drink' signify perfect happiness in the Word who is milk, that is, knowledge of the truth?

---
37 Apoc. 1.8; 21.6.
38 *Iliad* 13.6.
39 1 Cor. 3.1.
40 Rom. 8.5.
41 1 Cor. 3.3.
42 John 6.57.

The rest of the passage, 'not solid food, for you were not yet ready for it,' can signify the full revelation, face to face, in the world to come, likened to solid food. 'We see now through a mirror,' the same Apostle says, 'but then, face to face.'[43] That is why he adds to the first sentence: 'but you are not yet ready for it, for you are still carnal.' He means that you think, love, desire, seek, are angry and envious over the things of the flesh. It is not only that we are still in the flesh, as some have thought. For then, in the flesh, possessing an appearance like the angels', we shall see face to face what we have been promised. (37) But if, after our departure from this life, the promise really is that 'which eye has not seen, nor has it entered into the mind of man,'[44] how can we be said to see, if the meaning is not that we contemplate it in spirit, but that we receive in instruction 'what ear has never heard,' save only he who was rapt to the third heaven,[45] and even he was bidden to hold his peace?

But, if it is human wisdom which is the crowning boast of knowledge, as we are now to consider, listen to the command laid down in the Scripture: 'Let not the wise man boast in his wisdom, and let not the strong man boast in his strength.'[46] We, however, are they who are 'taught of God,'[47] and who boast in the name of Christ. Is there any reason, then, that we should not understand the Apostle to be referring to this when he speaks of the 'milk of little ones'? Whether we are the shepherds who rule the churches in imitation of the Good Shepherd,[48] or the sheep, should we not understand

---

43 1 Cor. 13.12.
44 1 Cor. 2.9.
45 2 Cor. 12.1-4.
46 Jer. 9.23; cf. 1 Cor. 1.31; 2 Cor. 10.17.
47 1 Thess. 4.9.
48 John 10.11,14. A. de la Barre sees in this passage an indication that Clement had received priestly orders ('Clément d'Alexandrie,' *Dictionnaire de Théologie Catholique* III col. 137).

that in speaking of the Lord as the milk of the flock, he is merely safeguarding the unity of his thought by a metaphor? Certainly, the passage, 'I gave you milk to drink, not solid food, for you were not yet ready for it,' can be adapted to this sense, too, if we only take 'solid food' as substantially the same thing as milk, not something superior to it. Either way, it is the same Word, whether light and mild as milk or become firm and solid as food.

(38) Still, taking it in this sense, we can also consider preaching as milk, poured out far and wide, and faith as food, made solid by instruction as the foundation. Faith is more substantial, in fact, than hearing, and is assimilated into the very soul and is, therefore, likened to solid food. The Lord presents the same foods elsewhere as symbols of another sort, when He says in the Gospel according to John: 'Do you eat My flesh and drink My blood.'[49] Here He uses food and drink as a striking figure for faith and for the promise. Through these, the Church, made up of many members, as man is, takes her nourishment and grows; she is welded together and formed into a unit[50] out of both body, which is faith, and soul, which is hope; just as the Lord, out of flesh and blood. Hope, indeed, which holds faith together as its soul, is the blood of faith. Once hope is extinguished, then the life-principle of faith expires, as when blood is drawn from the veins.

(39) If there are any contentious objectors who think to rise to a higher knowledge, and insist that milk means primary instructions in the sense of primary food, and that meat means spiritual knowledge, let them understand this: when they claim that solid food, meat, is the Body and Blood of Jesus,

---
49 John 6.55.
50 Cf. Eph. 2.21; 4.16.

they are being carried away by their boastful wisdom, contrary to the simple truth. For blood is the first substance produced in a man; some go so far as to call it the very substance of the soul. It is blood which is changed by the heat of the body once the mother has conceived, and in a maternal response develops and matures, for the well-being of the child. Blood is more liquid than flesh—in fact, it is a sort of liquid flesh—yet milk is more nourishing than blood and more finely broken down. At any rate, whether it is a question of the blood supplied to the embryo, flowing directly through the umbilical cord from the mother, or of the menstrual flow which by the command of the All-nourishing God, Author of life, is prevented from following its normal course and made to course to the already swelling breasts by a process of physical diffusion, and there, changed by the heat of the spirit, is provided the infant as his eagerly desired nourishment, in either case, what is changing is blood.

Of all the organs of the body, the breasts are the most sensitive to the condition of the womb. After childbirth, when the vein through which the blood was carried to the embryo has been cut off, then, with the passage obstructed, the blood is forced up into the breasts. As the blood accumulates, the breasts begin to distend and the blood begins to turn into milk, like its change in an infected wound into pus. Then, either the blood is drawn out into the natural pores of the breasts from the veins located there and dilated by the natural effects of pregnancy, or, mixed with air absorbed from the lungs near by, it becomes white as it is cast off, and though remaining blood in substance, turns into something different, much like foam spumed off from the sea which 'belches forth foam'[51] when mixed with air, as the poets tell us. Regardless of

---
51 *Iliad* 4.426.

CHRIST THE EDUCATOR 39

which explanation is true, milk retains its underlying substance of blood. (40) It is like a river which is churned into froth as it rushes along, swallowing air and letting out its roar, or like saliva in our mouth which turns white from contact with air. Is it unreasonable, then, to say that blood, united with air, is transformed into the lightest and whitest of all substances? It suffers change in its qualities, but not in its substance. There can be no doubt that we can find nothing more nourishing, more palatable, or whiter than milk. But heavenly food is similar to milk in every way: by its nature it is palatable through grace; nourishing, for it is life; and dazzling white, for it is the light of Christ. Therefore, it is more than evident that the Blood of Christ is milk.

(41) Thus is milk supplied to the infant, and it derives its purpose from its function in childbirth. The breasts which up to then had been pointing out, straight toward the husband, now begin to incline in the direction of the child, indicating that the nourishment produced by nature to sustain health is easy to obtain. The breasts, unlike springs, are not always full of milk ready to be drawn off, but manufacture milk by changing the nourishment stored up in them and then they become dry. There is a spiritual nourishment corresponding to this [physical] food, a food satisfying the needs of the re-created, reborn child; it also is prepared by God, the Nourisher and Father not only of those who are born, but also of those who are born again. This food is of the same kind as the manna which He made to rain down from heaven upon the ancient Hebrews, the celestial food of angels. In fact, even to this day, nurses still call the first flow of milk by the name manna,[52] but, even though women continue

---

52 This Greek noun, however, has apparently no etymological connection with the Hebrew word.

to give a flow of milk after they have conceived and given birth, it was not the breasts of women that were blessed by the Lord,⁵³ the fruit of a Virgin, or named as the true nourishment. No, because now that the loving and kind Father has rained down the Word, it is He Himself who has become the spiritual nourishment of the saints.

(42) O mystic wonder! The Father of all is one, the Word who belongs to all is one, the Holy Spirit is one and the same for all. And one alone, too, is the virgin Mother. I like to call her the Church. She alone, although a mother, had no milk because she alone never became a wife. She is at once virgin and mother: as virgin, undefiled; as mother, full of love. Calling her children about her, she nourishes them with milk that is holy: the Infant Word. That is why she has no milk,⁵⁴ because this Son of hers, beautiful and all hers, the Body of Christ, is milk. The new people she fosters on the Word,⁵⁵ for He Himself begot them in throes of His flesh and wrapped them in the swaddling clothes of His precious blood. What a holy begetting! What holy swaddling clothes! The Word is everything to His little ones, both father and mother, educator and nurse. 'Eat My flesh,' He says, 'and drink My blood.'⁵⁶ He is Himself the nourishment that He gives. He delivers up His own flesh and pours out His own blood. There is nothing lacking His children, that they may grow. (43) What a mysterious paradox! He bids us put off the former mortality of the flesh and, with it, the former nourishment, and receive instead this other new life of Christ, to find place in ourselves for Him as far as we can, and to

---

53 Cf. Luke 11.27,28.
54 The text is defective here.
55 The reading is obscure here. Stählin's text differs from that of Schwartz, but both are very difficult.
56 John 6.55.

enshrine the Saviour in our hearts that we may be rid of the passions of the flesh.

Yet, possibly you do not relish this turn of thought, but prefer to be more down to earth. Then listen to this interpretation: the flesh is a figure of speech for the Holy Spirit, for it is He, in fact, who created the flesh; the blood means the Word, for He has been poured forth as precious blood to give us life; the union of the two is the Lord, nourishment of little ones: the Lord, both Spirit and Word. Our nourishment, that is, the Lord Jesus, the Word of God, is Spirit become flesh, flesh from heaven made holy. This is our nourishment, the milk flowing from the Father by which alone we little ones are fed. I mean that He, the 'well-beloved,'[57] the Word, our provider, has saved mankind by shedding His blood for us. Therefore, we fly trustfully to the 'care-banishing breast'[58] of God the Father; the breast that is the Word, who is the only one who can truly bestow on us the milk of love. (44) Only those who nurse at the breast are blessed. Peter tells us: 'Lay aside therefore all malice and all deceit and all pretense, and envy and slander. Crave, as new-born babes, spiritual milk, that by it you may grow to salvation; if indeed, you have tasted that the Lord is sweet.'[59]

But, if we concede to our critics that 'solid food' is something more than milk, then we are creating confusion for ourselves and we prove that we have little understanding of nature. The truth is that, when the atmosphere becomes heavier during the winter, and, retaining the heat within the body, prevents it from passing off, then food is more readily digested by natural heat and changed into blood, which flows

---

57 Matt. 3.17.
58 *Iliad* 22.83.
59 1 Peter 2.1-3.

out through the veins. The veins, which had not been full before, now begin to pulse and to enlarge, and those who are nursing yield a greater abundance of milk precisely during this season. We have already shown that it is blood that changes into milk, but not in its substance, very much like light hair which, as we know, turns gray with the passing of the years. During the summer, however, the body is more porous, so that food is passed off much more quickly in perspiration; for that reason, since less food is retained, there is less blood and less milk. (45) But, if food that is retained turns into blood, and the blood into milk, then blood is the source of milk, just as semen is of man, and the grape-stone is of the vine.

We are nourished with milk, the Lord's own nourishment, as soon as we leave our mother's womb; and as soon as we are born anew we are favored with the good tidings of hope of rest, that heavenly Jerusalem in which, as it is written, 'milk and honey rain down.' In this material figure,[60] we are given a pledge of the food of holiness, for, though solid food must be put away sooner or later, as the Apostle says, the nourishment that we derive from milk leads us directly to heaven, since it educates us to be citizens of heaven and companions of the angels. If the Word is an overflowing fountain of life,[61] and is also called a river of oil,[62] then certainly Paul can use a similar figure of speech and call Him 'milk,' adding: 'I gave you to drink.' We do drink the Word, nourishment of truth. As we know, drink is called liquid food, for the same thing can possess the qualities of both solid food and of drink if we consider it from different

---

60 Cf. Exod. 3.8,17. Echle sees in this passage a reference to the milk and honey that was given to the newly baptised (*op. cit.* 88-89).
61 Cf. Apoc. 21.6.
62 Cf. Deut. 32.13.

aspects, as cheese which may be considered either a solid made from milk, or milk become solid. Now, I am not interested in splitting hairs; I am only trying to show that the one substance can serve as both kinds of nourishment. For instance, infants at the breast find in milk alone all the food and drink they need.

The Lord said: 'I have a food to eat of which you do not know. My food is to do the will of Him who sent Me.'[63] Here is another food, a figure very similar to that of milk: it is the will of God. (46) And He called the accomplishment of His sufferings a 'chalice,'[64] in the sense that He had to drain it, by Himself, to the dregs. Just as the fulfillment of His Father's will was food for Christ, so, for us little ones who draw milk from the breast, that is, the Word of Heaven, it is Christ Himself who is our food. Again, the Greek word for 'seeking' also means 'craving,'[65] implying that to little ones who seek the Word the craved-for milk is given from the Father's breasts of love for man.

There was another time that the Word proclaimed Himself Bread from heaven: 'Moses did not give you the bread from heaven,' He said, 'but My Father gives you the true bread from heaven. For the bread of God is that which comes down from heaven and gives life to the world. And the bread which I will give is My flesh for the life of the world.'[66] In this passage, we must read a mystic meaning for bread. He says that He is flesh, and very likely means flesh that has risen after having passed through the fire,[67] as wheat

---

63 John 4.32,34.
64 Matt. 20.22; 26.39.
65 *Másteusai*, which Clement suggests here as etymologically related to the word for 'breast,' *mastós*.
66 John 6.32,33,52.
67 This passage becomes clearer when we note Clement's play on words: fire is *pûr*, while wheat is *purós*.

destined to become bread rises from the destruction of the seed, and flesh which yet has gathered all the churches together in gladness of heart through fire, as the wheat is gathered together and baked by fire to become bread. But we will treat this more clearly and in greater detail in a treatise *On the Resurrection*.[68]

(47) 'And the bread which I will give you,' the Lord said, 'is My flesh.'[69] But flesh is nourished by blood, and blood is spoken of under the figure of wine. Therefore, we must understand Him to mean that just as bread dipped in a mixture of water and wine absorbs the wine and leaves the water, so the flesh of the Lord, Bread of heaven, absorbs the blood, that is, it raises to immortality those among men who are heavenly minded, and leaves for corruption only the desires of the flesh.

In all these various ways and figures of speech is the Word spoken of: solid food, flesh, nourishment, bread, blood and milk. The Lord is all these things for the refreshment of us who believe in Him. Let no one think it strange, then, that we speak of the blood of the Lord also under the figure of milk. Is it not named wine, metaphorically? 'He washes his garment in wine,' Scripture says, 'and his robe in the blood of the grape.'[70] That means He will attire the body of the Word with His own blood, just as He will nurture those who hunger for the Word with His own Spirit.

The blood of just Abel, too, pleading before the throne of God,[71] gives evidence that the Word is blood, because blood, of itself, could never plead, unless it were considered a word.

---

68 If Clement ever wrote such a work, it is not extant.
69 John 6.52.
70 Gen. 49.11.
71 Cf. Gen. 4.10; Heb. 11.4.

The man of ancient times is, indeed, a type of the new just Man, and the blood that once made its plea, in reality, was pleading as a symbol of the new Blood. The blood, as the Word, sent up its cry, foreshadowing that the Word would suffer.

(48) This flesh and the blood it contains, fostering one another mutually, are fed and made to increase by milk. In fact, the development of a fetus after it has been conceived comes about by contact with the pure blood left from the monthly purification; just as the beestings of the cow cause its milk to coagulate, so, by congealing the blood, the power contained in the fetus accomplishes the substance of that development. The union of the two thrives, but an excess of either is likely to end in barrenness. Certainly, a seed planted in the ground will be laid bare by a heavy downpour of rain, while, even during a drought when moisture dries up, a viscous-like juice holds the seed together and makes it germinate. There are those who hold that the animal semen is substantially foam of its blood, violently agitated in the act of intercourse by the natural heat of the male, and in its agitation, turned into foam and then deposited in the spermatic ducts. According to Diogenes Apolloniates, this is the derivation of the Greek word for sexual pleasure, *aphrodísia*.[72]

(49) From all these arguments it becomes clear that blood is the fundamental matter of the human body. Recall that the first substance in the womb is a milk-like liquid that gathers there and turns into blood and then into flesh and finally, when the heat of the spirit which forms the embryo solidifies this composite, develops into a living being. Even

---

72 Clement falsely believed that *aphrodísia* is derived from *aphrós* ('foam').

after birth, the infant is still nurtured on the same blood, for the flow of milk possesses the nature of blood.

Milk is the spring that gives nourishment. By its presence, a woman is known to have given birth and become a mother, and therefore, it bestows on her a certain lovableness that arouses reverence. That is the reason the Holy Spirit mystically puts these words of the Apostle on the lips of the Lord: 'I have given you milk to drink.' For, if we have been reborn to become members of Christ, then He who gives us this new birth nurtures us with milk flowing from Himself, the Word.[73] Anyone who begets naturally provides sustenance for him whom he has begotten; with man, his sustenance, as his rebirth, must needs be spiritual. Doubtless, then, we belong entirely to Christ as His property from every point of view: by reason of relationship, because His blood has redeemed us; by our resemblance to Him, through the upbringing we receive from the Word, and in immortality, because of the guidance He imparts. 'Raising children, for mortals, is often the cause of greater affection than begetting them.'[74] So, too, the blood and the milk of the Lord are a symbol of His sufferings and of His teachings. (50) Accordingly, each of us little ones may make our boast in the Lord, crying out: 'From out a noble father and noble blood, I make my claim to be.'[75]

Surely, it is clear by now that milk is developed from blood by some sort of change. But that is not to say that we cannot learn something more, from sheep-folds and ox-stalls. During the time of year called spring, when the climate has a higher degree of humidity and when the grass and the

---
[73] A veiled reference, again, to the rite of baptism.
[74] Biotus, *Fragment* 1, TGF 825.
[75] *Iliad* 14.113.

CHRIST THE EDUCATOR   47

meadows become green and filled with the sap of life, then the sheep and the oxen right away take on a greater abundance of blood, as the protuberance of their veins prove, and so, because of more blood, they yield milk in more copious supply. But in summertime, their blood is warmed and dried up by the scorching heat, and so does not form into milk, so that these animals yield much less milk.

Milk has a real physical relationship with water, just as the spiritual water of cleansing has with spiritual nourishment, as we know. This may be proved by the fact that one who swallows a bit of cold water, along with the milk we are talking about, immediately feels the good effects; actually, the water keeps milk from turning sour, not because it reacts on it adversely, but because it is so much akin to what is being consumed with it. In fact, milk has the same intimate relationship with water that Christ has with the waters of baptism. For, milk is the only liquid that absorbs water into itself, and is used as a cathartic when so mixed, just as baptism purifies us from sin.

(51) On the other hand, milk is mixed with honey, too, with good results, again as a cathartic that is also a sweet-tasting food. In the same way, the Word, penetrated with love for man, heals sicknesses and purifies from sin. The expression, 'the word flows sweeter than honey,'[76] is said, I believe, of the Word who is also honey, for the inspired word so often praises Him 'above honey and the honeycomb.'[77]

Again, we find that milk is mixed with sweet wine. Such a mixture is very beneficial, just as suffering tempers men to gain immortality. The reason is that milk is curdled by wine and separated into its component parts, so that the whey can

---

76 *Iliad* 1.249.
77 Cf. Ps. 18.11; 118.103.

then be drawn off as a less essential part of the milk. In the same way, the spiritual intermingling of faith with the passions of men curdles their carnal lusts and raises them to eternity, making them divine with the qualities of divinity.

Then there are many people who use the oily part of milk, the part called butter, for light. This is an unmistakable analogy for the rich oil of the Word who is the only one who can give to little ones both nourishment and growth and light. (52) And so, Scripture says of the Lord: 'He fed them with the fruits of the fields, and He suckled them with honey from rocks and oil from out the hardest rocks, butter of the herd and milk of the sheep, with the fat of lambs,'[78] and He gave them, too, all the other things it mentions. The Prophet, too, used the same words when he referred to the birth of the Child: 'And he will eat butter and honey.'[79]

It is a matter for wonder to me that some people dare to call themselves perfect and Gnostics, laying claim in their inflated pride to a loftier state than the Apostle. Paul himself made only this claim: 'Not that I have already obtained this, or already been made perfect, but I press on hoping that I may lay hold of that for which Christ Jesus has laid hold of me. But one thing I do: forgetting what is behind, I strain forward to what is before, I press on toward the goal, to the prize of God's heavenly call in Christ Jesus.'[80] He considers himself perfect in the sense that he has changed his old way of life and follows a better one, but not in the sense that he is perfect in knowledge. He only desires what is perfect. That is why he adds: 'Let us then, as many as are perfect, be of this mind,'[81] meaning simply that perfection is

---
78 Cf. Deut. 32.13,14.
79 Isa. 7.15.
80 Phil. 3.12-14.
81 Phil. 3.15.

turning away from sin and being reborn, after we have forgotten the sins that are behind, to faith in the only Perfect One.

Chapter 7

(53) We have now shown that not only does Scripture call all of us children, but also it figuratively calls us who follow Christ, little ones, and that the only perfect being is the Father of all (in fact, the Son is in Him, and the Father is in the Son). If we would follow right order, we should now speak of the Educator of little ones and explain who He is.

He is called Jesus. On occasion, He speaks of Himself as a Shepherd, as when He says: 'I am the Good Shepherd.'[1] In keeping with this metaphor of shepherds leading their sheep, He leads His children, the Shepherd with the care of His little ones. The little ones, in their simplicity, are given the figurative name of sheep; 'And there shall be one sheep-fold,' He says, 'and one Shepherd.'[2]

Therefore, the Word who leads us His children to salvation is unquestionably an Educator of little ones. In fact, through Osee, the Word says plainly of Himself: 'I am your Educator.'[3] The material He educates us in is fear of God, for this fear instructs us in the service of God, educates to the knowledge of truth, and guides by a path leading straight up to heaven.

(54) Education is a word used in many different senses. There is education in the sense of the one who is being led and instructed; there is that of the one who leads and gives instruction; and thirdly, there is education in the sense of

---

1 John 10.11,14.
2 John 10.16.
3 Osee 5.2. The word used is *paideutés*.

the guidance itself; and finally, the things that are taught, such as precepts. The education that God gives is the imparting of the truth that will guide us correctly to the contemplation of God, and a description of holy deeds that endure forever. Just as the general directs a line of battle with the safety of his soldiers in mind, and as the helmsman pilots his ship conscious of his responsibility for the lives of his passengers, so the Educator, in his concern for us, leads His children along a way of life that ensures salvation. In brief, all that we could reasonably ask God to do for us is within the reach of those who trust in the Educator of little ones. Again, just as the helmsman does not always sail with the wind, but sometimes when there is a squall, sets his prow head on against it, so, too, the Educator never falls in with the winds sweeping through this world, nor does He suffer His children to be driven like a ship into a wild and unregulated course of life. Rather, assisted only by the favorable breeze of the Spirit of truth, He holds steadfastly to the rudder, that is, the hearing of His children, until He brings them safely to anchor in the port of heaven.

The habits that men speak of as hereditary, for the most part pass away, but the education God gives is a possession that endures forever. (55) It is related how Phenix was the pedagogue of Achilles; Adrastrus, of the sons of Croesus; Leonides, of Alexander; and Nausithoon, of Philip. Yet one of them, Phenix, was mad with lust; another, Adrastrus, was a fugitive; Leonides did not rid his Macedonian pupil of his vanity, and Nausithoon did not cure the Pellean of his drunkenness. Again, the Thracian Zoporus was unable to restrain Alcibiades from immorality, and, besides, he was a bought slave. The pedagogue of the children of Themistocles, Sicinnos, was a spineless menial. The story goes that he used to dance and invented the dance step called the Sicinnis. We must not forget, either, the so-called royal pedagogues of the Persian court, four in number, whom the Persian kings chose from all the Persians according to merit and set over their children; but the children learned only how to use the bow and arrow, and once they come of age begin to have intercourse with sister and mother, with married women and others without number, like wild boars well-practised in sexual indulgence.

But our Educator is the holy God, Jesus, the Word guiding all mankind. God Himself, in His love for men, is our Educator. (56) The Holy Spirit says about Him somewhere in a canticle: 'He founded the people in a desert land, in a drought of burning heat, in a place without water: He encircled him and taught him: and He kept him as the apple of His eye. As an eagle might shelter its brood, and yearn after its young, and having flown about, show them its wings and take them upon its shoulders. The Lord alone was their leader, and there was no strange god with them.'[4] As far as I can see, Scripture is undoubtedly presenting a picture of the Educator of children, and describing the guidance He imparts. When He speaks in His own person, He also confesses Himself to be the Educator: 'I am the Lord thy God, who brought thee out of the land of Egypt.'[5] But who has the authority to lead in or out? Is it not the Educator? It is He who 'appeared to Abraham and said to him: 'I am your God: be pleasing before Me.'[6] He fashioned Moses by a gradual process into a worthy child, truly as an educator would, commanding him: 'Be without blame. And I will establish My covenant between Me and your descendants.'[7] Here is a share, indeed, in friendship that is undying.

---
4 Deut. 32.10-12 (Septuagint).
5 Exod. 20.2. For this more literal sense of 'Educator,' cf. Introd.
6 Cf. Gen. 17.1,2.
7 Gen. 17.7.

He manifests Himself plainly as the Educator of Jacob, too. For example, He said to him: 'I will be with you and protect you wherever you go. I will bring you back to this land; indeed I will not forsake you till I fulfill My promise'[8] to you. He is also said to have wrestled with him: 'Jacob remained behind, all alone. Someone wrestled with him,' that is, the Educator, 'until the break of dawn.'[9] (57) This is the Man who leads and who carries, He who wrestled with Jacob and anointed him for his toil as an athlete. But because the Word was not only the wrestling Master of Jacob, but also the Educator of all mankind, when 'Jacob asked,' as Scripture says, 'What is your name? He answered: Why do you ask My name?'[10] He was saving His new name for His new people, the little ones. The Lord God still remained without a name, since He had not yet become man. However, 'Jacob named the place Phanuel, saying: I have seen a heavenly being face to face, yet my life has been saved.'[11] The face of God is the Word, for God is revealed by Him and made known. Jacob also received the name Israel from the time that he had seen the Lord.[12] It was God the Word, the Educator, who said to him on another occasion: 'Do not fear to go down to Egypt.'[13] See how the Educator follows a just man, anoints the athlete, and teaches him how to overcome his adversary.

It was He who taught Moses also to act the part of educator. For the Lord said: 'He that hath sinned against Me, him will I strike out of My book: but go there, and lead the

---
8 Gen. 28.15.
9 Gen. 32.25.
10 Gen. 32.30.
11 Gen. 32.31.
12 Gen. 32.29.
13 Gen. 46.3.

people whither I have told thee.'¹⁴ (58) In this passage, He teaches him the art of educating. And well He might, for it was through Moses, in fact, that the Lord of the ancient people was the Educator of His children. It is in His own person, however, face to face, that He is the guide of the new people.

He said to Moses: 'Behold, My angel shall go before thee,' to establish the Gospel and the authority of the Word to guide; and then, adhering to His own divine decree, He adds: 'On the day I shall visit, I shall bring down on them their sin,'[15] that is, on the day I shall sit as Judge, I shall mete out the punishments due to sin. He passes sentence on those who disobey Him, both as Educator and as Judge; the Word, with all His love for man, does not pass over their sin in silence, but punishes that they may repent. 'The Lord, indeed, desires the conversion of the sinner more than his death.'[16] Let us little ones, then, attending to the story of the sins of others, refrain from like offenses, from fear of the threat of suffering like punishment. What sin did they commit? 'In their fury, they slew men, and in their willfulness, they hamstrung oxen. Cursed be their fury.'[17]

(59) Who could teach with greater love for men than He? In other times, the older people[18] had an old Covenant: as law, it guided them through fear; as word, it was a messenger. But the new and young people have received a new and young Covenant: the Word has become flesh, fear has been turned into love, and the mystic messenger of old has

---
14 Exod. 32.33.
15 Exod. 32.34 (Septuagint).
16 Cf. Ezech. 18.23; 33.15.
17 Gen. 49.6,7 (Septuagint).
18 The Scholion sees in this passage a reference to the elder son Ruben, disinherited for his sin. Cf. Gen. 49.3,4.

been born, Jesus. Of old, this same Educator proclaimed: 'Thou shalt fear the Lord, thy God.'[19] But to us He appeals: 'Thou shalt love the Lord thy God.'[20] And so He gives command: 'Cease from thy deeds,' that is, your old sins, 'and learn to do well; turn away from evil and do good. Thou hast loved justice and hated iniquity.'[21] This is My new Covenant, written with the letters of the old.

But the newness of the Word does not at all lessen respect due Him. The Lord says through Jeremias: 'Say not, I am a child. Before I formed thee in the bowel of thy mother, I knew thee: and before thou camest forth out of the womb, I sanctified thee.'[22] In this passage, possibly the inspired Word refers to us who before the foundation of the world have been destined by God for the faith, and now, by the will of God just being fulfilled, are little ones, in that we have become newborn into the calling and into salvation. (60) For that reason, Scripture adds these words: 'I have made thee a prophet unto the nations,'[23] meaning that he must needs begin to prophesy and that the name 'young' ought not to seem a reproach to those who are called little ones.

The Law is the old gift bestowed by the Word through Moses. So Scripture says: 'The law has been given through Moses' (not by Moses, but by the Word through Moses His servant; and at that, given only for a time), 'but everlasting grace and truth was through Jesus Christ.'[24] Notice the wording of Scripture: in speaking of the Law, it says it was only given, but the truth, being the gift of the Father, is the

---

19 Deut. 6.2.
20 Matt. 22.37.
21 Cf. Isa. 1.16-17; Ps. 33.15.
22 Jer. 1.7.
23 Jer. 1.5.
24 John 1.17.

eternal achievement of the Word, and so is no longer said to be given, but rather 'was, through Jesus Christ, without whom was made nothing.'[25]

For his part, Moses made way for the perfect Educator, the Word, prophesying both His name and His method of educating, and placed Him in charge of the people with the command to obey Him. He said: 'God will raise up to thee a prophet of thy brethren like unto me,'[26] meaning Jesus, son of Naim, but implying Jesus, the Son of God. That name, Jesus, already predicted in the law, described the Lord, for Moses, taking thought for the best interests of the people, said: 'Him thou shalt hear: and he that will not hear this prophet, him He threatens.'[27] (61) The name that He has tells us by divine inspiration that the Educator will save. It is for this reason that the Scripture associates Him with a rod that suggests correction, government and sovereignty. Scripture seems to be suggesting that those whom the Word does not heal through persuasion He will heal with threats; and those whom threats do not heal the rod will; and those whom the rod does not heal fire will consume. 'And there shall come forth,' it is said, 'a rod out of the root of Jesse.'[28]

Consider the carefulness and the wisdom and the power of this Educator: 'He shall not judge according to appearance, nor reprove according to gossip, but He shall judge judgment with humility, and shall reprove the sinners of the earth.'[29] And through the lips of David, He says: 'The Lord chastising has chastised me, but He hath not delivered me over to death.'[30] Indeed, the very act of being chastised, and

---
25 John 1.3.
26 Deut. 18.15.
27 Cf. Deut. 18.15,19.
28 Isa. 11.1.
29 Isa. 11.3.
30 Ps. 117.18.

being educated by the Lord as a child, means deliverance from death. Again, He says through the same Psalmist: 'Thou shalt rule them with a rod of iron.'[31] Similarly, the Apostle exclaimed when he was aroused by the Corinthians: 'What is your wish? Shall I come to you with a rod, or in love and in the spirit of meekness?'[32] By another Psalmist, the Lord says again: 'The Lord will send forth the rod of power out of Sion.'[33] This 'rod and staff of Thine,' bespeaking education, 'they have comforted me,'[34] another says.

Such, then, is the authority wielded by the Educator of children, awe-inspiring, consoling, leading us to salvation.

Chapter 8

(62) Thereupon certain persons[1] have arisen denying that the Lord is good, because of the rod and threats and the fear that He resorts to. First of all, it seems to me that such an attitude turns deaf ear to the Scripture which says somewhere: 'And he that feareth God will turn to his own heart.'[2] It is to forget, too, the supreme proof He has given of His love for men, in that He has become man on our account. Surely, the words the Prophet uses in his prayer to God are very appropriate: 'Remember us, that we are dust,'[3] that is, sympathize with us because by Thy own experience Thou hast made trial of the weakness of our flesh. The Lord our

---

31 Ps. 2.9.
32 1 Cor. 4.21.
33 Ps. 109.2 (Septuagint).
34 Ps. 22.4.

---

1 The Marcionites.
2 Eccli. 21.7.
3 Ps. 102.14.

Educator is completely good and blameless, for out of the excess of His love for man He has Himself experienced the sufferings which are common to every man by his nature.

There is nothing that the Lord hates.[4] Surely, He does not hate a thing and still at the same time will it to exist; nor does He will something not to exist and yet cause what He does not will to exist to come into being; and, most surely, it does not happen that He wills a thing not to be and that nevertheless it is. Remember that if the Word hates anything, His will is that it not exist: there is nothing in existence for which God is not the cause. It must be, then, that there is nothing that God hates, nothing that the Word hates. Both are one, and both are God, because Scripture says: 'In the beginning was the Word, and the Word was in God, and the Word was God.'[5] But if He does not hate any of the things He has made, then it follows that He loves them. (63) But He loves man with a great love above all others, since man is the living being that is the noblest of those He has made, and the one dearly beloved of God. Therefore, God loves man; therefore, the Word loves man.

But he who loves desires to benefit the object of his love. Now, there can be no doubt that the one who benefits must be better than the one who does not; nothing is better than goodness; therefore, goodness must render benefit. But, God is admitted to be good; therefore, God confers benefits. But goodness, as goodness, does nothing else but confer benefits; therefore, God is beneficent to all things. If God does not do good to man in any way, then, naturally, He is not interested in him; and if He is not interested in man, then He does not take care of him. But one who deliberately does good is better

---
4 Cf. Wisd. 11.25.
5 Cf. John. 1.1. For the change in the text, cf. E. L. Titus, *op. cit.* 28.

than one who deliberately neglects doing so. But, nothing is better than God. Yet, doing good to man deliberately is simply taking care of him; therefore, God must be interested in man and take care of him. He manifests this care, in deed, by educating him by His Word, who shares by nature in His love for man.

Being good does not deserve the name of good simply because a person possesses virtue. Justice, for example, is spoken of as good, not because it possesses virtue (for it is itself a virtue), but because it is good in itself and of itself. (64) The useful is called good, too, but in another way, because it gives, not pleasure, but service. Actually, justice is all these things: it is good because it is a virtue, because it is something desirable in itself, and because it does more than give pleasure. For, it does not judge with an eye to please, but is a disposition to distribute to each according to his merit, and renders service because it is also useful. As a consequence, justice is typified by all the different things which goodness embraces, both of them sharing the same things in the same way. But, equals that are characterized by equals are similar to each other; therefore, justice must be good.

But, if the Lord loves man and is good, some object, then how is it that He becomes angry and inflicts punishments? We want to be as brief as possible in our reply, for a concise style gains much in the correct training of children when it restricts itself to the help needed.

Many passions are healed by punishment and by the imposition of severe commands and, more particularly, by the teaching of certain principles. Reproof is like surgery performed on the passions of the soul; the passions are like a disease of truth, which need to be removed by the surgeon's knife. (65) Rebuke is like a physic, dissolving the hardness of passion and purging the lusts, the impurities of life; besides, it levels the swelling of pride and restores man to normalcy and health. Then there is admonition which is like the diet given one who is sick, counseling what should be taken and forbidding what should not. All these things tend to salvation and eternal good health.

When a general inflicts upon evil-doers pecuniary fines and confinement in chains affecting the body as well, and complete disgrace, and even when he exacts the death penalty, it is for a good purpose: he is using his authority as general to serve warning to his subjects. Similarly, when that mighty General of ours, the Word, Guide of the whole world, serves notice on those who disobey the law to restrain the passions of their heart, it is to release them from error and from slavery and captivity to the enemy, and to guide them in peace to a holy concord of life.

(66) Just as exhortation and encouragement are types of discourse allied to the type called advice, so the type called encomium is allied to that of reproach and blame. This last is the art of rebuke; it indicates, not hatred, but good will. Both he who is friendly and he who is not express disapproval: the one who is hostile does so out of contempt; the friend, in good will. Therefore, it is not from hatred that the Lord reproves men, for instead of destroying him because of his personal faults, He has suffered for us. Because He is the good Educator, He wisely assumes the task of correcting by means of reproach, as though to arouse by the whip of sharp words minds become sluggish, and then He attempts to encourage the same men. Those whom praise does not stimulate blame arouses; and those whom blame does not stir up to seek salvation, as if they were already dead, denunciation raises to the light of truth. 'The stripes and instruction of wisdom are

never out of time. He that teacheth a fool is like one that glueth a potsherd together,[6] Scripture remarks, seeking to make the earth attend and to arouse those without hope to understand. So it is that it dramatically adds: 'like one that waketh out of a deep sleep,' which of all things is most like death.

The Lord, in fact, presented Himself in the same light very clearly when He described under an allegory the many different ways in which He benefits us, saying: 'I am the true Vine, and My Father is the Vine-dresser,' and then adding: 'Every branch in Me that bears no fruit He will take away; and every branch that bears fruit He will cleanse that it may bear more fruit.'[7] For, unless the vine's branches are pruned, it turns into a mere mass of branches; so, too, does man. The pruning-knife, the Word, cuts away excessive offshoots, and so restricts the efforts of man to bring forth fruit, not merely desires.

The punishments that are inflicted on those who sin aim at their salvation. The Word adapts Himself completely to the disposition of each, being strict with one, forgiving another. (67) In fact, He says very plainly, through Moses: 'Be of good heart, for God has come to prove you, that the dread of Him might be in you, that you may sin not.'[8] Similarly, Plato teaches beautifully: 'Now all who are punished, in reality suffer what is good. For they are benefitted by those who punish justly, in that their soul is improved.'[9] But if they who are corrected suffer what is good, even according to Plato, then, admittedly, justice is good. Even fear, indeed,

---
6 Eccli. 22.7.
7 John 15.1.
8 Exod. 20.20.
9 Gorg. 477A.

is beneficial, and has a good effect upon men, because 'the spirit fearing the Lord will live, for his hope is upon Him who saveth him.'[10]

This same Word is the Judge passing sentence, for Isaias says of Him: 'The Lord hath laid on Him the iniquity of us all,'[11] that is, to correct our iniquities and set them right. (68) For that reason, He alone is able to forgive our sins, He who has been appointed by the Father of all as our Educator, for He alone is able to separate obedience from disobedience.

It is clear that He who threatens desires to do nothing that will harm us, or to execute none of His threats. Yet, by giving us cause for fear, He takes away any inclination to sin, and at the same time reveals His love for men by delaying over and over, and repeatedly manifesting to them, what they will suffer if they continue in their sins, unlike the serpent that bites without delay. Therefore, God is good.

The Lord frequently turns to words before He acts. 'I will spend My arrows among them,' He says. 'They shall be consumed with famine, and by the bite of birds, and the bending of their back shall be incurable; I will send the teeth of beasts upon them, with the fury of creatures that trail upon the ground. Without, the sword shall destroy their children and there will be fear within the storehouse.'[12] Really, then, the Divinity is not angry, as some suppose, but when He makes so many threats He is only making an appeal and showing mankind the things that are to be accomplished. Such a procedure is surely good, for it instils fear to keep us away from sin. 'The fear of the Lord driveth out sin: for

10 Eccli. 34.14 (Septuagint).
11 Isa. 53.6.
12 Deut. 32.23-25 (Septuagint).

he that is without fear cannot be justified.'[13] The punishment that God imposes is due not to anger, but to justice, for the neglect of justice contributes nothing to our improvement.

(69) It is each one of us who makes the choice to be punished, for it is we who deliberately sin. 'The blame belongs to the one who makes the choice; God is blameless.'[14] 'But if our wickedness shows forth the justice of God, what shall we say? Is God unjust who inflicts punishment? By no means!'[15] For instance, He makes this threat: 'I shall whet My sword, and My hand will take hold of judgment, and I will render vengeance to My enemies, and will render vengeance to them that hate Me. I will make My arrows drunk with blood, and My sword shall devour flesh of the blood of the wounded.'[16] Obviously, then, unless a man were an enemy of the truth and hostile to the Word, he would not be indifferent to his own salvation, but would seek to escape the penalties for such hostility. 'The crown of wisdom,' says Wisdom, 'is the fear of the Lord.'[17]

Through the Prophet Amos, the Word explains His own conduct fully: 'I destroyed you,' He says, 'as God destroyed Sodom and Gomorrha, and you were as a fire-brand plucked out of the burning. Yet you returned not to Me, saith the Lord.'[18] (70) Notice how God seeks their conversion in loving kindness and, in the very words with which He makes His threats, sweetly reveals the love He has for men. 'I will hide My face from them,' He says, 'and I will show what will happen to them.'[19] There is peace and joy in the hearts of those

---

13 Eccli. 1.27,28.
14 Plato, *Repub.* X 617E.
15 Rom. 3.5,6.
16 Deut. 32.41.
17 Eccli. 1.22.
18 Amos 4.11.
19 Deut. 32.20.

upon whom the face of the Lord looks, but for those from whom He turns away there is an accumulation of evils.

He does not desire to look upon evil, because He is good. But, if He deliberately overlook it, then wickedness takes root, because of mankind's infidelity. 'See then,' Paul says, 'the goodness and the severity of God: His severity toward those who have fallen, but the goodness of God toward thee, if thou abidest in His goodness,'[20] that is, in faith in Christ. It is of the very nature of goodness that it arouse a hatred for what is evil. I can readily grant, then, that He punishes those who are faithless (punishment inflicted for the greater good and for the advantage of the one punished is a corrective of the one who resists), but I can never grant that He wishes to exact revenge. Revenge is returning evil for evil, imposed for the satisfaction only of the one taking vengeance, but He would never desire revenge who has taught us to pray for those who calumniate us.[21]

(71) Now, everyone admits that God is good, even if they do so reluctantly. That the same God is also just, I need no further argument than the words used by the Lord in the Gospel when He claimed that He was one [with the Father]: 'That all may be one, even as Thou, Father, in Me and I in Thee, that they also may be one in Us, that the world may believe that Thou hast sent Me. And the glory that Thou hast given Me, I have given to them, that they may be one, even as We are one: I in them, and Thou in Me; that they may be perfected in one.'[22] God is one, and He is more than one, beyond unity. The point is that the pronoun 'Thou,' with its vocative force, refers to God, He who alone is, that

---

20 Rom. 11.22.
21 Cf. Matt. 5.44; Luke 6.28.
22 John 17.21-23.

is, who was and who is and who will be, according to the three different time values that the one phrase 'He who is' connotes. In the same passage, the Lord goes on to say that this same God, the only one who fully is, is also just (that is, the same and only one Being): 'Father, I will that where I am, they also whom Thou hast given Me may be with Me; in order that they may behold My glory, which Thou hast given Me, because Thou hast loved Me before the creation of the world. Just Father, the world has not known Thee, but I have known Thee, and these have known that Thou hast sent Me. And I have made known to them Thy name, and will make it known.'[23]

This is He who 'visits the iniquity of the fathers upon the children of them that hate and shews mercy upon those that love.'[24] He who makes some to stand on His right hand, and others on His left,[25] if He is considered as the Father, who is good, is called that very thing which He alone is—good; but if He is thought of as being the Son, His Word, who is in the Father, then He is given the title, just, because of their relationship of love, one for the other, since justice is the term to describe equality of degree. 'He judgeth a man,' Scripture says, 'according to his works,'[26] for God makes known to us the countenance of the good scale of justice, Jesus, through whom we know God as by a perfectly balanced scale.

(72) Therefore, Wisdom expressly declares: 'Mercy and wrath are with Him.'[27] He alone is the Lord of both. 'He is mighty to forgive and to pour out indignation. According as

---
23 John 17.24-26.
24 Exod. 20.5.
25 Cf. Matt. 25.33.
26 Cf. Eccli. 16.13.
27 Eccli. 16.12.

His mercy is, so is His correction.'[28] The aim of both mercy and of correction is the salvation of the one being corrected. In fact, the Word Himself, on His part, declares that 'the God and Father of our Lord Jesus'[29] is good, because 'He is kind toward the ungrateful and the evil'; again, He says: 'Be merciful even as your Father is merciful.'[30] Besides, on one occasion, He explicitly states: 'No one is good but My Father in heaven,'[31] and, again: 'My Father makes His sun to shine upon all.'[32] It is easy to go on to show how He declares that His Father, who is good, is also the Creator, and it cannot be denied that the Creator is just. Another time, He did say: 'My Father sends His rain upon the just and the unjust.' He sends rain, because He is the Creator of the waters and of the clouds; and He sends them upon all, because He portions out an equal share of virtue justly; He is good, because He sends it upon the just and the unjust alike.

(73) We conclude unhesitatingly, then, that one and the same God is both of these things, because, as the Holy Spirit says in the Psalms: 'We shall see the heavens, the work of Thy hands,'[33] and 'He who founded the heavens, dwells in the heavens,'[34] and 'Heaven is Thy throne.'[35] The Lord also says in His prayer: 'Our Father, who art in heaven.'[36] The heavens belong to Him who founded the world. Yet, it is certainly undeniable that the Lord is the Son of the Creator; if all admit that the Creator is just, and that the Lord is

---
28 Eccli. 16.12,13.
29 2 Cor. 1.3.
30 Luke 6.35,36.
31 Matt. 19.17.
32 Matt. 5.45.
33 Ps. 8.4.
34 Ps. 2.4.
35 Ps. 10.4; 102.19.
36 Matt. 6.9.

the Son of the Creator, then the Lord is also the Son of the Just One. Paul says: 'But the justice of God has been made manifest independently of the Law,' and, to make us regard Him as God: 'the justice of God, through faith in Jesus Christ, upon whom all believe; for there is no distinction.' After a few lines, testifying to the truth, he adds: 'in the patience of God, to manifest that He Himself is just and makes just him who has faith in Jesus.'[37] Paul proves also that he considers justice good when he places these two virtues together in the same context, saying somewhere: 'So that the Law indeed is holy, and the commandments holy and just and good.'[38]

(74) Yet, 'No one is good except His Father';[39] He describes this same Father of His under many different qualities. That is the meaning of His words: 'No one knows the Father,'[40] that is, how He can be all these different things, until the Son came. It is more than clear, then, that the one only God of the whole world is truly good and just and the Creator, and the Son is in the Father, to whom be glory for ever and ever. Amen.

It is not inconsistent that the Word who saves should make use of reproof in His care for us. As a matter of fact, reproof is simply the antidote supplied by the divine love for man, because it awakens the blush of confusion and shame for sins committed. And if there is need for reproach and for harsh words, then there is also occasion to wound, not to death, but to its salvation, a soul grown callous; in such a way He inflicts a little pain, but spares it eternal death.

---

37 Rom. 3.21,22,26.
38 Rom. 7.12.
39 Cf. Matt. 19.17; Mark 10.18.
40 Matt. 11.27.

His wisdom is profound in His education of His children; His method of conducting them to salvation is manifold. He furnishes proofs for the good; He summons the elect to a more excellent life; and those who are bent on evil He restrains from their course and encourages to turn to a better life. Neither way of life lacks its testimony; in fact, the one supplies testimony to the other. Our gratefulness for the testimony is unbounded, especially when the motive of His wrath—if we can call His words of warning, wrath—is really love for man. It is God falling into a passion for the sake of man, for whom the Word of God also became man.

Chapter 9

(75) Truly, the Educator of mankind, the divine Word of ours, has devoted Himself with all His strength to save His little ones by all the means at the disposal of His wisdom: warning, blaming, rebuking, correcting, threatening, healing, promising, bestowing favors—in a word, 'binding as if with many bits'[1] the unreasonable impulses of human nature. In fact, the Lord acts toward us just as we do toward our children: 'Hast thou children? Chastise them,' Wisdom advises, 'and hast thou daughters? Have a care of their body and shew not thy countenance gay toward them.'[2] Yet we have a great love for our children, sons or daughters, more than that we have for anything else. Indeed, those who are very affable in their relations with others really show less love simply because they never become provoked, while those who administer rebuke for the good of someone else, although they

---
1 Plato, *Laws* VII 808D.
2 Eccli. 7.25.

are disagreeable at the moment, render a service that affects the life after the grave. So, too, the Lord is interested, not in promoting our present pleasure, but the happiness that is to come. Let us consider the nature of the loving education which He imparts, together with the testimony which the Prophets have made concerning it.

(76) Admonition is solicitous disapproval, seeking to arouse the mind. The Educator uses admonition when He says in the Gospel: 'How often would I gather thy children together, as a hen gathers her young under her wings, but thou wouldst not.'[3] Another time, Scripture admonishes: 'They fornicated with sticks and stones, and they lusted after Baal.'[4] Surely, the proof of His love for men is striking, for, although He sees clearly the shamelessness of His people in their reveling and merry-making, He calls them to conversion and says to Ezechiel: 'O son of man, thou dwellest with scorpions, thou shall speak my words to them, if perhaps they will hear.'[5] He said to Moses: 'Go and speak to Pharaoh, that he may let My people go, but I know that he will not let them go.'[6] In both these passages, He manifests His divinity by foreseeing what is to happen, and also His love for man by offering to the free will of man an opportunity to repent. In His concern for His people, He admonishes through Isaias, also: 'This people honor Me with their lips, but their hearts are far from Me' (this is really to correct them), 'but in vain do they worship Me, teaching for doctrine precepts of men.'[7] Therefore, while His solicitude lays their sin bare, at the same time He points out the way to salvation.

---

3 Matt. 23.37.
4 Jer. 3.9.
5 Ezech. 2.6.
6 Exod. 6.11; 3.19.
7 Isa. 29.13; cf. Matt. 15.8.

(77) Censure is disapproval of something that is shameful, seeking to dispose the individual to perform good deeds. This is what He expresses in the words of Jeremias: 'They are become as amorous horses: every one neighed after his neighbor's wife. Shall I not visit for these things, saith the Lord? And shall not My soul take revenge on such a nation?'[8] He weaves the thread of fear into everything because 'fear of the Lord is the beginning of understanding.'[9] Another time, He says through Osee: 'I will not visit upon them, because they themselves conversed with harlots, and offered sacrifice with the initiate, and the people that does not understand shall have intercourse with the harlot.'[10] Here He describes their sin in unmistakable language and implies that they understand that they are sinning deliberately. Understanding is the sight of the soul, just as the name Israel means 'he who sees God,'[11] that is, with his understanding.

Complaint is disapproval of those who manifest unconcern or indifference. This kind of education He employs when He says through Isaias: 'Hear, O ye heavens, and give ear, O earth, for the Lord has spoken. I have brought up children and exalted them: but they have despised Me. The ox knoweth his owner and the ass his master's crib. But Israel hath not known Me.'[12] Now, is it not a fearsome thing that one who knows of God will not acknowledge the Lord, or that, while the ox and ass, dumb and unreasoning beasts that they are, recognize the one who feeds them, Israel is more unreasoning than they? He makes many complaints of His people through

8 Jer. 5.8.
9 Cf. Prov. 1.7.
10 Osee 4.14.
11 Cf. Gen. 32.28,30; cf. above, p. 52.
12 Isa. 1.2.

Jeremias, also, and concludes: 'They have forsaken Me, saith the Lord.'[13]

(78) Reprimand is disapproval expressed in correction, or strongly worded blame. The Educator resorts to this method of training when He says through Isaias: 'Woe to you, apostate children, saith the Lord, that you would take counsel and not of Me, and make treaties, and not of My Spirit.'[14] He flavors each pronouncement in turn with the tart spice of fear, to whet the appetite of His people for salvation and make them more aware of it, just as wool to be dyed is usually steeped first in an astringent to prepare it to preserve the dye.

Correction is rebuke for sin expressed publicly. He employs it in a special way, as a necessity in our education, because of the weakness of faith of so many. For example, He says through Isaias: 'You have forsaken the Lord, you have provoked the Holy One of Israel.'[15] And through Jeremias He declares: 'Be astonished, O ye heavens, at this, and O earth, be very desolate. For My people have done two evils. They have forsaken Me, the fountain of living water, and have digged broken cisterns that can hold no water.'[16] And again, through the same Prophet: 'Jerusalem has grieviously sinned, therefore is she become unstable. All that honored her have despised her, because they have seen her shame.'[17] Then, to soften the severity of the correction and weaken its sting, He advises through Solomon (suggesting His love for us as our Educator by the very fact that He does not expressly mention it): 'My son, reject not the correction of the Lord, and do

---

13 Jer. 1.16; 2.13,19.
14 Isa. 30.1.
15 Isa. 1.4.
16 Jer. 2.12.
17 Lam. 1.8.

not faint when thou art chastised by Him. For whom the
Lord loveth, He chastiseth: and He scourges every son whom
He receives.'[18] As a natural consequence, Scripture remarks:
'Let a just man correct me and reprove me, but let not the
oil of the sinner anoint my head.'[19]

(79) Caution is disapproval that brings a man to his
senses. He does not neglect this manner of educating, either,
but exclaims through Jeremias: 'To whom shall I cry out and
they will not listen? Behold their ears are uncircumcised.'[20]
What blessed long-suffering! Again, through the same Prophet He says: 'All the nations are uncircumcised in the flesh,
but this people is uncircumcised in the heart,'[21] 'for it is a
disobedient people, sons in whom there is no fidelity.'[22]

Retribution is very severe rebuke. This kind He resorts to
in the Gospel: 'Jerusalem, Jerusalem, thou who killest the
prophets and stonest those who are sent to thee.' (He repeats
the name to make His rebuke emphatic, for how is it possible
that one who has known God should persecute the ministers
of God? Therefore, He continues:) 'Your house is left to you
desolate. For I say to you, you shall not see Me henceforth
until you shall say: Blessed is He who comes in the name of
the Lord.'[23] If you do not accept His love, you will experience
the might of His power.

(80) Excoriation is disapproval expressed in vigorous
terms. He made use of excoriation as a remedy when He said
through Isaias: 'Woe to the sinful nation, lawless sons, a
people laden with iniquity, a wicked seed.'[24] And in the

18 Prov. 3.11.
19 Ps. 140.5.
20 Jer. 6.10.
21 Jer. 9.26.
22 Isa. 30.9.
23 Matt. 23.37-39.
24 Isa. 1.4.

Gospel, through John, He calls them 'serpents, brood of vipers.'[25]

Reprobation is disapproval of evil-doers. He uses this sort of education when He says through David: 'A people which I knew not have served Me and at the hearing of the ear they have obeyed Me. The children that are strangers have lied to Me and have halted from their paths.'[26] And through Jeremias: 'And I gave to her a bill of divorce, yet treacherous Judah was not afraid.'[27] And again: 'And the house of Israel has rebelled against Me, and the house of Judah has denied the Lord.'[28]

Lamentation is implied disapproval, contributing to salvation also by the influence it exerts, although as if under a veil. He avails Himself of it in the words of Jeremias: 'How did the city sit solitary that was full of people! She has become as a widow. Ruling over provinces, she has become tributary. Weeping, she hath wept in the night.'[29]

(81) Derision is scornful disapproval. This also the divine Educator uses to aid us, in the passage of Jeremias: 'Thou hast the look of a harlot without shame before all. And you did not call Me to the house, your Father and the Guide of thy virginity.'[30] And, 'a harlot beautiful and agreeable that made use of witchcraft.'[31] By shaming the virgin in calling her a harlot, He skillfully calls her back to holiness.

Righteous indignation is justified rebuke, or the rebuke of paths that are exalted beyond measure. He educates in this way, saying through Moses: 'Children to be blamed, wicked

---

25 Matt. 23.33.
26 Ps. 17.45,46.
27 Jer. 3.8.
28 Jer. 5.11.
29 Lam. 1.1.
30 Jer. 3.3.
31 Nah. 3.4.

and perverse generation. Is this the return thou makest to the Lord? This is a foolish and senseless people! Is He not thy Father that has possessed thee?'[32] And, in the words of Isaias: 'Thy princes are faithless, companions of thieves; they all love bribes, they run after rewards. They judge not for the fatherless.'[33]

Generally speaking, His use of fear is a device for saving us, but to save proves that a person is good. 'The mercy of God is upon all flesh. He corrects and chastises and teaches as a shepherd does his flock. He hath mercy on those that receive chastisement and that eagerly seek His friendship.'[34] With such guidance He watched over 'the six hundred thousand wanderers that were gathered together in the hardness of their heart,'[35] with pity and with chastisement, scourging, showing mercy, striking and healing. 'According to the greatness of His mercy, so also is His correction.'[36] It is a wonderful thing, indeed, not to sin at all, but it is good also that the sinner repents; just as it is better to remain healthy always, but good, too, to recover from an illness. (82) So He counsels through Solomon: 'Thou shalt beat thy son with a rod and deliver his soul from death.' And again: 'Withhold not correction from a child; for if thou strike him with the rod, he shall not die.'[37]

Correction and chastisement, as their very name implies, are blows inflicted upon the soul, restraining sin, warding off death, leading those enslaved by vice back to self-control. Thus, Plato, recognizing that correction has the greatest influence and is the most effective purification, echoes the

32 Deut. 32.5.
33 Isa. 1.23.
34 Eccli. 18.12,13 (Septuagint).
35 Eccli. 16.11.
36 Eccli. 16.13.
37 Prov. 23.14,13.

Word when he claims that one who is notably lacking in purification becomes undisciplined and degenerate because he was left uncorrected, while one who is to be truly happy should be the most purified and virtuous.[38] For, if 'rulers are a terror not to the good work,'[39] how can He who is by nature good, God, be a terror to one who does not sin? 'But if thou dost what is evil,' as the Apostle says, 'fear.' (83) So it is that the Apostle himself, in imitation of the Lord, after he had rebuked each of the churches in turn, takes into account his own boldness of speech and their weakness, and asks the Galatians: 'Have I then become your enemy, because I tell you the truth?'[40]

Just as those who are well do not need a physician in that they are strong, but only those who are sick[41] and in need of his skill, so, too, we need the Saviour because we are sick from the reprehensible lusts of our lives, and from blameworthy vices and from the diseases caused by our other passions. He applies not only remedies that soothe, but also others that sear, such as the bitter herb of fear which arrests the growth of sin. Fear, then, is bitter, but it confers health. Truly, then, we need the Saviour, for we are sick; the Guide, for we are wandering; Him who gives light, for we are blind; the lifegiving Spring, for we are parched with thirst, and, once we have tasted of it, we will never thirst again. We are in need of Life, for we are dead; of the Shepherd, for we are sheep; of the Educator, for we are children. In a word, throughout the whole of our human lives, we need Jesus that we may not go astray and at length merit condemnation as sinners, but may be separated from the chaff and gathered into the storehouse of

---

38 Cf. Plato, *Soph.* 230DE.
39 Rom. 13.3.
40 Gal. 4.16.
41 Cf. Luke 5.31.

the Father. 'For the winnowing-fan is in the hand of the Lord,'[42] with which He will separate the chaff destined for the fire from His wheat.

(84) To make it easy for us to understand the supreme wisdom, if you will, of the all-holy Shepherd and Guide, the almighty Word of the Father, He makes use of a metaphor, calling Himself the Shepherd of his sheep. He is truly the Educator of His children, who are little ones. In fact, through Ezechiel, He makes a long address to the rulers in which He presents a helpful description of His wise care: 'The lame I shall bind up and the wounded I shall heal and the wandering I shall bring back, and I shall feed them on My holy mountain.'[43] This is the promise of Him who is the Good Shepherd.

Feed us, Thy little ones, for we are Thy sheep! Yes, O Master, fill us with Thy food, Thy justice. Yes, O Educator, shepherd us to Thy holy mountain, the Church, which is lifted up above the clouds, touching the heavens. 'And I shall be their shepherd,' He says, 'and I will be near them,'[44] as the garment is to the skin. He wills to save my body by clothing it with the cloak of immortality, and my flesh He has anointed. 'They will call to Me and I shall say: Behold I am near.'[45] More quickly did You answer me than I expected, O Master. 'Even if they cross over, they shall not slip, saith the Lord.'[46] We shall not slip into corruption, we who are crossing over into incorruption, because He Himself will support us. For so He Himself has said and so He has willed.

(85) Such is our Educator, good beyond a doubt. 'I have not come,' He declared, 'to be ministered unto, but to

---
42 Matt. 3.12.
43 Cf. Ezech. 34.11-16.
44 *Ibid.;* Isa. 51.5; Ps. 118.151.
45 Isa. 53.9.
46 Isa. 43.2.

minister.' For that reason He is represented in the Gospel as afflicted, for He is afflicted on our account and undertakes 'to give His life as a redemption for many.'[47] He alone, He asserts, is the Good Shepherd.[48] He is generous indeed who gives us the greatest thing He has, His own life, and liberal and kind because He willed to be man's brother, though He could have been His Lord; so good that He even died for our sake.[49]

His justice, however, also cries out: 'If you come to Me upright, I will come to you also upright; but if you walk perversely, I also will be perverse, saith the Lord of princes.'[50] By perverse, He means He will chastize sinners. For His natural uprightness, which the 'I' of Jesus[51] suggests, and His goodness toward those who believe obediently, are immovable and unshakable. 'Because I called and you did not obey, saith the Lord, you have despised all My counsel and have neglected My reprehensions.'[52] So, the correction of the Lord is very beneficial. (86) He calls the same people, through David, also, 'a perverse and exasperating generation, a generation that set not their heart aright: and whose spirit was not faithful to God. They kept not the convenant of God: and in His law they would not walk.'[53] These are the reasons for His exasperation, and for these reasons He will come as Judge to pass sentence on those who are unwilling to preserve goodness in their lives. Therefore, He treats them severely in the hope that perhaps He might curb their impulse toward death. At least He speaks very plainly of the reason for His threats

---

47 Matt. 20.28.
48 John 10.11,12.
49 Cf. 1 Thess. 5.10.
50 Cf. Ps. 17.26,27.
51 That is, the first letter of *Iēsoûs*.
52 Prov. 1.24,25.
53 Ps. 77.8-10.

when He says through David: 'They believed not for His wondrous works. When He slew them, then they sought Him: and they returned and came straight to God and they remembered that God was their helper, and the most high God, their redeemer.'[54] He knew that they repented out of fear, after neglecting His love; as a general rule, men always neglect the good that is kind, but serve it with loving fear if it keeps recalling justice.

(87) There are two sorts of fear, one of which is accompanied by reverence. This sort citizens feel toward their rulers if they are good, and we toward God, as well-trained children do toward their father. 'A horse not broken,' Scripture says, 'becomes stubborn, and a child left to himself will become headstrong.'[55] The other kind of fear is mixed with hate: this is the way slaves feel toward harsh masters, and the Hebrews when they looked on God as their Master and not their Father. It seems to me that what is done willingly and of one's own accord is far more excellent from every point of view than that which is done under duress in the service of God.

'He is merciful,' it is said, 'and will forgive their sins, and will not destroy them. And many a time did He turn away His anger; and did not kindle His wrath.'[56] Notice how the justice of the Educator is manifest in His chastisements and the goodness of God in His mercies. That is why David, or rather, the Spirit through him, includes both when he says, in the psalm, of the same God: 'Justice and judgment are the preparation of Thy throne. Mercy and truth shall go before Thy face.'[57] He is suggesting that judging and doing good are acts of the same faculty, for judging what is just, distin-

---
54 Ps. 77.32-35.
55 Eccli. 30.8.
56 Ps. 77.38.
57 Ps. 88.15.

guishing it from what is not just, is the basis for both. (88) And so, the same person is both just and good, He who is truly God, who is Himself all things, and all things are He, because He is Himself God, the only Good.

As the mirror is not unjust to an ugly man for showing him exactly as he is, and as the doctor is not unjust to the sick man for diagnosing his fever (for he is not responsible for the fever, but simply states it is present), so he who corrects is not ill disposed toward one sick of soul. He does not put the sins there, but only shows that they are present, so that similar sins may be avoided in the future. Therefore, God is good of Himself, but just for our sake and because He is good. His justice is revealed to us through His Word who has descended from above where the Father has always been. Before becoming the Creator, He was God, and good; that is why He wished to become Creator and Father. The nature of His love is the origin of His justice, making His sun to shine and sending down His own Son. The Son was the first to proclaim the good justice which is from heaven, for He said: 'No one knows the Son but the Father, and no one knows the Father but the Son.'[58] This balanced reciprocity of knowledge is a symbol of the justice that existed at the beginning. Afterwards, justice came down among men, both in the Scriptures and in the flesh: in the Word and in the Law,[59] drawing men to salutary repentance; for it is good.

But you do not obey God. Then blame yourself if you draw down upon yourself the judgment of the Judge.

---

58 Luke 10.22.
59 Cf. C. Mondésert, *Clément D'Alexandrie* (Paris 1944) 99-100: 'Clement speaks . . . of a sort of first incarnation of the Logos in letters, preceding that in the flesh and already realizing, in the midst of men, a presence of the justice of God which works for their salvation.'

Chapter 10

(89) We have shown that the correction of men is a good thing, contributing to their salvation, and that it has been assumed by the Word, necessarily, because it is the most effective means to lead them to repentance and to restrain them from sin.

The next point that we should consider is the gentleness of the Word. He has been pictured as just, but He also offers us sentiments characteristic of Him, that encourage us on the way to salvation, and by which He intends to make us know what is good and useful in the light of His Father's will. Now, this is a point to keep in mind: all that is good is the proper subject matter of encomium, and whatever is useful, of advice. The nature of advice extends to both persuasion and dissuasion; encomium to both praise and blame. If the intention of advice is directed one way, it is persuasion, but if in the opposite way, it is dissuasion; similarly, if encomium is expressed in one way, it is blame, but if in contrary way, it is praise. The just Educator, desiring our improvement, concerns Himself with these forms of speech. But, since blame and dissuasion have already been discussed in the previous chapter, let us now turn our attention to praise and persuasion, and balance as though on scales the evenly matched, contrasting parts of justice.

(90) When the Educator says in one of the passages of Solomon's work: 'O ye men, to you I call, and My voice is to the sons of men. Hear, for I will speak of great things,' and the rest of the passage,[1] He is making use of persuasion, persuasion to something that is useful. Since advice is called for when there is a question of free acceptance or rejection, He is

---
1 Prov. 8.4,6.

here advising what will lead to salvation. He does the same thing when He says through David: 'Blessed is the man who hath not walked in the counsel of the ungodly, nor stood in the way of sinners, nor sat in the chair of pestilence. But his will is in the law of the Lord.'[2]

There are three possible methods of giving advice. The first is to take examples from times gone by, such as the punishments the Jews met with after they had worshiped the golden calf,[3] or when they had committed fornication,[4] or after similar misdeeds. The second method is to call attention to some conclusion drawn from present events, as a conclusion readily grasped by the mind; such was the answer given by the Lord to those who asked Him: 'Art thou the Christ or look we for another?' 'Go,' He said, 'report to John that the blind see, the lame walk, the lepers are cleansed, the dead rise, and blessed is he who is not scandalized in Me.'[5] Truly, David had already said, by divine inspiration: (91) 'As we have heard, so we have seen.'[6] Finally, the third method of advice is drawn from future events, in which things that are to come put us on our guard; an example is that saying that those who fall into sin 'will be put forth into the darkness outside, there will be weeping and the gnashing of teeth,'[7] and sayings of the same import. Therefore, it can be clearly seen that the Lord calls mankind to salvation by using progressively every kind of treatment.

He uses encouragement to alleviate sin, for by it He mitigates concupiscence and at the same time instils hope of salvation. Through the mouth of Ezechiel He says: 'If you

---

2 Ps. 1.1.
3 Cf. Exod. 32.26-28.
4 Cf. Num. 25.4-9.
5 Cf. Matt. 11.3-6.
6 Ps. 47.9.
7 Matt. 8.12.

be converted with all your heart and say: Father, I will hear you as a holy people.'[8] And another time, He says: 'Come to Me all you who labor and are burdened and I will give you rest,'[9] and the words that follow which the Lord Himself said. As plainly as He can, He invites us to goodness when He says through Solomon: 'Blessed is the man that findeth wisdom, and the mortal who findeth prudence,'[10] and 'Goodness is found by him who seeks it, and is easily seen by him that has found her.'[11] He explains what He means by prudence in the words of Jeremias: 'We are happy, O Israel, because the things that are pleasing to God are made known to us,'[12] made known through the Word who makes us both prudent and happy. For, knowledge is prudence, according to the words of the same Prophet: 'Hear, O Israel, the commandments of life: give ear that thou mayest learn wisdom.'[13] And, again, in His love for men, He generously gives further promises to those laboring for salvation, through Moses, when He says: 'I will bring you into the good land, for which I swore to your fathers,'[14] and He adds, in the words of Isaias: 'I will bring you unto My holy mount, and will make you joyful.'[15]

(92) There is still another sort of education He resorts to, that is, blessing. 'Blessed is he who does not sin,' He declares through David; 'he shall be like a tree which is planted near the running waters, which shall bring forth its fruit in due season. And his leaf shall not fall off' (refer-

---
8 Not in Ezechiel, but cf. Ezech. 18.21-23; 33.11; Deut. 30.1-5.
9 Matt. 11.28.
10 Cf. Prov. 3.13 (Septuagint).
11 Cf. Wisd. 6.13.
12 Bar. 4.4.
13 Bar. 3.9.
14 Cf. Deut. 31.20.
15 Isa. 56.7.

ring to the resurrection), 'And all whatsoever he shall do shall prosper.'[16] This is what He wants us to be, blessed. Then, by way of contrast, to manifest the balance of the scales of justice, He continues: 'Not so the wicked, not so; but like the dust which the wind driveth from the face of the earth.'[17] Our Educator seeks to turn His children from sin and punishment by disclosing the punishment inflicted on sinners, and their insecurity and instability. When He reveals the punishment they deserve, He is suggesting the advantages of doing good, and adroitly urging us to acquire and to practise virtue.

Even more, He calls us to knowledge[18] by saying through Jeremias: 'If thou hast walked in the way of God, thou hast surely dwelt in peace for ever.'[19] He encourages the prudent to embrace knowledge by indicating in these words the reward for it, and by offering pardon to those who have erred, in these words: 'Turn back, turn back, as a grape-gatherer into his basket.'[20] Do you not detect the goodness in that justice as He counsels repentance? (93) Another time, He causes the light of truth to be shed upon the erring when He says through Jeremias: 'Thus saith the Lord: Stand ye on the ways and see, and ask for the eternal paths of the Lord, which is the good way, and walk ye in it: and you shall find refreshment for your soul.'[21] He desires to draw us to repentance that we might be saved, and therefore says: 'If thou repent, the Lord will circumcize thy heart, and the heart of thy seed.'[22]

To corroborate our argument, we might possibly include the philosophers[23] who hold that only he who is perfect

---

16 Ps. 1.1-3.
17 Ps. 1.4.
18 That is, *gnōsis*. Cf. Introduction, pp. ix-x.
19 Bar. 3.13.
20 Cf. Jer. 6.9.
21 Jer. 6.16.
22 Deut. 30.6.
23 Probably the older Stoics and Cynics.

deserves praise and he who is imperfect deserves blame. But, since there are those[24] who misconstrue happiness by maintaining that it does not ever become disturbed, or disturb anyone else, not understanding the love for man that happiness implies, therefore, because of them as well as of those who separate justice from goodness, we add the following remark. Since they hold that all men are bad, it follows that we should admit that only the sort of education that makes use of correction and discipline is suitable for men. And since God alone is wise, from whom wisdom proceeds, and He alone is perfect, He alone deserves praise. (94) But I do not agree with the reasoning. I hold that praise and blame, or something very similar to praise and blame, are the remedies more necessary for men than any other sort. The apathetic need to be forged as iron is with fire and hammer and anvil, that is, fired by threats and reproach and punishment, while others who adhere to faith for its own sake, almost instinctively and of their own choice, will expand if they are praised. 'Virtue, if it be praised, like a tree doth grow.'[25] And Pythagoras the Samian agrees, I believe, for he gives this advice: 'If you have done evil deeds, correct them; if noble deeds, rejoice in them.'[26] Correction is also called in Greek *nouthetein*, whose etymology[27] means placing something in the mind; therefore, correction is really transformation of the mind.

There are, indeed, countless words of advice to be found, directing us to acquire what is good and to avoid what is

---

24 The Scholion says he means Epicurus.
25 Cf. Pindar, *Nem.* 8.40, or Bacchylides, cf. Blass, *Hermes*, 36 (1901) S.285.
26 Pythagoras, *Carm. aur.* 44.
27 *nouthetein* is derived from *noûs* ('mind') and *tithēmi* ('place'). For once, Clement's etymological analysis is correct.

evil. 'There is no peace to the wicked, saith the Lord.'[28] Therefore, He advises His little ones to be on their guard, in the words of Solomon: 'My son, let not sinners lead thee astray, walk not thou with their ways. Do not walk if they entice you saying: Come with us, let us share innocent blood: let us hide the just man in the earth unjustly, let us swallow him up alive as in hell.'[29] (95) (This last passage is also a prophecy of the Passion of the Lord.) In the words of Ezechiel, even life is dependent upon the commandments: 'The soul that sinneth, the same shall die. And if a man be just and do justice, and hath not eaten upon the mountain, nor lifted up his eyes to the idols of the house of Israel; and hath not defiled his neighbor's wife, nor come near to a menstrous woman; and hath not wronged any man; but hath restored his pledge to the debtor, hath taken nothing away by violence; hath given his bread to the hungry, and hath covered the naked, hath not lent upon usury, nor taken any increase; hath withdrawn his hand from iniquity, and hath executed true judgment between man and his neighbor; hath walked in My commandments, and kept My judgments to do them: he is just, he shall surely live, saith the Lord.'[30] These words present a complete description of the Christian life and are a wonderful encouragement to work for the blessed life, which is the reward of good living, that is, life everlasting.

Chapter 11

(96) The nature of His love for men and of His method of educating His little ones we have described as far as lay

---

28 Isa. 48.22; 57.21.
29 Prov. 1.10-15.
30 Ezech. 18.4-9.

in our power. He pictures Himself cogently by likening Himself to a 'grain of mustard-seed.'¹ With such a figure, He depicts the spiritual nature of the word that is sown, the productiveness it has by nature, and the growth and the greatness latent in the power of the word. By the bitterness of the mustard-seed he suggests, too, that the unpleasantness and the purgative nature of correction are all to our advantage. At any rate, through this allegory of the small mustard-seed, applicable in so many ways, He proves that He bestows salvation on all mankind.

Honey, because it is so sweet, gives rise to bile just as virtue to derision, which in its turn is the cause of sin. But mustard diminishes bile, that is, wrath, and dispels morbid humors, that is, pride. From the Word comes true health of soul and immortal robustness.

Of old, the Word educated through Moses, and after that through the Prophets; even Moses was in fact a Prophet. For the Law was the education of children difficult to control. 'Having eaten their fill,' Scripture says, 'they got up to play,'² using a Greek word which means, not food, but cattle-fodder, because of their irrational gorging. (97) And since they were continually filling themselves without obeying reason, and playing without listening to reason, the Law and fear followed them to restrain them from sin and to encourage them to reform themselves. So it disposed them to give ready obedience to the true Educator; then the one same Word directed their docility toward what was of obligation. 'The Law has been given,' Paul says, 'as our educator in Christ.'³ Then it is obvious that the one person

---

1 Matt. 13.31.
2 Exod. 32.6. The word referred to is *chórtasma*.
3 Cf. Gal. 3.24.

who is alone reliable, just, good, Jesus, the Son of the Father as His image and likeness,[4] the Word of God, is our Educator. It is to Him that God has entrusted us, as a loving Father delivering His children to a true Educator, for He expressly commanded us: 'This is My beloved Son: hear Him.'[5]

Our divine Educator is trustworthy, for He is endowed with three excellent qualities: intelligence, good will and authority to speak. With intelligence, because He is the Wisdom of the Father: 'All wisdom is from the Lord and hath been always with Him.'[6] With authority to speak, because He is God and Creator: 'All things were made through Him, and without Him was made nothing.'[7] With good will, because He is the only one who has given Himself as a sacrifice for us: 'The Good Shepherd lays down His life for His sheep,'[8] and in fact He did lay it down. Surely, good will is nothing else than willing what is good for the neighbor for his own sake.

Chapter 12

(98) From the subjects that we have already discussed it must be concluded that Jesus, our Educator, has outlined for us the true life, and that He educates the man who abides in Christ. His character is not excessively fear-inspiring, yet neither is it overindulgent in its kindness. He imposes commands, but at the same time expresses them in such a way that we can fullfill them.

It seems to me that the reason that He formed man from dust with His own hands, gave him a second birth through

---
4 Cf. Col. 1.15.
5 Matt. 17.5.
6 Eccli. 1.1.
7 John 1.3.
8 John 10.11.

water, increase through the Spirit, education by the Word, thereby guiding him surely to the adoption of sons and to salvation with holy precepts, was precisely that He might transform an earth-born man into a holy and heavenly creature by His coming, and accomplish the original divine command: 'Let us make mankind in our image and likeness.'[1] It is Christ, in fact, who is, in all its perfection, what God then commanded; other men are so only by a certain image.

As for us, O children of a good Father, flock of a good Educator, let us fulfill the will of the Father, let us obey the Word, and let us be truly molded by the saving life of the Saviour. Then, since we shall already be living the life of heaven which makes us divine, let us anoint ourselves with the never-failing oil of gladness, the incorruptible oil of good odor. We possess an unmistakable model of incorruptibility in the life of the Lord and are following in the footsteps of God.

His main concern is to consider the way and the means by which the life of man might be made more conformable to salvation. He does truly make this His concern. He seeks to train us to the condition of a wayfarer, that is, to make us well girded and unimpeded by provisions, that we might be self-sufficient of life[2] and practise a moderate frugality in our journey toward the good life of eternity, telling us that each one of us is to be his own storehouse: 'Do not be anxious about tomorrow.'[3] He means to say that he who has dedicated himself to Christ ought to be self-sufficient and his own servant and, besides, live his life from day to day.

(99) We are educated not for war but for peace. In

---
1 Gen. 1.26.
2 *autarkeia,* a virtue the Stoics emphasized.
3 Matt. 6.34.

war, there is need for much equipment, just as self-indulgence craves an abundance. But peace and love, simple and plain blood sisters, do not need arms nor abundant supplies. Their nourishment is the Word, the Word whose leadership enlightens and educates, from whom we learn poverty and humility and all that goes with love of freedom and of mankind and of the good. In a word, through Him we become like God by a likeness of virtue. Labor, then, and do not grow weary; you will become what you dare not hope or cannot imagine.[4]

As there is one sort of training for philosophers, another for orators and another for wrestlers, so, too, there is an excellent disposition imparted by the education of Christ that is proper to the free will loving the good. As for deeds, walking and reclining at table, eating and sleeping, marriage relations and the manner of life, the whole of a man's education all become illustrious as holy deeds under the influence of the Educator. The education He gives is not overstrained, but in harmony [with man's needs]. (100) That is why the Word is called Saviour, because He has left men remedies of reason to effect understanding and salvation, and because, awaiting the favorable opportunity, He corrects evil, diagnoses the cause for passion, extracts the roots of unreasonable lusts, advises what we should avoid, and applies all the remedies of salvation to those who are sick.

This is the greatest and most noble of all God's acts: saving mankind.[5] But those who labor under some sickness are dissatisfied if the physician prescribes no remedy to restore their health; how, then, can we withhold our sincerest

---
4 Cf. 1 Cor. 2.9.
5 Cf. Isa. 33.22; Jer. 30.11; Matt. 18.11.

gratitude from the divine Educator when He corrects the acts of disobedience that sweep us on to ruin and uproots the desires that drag us into sin, refusing to be silent and connive at them, and even offers counsels on the right way to live? Certainly we owe Him the deepest gratitude.

Do we say, then, that the rational animal, I mean man, ought to do anything besides contemplate the divinity? I maintain that he ought to contemplate human nature, also, and live as the truth leads him, admiring the way in which the Educator and His precepts are worthy of one another and adapted one to the other. In keeping with such a model, we ought also to adapt ourselves to our Educator, conform our deeds to the Word, and then we will truly live.

Chapter 13

(101) Everything contrary to right reason is a sin. The philosophers,[1] for example, maintained that the more generic passions are defined in some such way as this: lust is desire disobedient to reason; fear, aversion disobedient to reason; pleasure, elation of mind disobedient to reason; and grief, depression of mind disobedient to reason. Now, if it is in its relationship with reason that disobedience is the origin of sin, is it not necessarily true that obedience to reason, or the Word,[2] which is what we call faith, is the very substance of what is called a person's duty?[3] This is said with good reason,

---

1 Principally, the Stoics.
2 That is, *lógos*. This whole chapter is a play on the twofold meaning of this word: according to the Stoics, sin is acting contrary to reason (*lógos*); according to Christians, this *lógos* is the Second Person of the Trinity, the Word.
3 *to kathēkon*, a familiar Stoic term.

for virtue itself is a disposition of soul attuned to the dictate of reason in the whole course of life. Besides, even philosophy is defined as the pursuit of right reason, so that an error arising from faulty reasoning is necessarily, and properly, called a defection.[4]

By way of illustration, when the first man sinned and disobeyed God, 'man became,' as Scripture puts it, 'like to the beasts,'[5] because he sinned against reason. With good cause was he considered unreasonable and likened to the beasts. (102) Similarly, Wisdom says: 'The pleasure-seeker and the adulterer is a stallion-horse,'[6] because they have become like the most unreasoning of animals. Therefore, it adds: 'He neighed under everyone that sitteth upon him.' Such a man is no longer said to speak, for he who sins against reason is no longer rational, but is an irrational animal wholly given up to lust, whom every sort of pleasure sits upon and drives.

The followers of the Stoics call virtuous action performed in obedience to reason 'the dutiful and the fitting.'[7] But what is a duty is also fitting, and obedience has as its foundation commands. Since these are the same as counsels, in the sense that both have the truth as their goal, they guide us to the final goal we desire, which is spoken of as the end.[8] The end of service of God is eternal rest in God; our end is the beginning of eternity. But, that which is done properly in the service of God fulfills in deeds the duty imposed on it. Therefore, duty consists not in words but in actions. But the deed of a Christian soul is the work of its reason accomplished

---

4 A play on words: 'error' is *diamartía*, or 'missing the goal'; 'sin' is *hamártēma*, or 'defection.'
5 Ps. 48.13,21.
6 Cf. Eccli. 33.6.
7 *kathēkon kai prosēkon*, a Stoic definition of virtue.
8 *télos*, end or purpose.

by means of its friend and companion, the body, obeying the dictate of an educated judgment and of a desire for the truth. But man's duty is to cultivate a will that is in conformity and united throughout his life to God and Christ, properly directed to eternal life. Indeed, the life of the Christian, in which we are now being educated, is a united whole made up of deeds controlled by reason; that is, it is the persevering accomplishment of the truths taught by reason, or rather, the Word, an accomplishment which we call fidelity. (103) The whole is the sum total of the Lord's commands which, as the sentiments of God, are prescribed for us as spiritual counsels, imposed upon ourselves and upon the neighbor for our greater good. But it must be borne in mind that, like an elastic ball that comes back to the one who throws it, they recoil upon us.

Therefore, in the divine education, it is necessary that duties be imposed upon us, as things commanded by God and provided for our salvation. But, since of things that are necessary, some are for this life alone, while others cause the soul to aspire after a good life in the next world, it is but right that some obligations be imposed merely for living, and others for living well. Whatever is imposed for material life is binding upon the multitude, but what is adapted to living well, that is, the things by which eternal life is gained, should be able to be gathered from the Scriptures by those who read them, gathered at least in their general outline.

BOOK TWO

Chapter 1

IN KEEPING WITH the purpose we have in mind, we must now select passages from the Scriptures that bear on education in the practical needs of life, and describe the sort of life he who is called a Christian should live throughout his life. We should begin with ourselves, and with the way we should regulate [our actions].

In the effort to maintain a proper proportion in this treatise, let us speak first of the way each should conduct himself in reference to his body, or, rather, of the manner in which he should exercise control over it. Now, whenever a man is drawn by reason away from external things and even from any further concern for his body to the realm of the understanding, and acquires a clear insight into the natural attributes of man,[1] he will understand that he is not to be eager about external things, but is to purify that which is proper to man, the eye of his soul,[2] and to sanctify even his

---
1 A Stoic phrase for the standard of virtuous living.
2 Cf. Plato, *Republic* VIII 533D.

body. For, if a man is completely purified and freed from the things that make him only dust, what could he have more serviceable for walking in the path that leads to the perception of God than his own self?[3]

Other men, indeed, live that they may eat, just like unreasoning beasts; for them life is only their belly.[4] But as for us, our Educator has given the command that we eat only to live. Eating is not our main occupation, nor is pleasure our chief ambition. (2) Food is permitted us simply because of our stay in this world, which the Word is shaping for immortality by His education. Our food should be plain and ungarnished, in keeping with the truth, suitable to children who are plain and unpretentious, adapted to maintaining life, not self-indulgence.

Viewed in this sense, life depends upon two things only: health and strength. To satisfy these needs, all that is required is a disposition easily satisfied with any sort of food; it aids digestion and restricts the weight of the body. Thus, growth and health and strength will be fostered; not the unbalanced and unhealthy and miserable state of men such as athletes fed on an enforced diet. Surely, excessive variety in food must be avoided, for it gives rise to every kind of bad effect: indisposition of body, upset stomach, perversion of taste due to some misguided culinary adventure or foolish experiment in pastry cooking. Men have the nerve to style such self-indulgence nourishment, even though it degenerates into pleasures that only inflict harm. Antiphanes, the Delian physician, has said that rich variety in food is one of the causes of disease. Yet, there are those who grow dissatisfied with the truth in their restless ostentation, and reject simplicity

---
3 Cf. Seneca, *Ep.* 23.6.
4 Cf. Phil. 3.19.

of diet to engage in a frantic search for expensive menus that must be imported from across the seas.

(3) I feel pity for their disease; but they themselves show no shame in flaunting their extravagances, going to no end of trouble to procure lampreys from the Sicilian straits and eels from Maeander, kids from Melos and mullets from Sciathos, Pelordian mussels and Abydean oysters, to say nothing of sprats from Lipara and Mantinean turnips and beets from Ascra. They anxiously search for Methymnian scallops, Attic turgots, laurel-thrushes, and the golden-brown figs for five thousand of which the notorious Persian sent to Greece. On top of all this, they buy fowl from Phasis, francolins from Egypt and peacocks from Medea. Gourmands that they are, they greedily yearn for these fowl and dress them up with sweet sauces, ravenously providing themselves with whatever the land and the depth of the sea and the vast expanse of the sky produce as food. Such grasping and excitable people seem to scour the world blunderingly for their costly pleasures, and make themselves heard for their 'sizzling frying-pans,' wasting the whole of their lives in hovering over mortar and pestle, omnivorous fellows who cling as close to matter as fire does. Why, they deprive even the stable food, bread, of its strength by sifting away the nourishing parts of wheat, turning a necessity of life into a dishonorable pleasure. (4) There is no limit to the gluttony that these men practise. Truly, in ever inventing a multitude of new sweets and ever seeking recipes of every description, they are shipwrecked on pastries and honey-cakes and desserts.

To me, a man of this sort seems nothing more than one great mouth. 'Be not desirous,' Scripture says, 'of the meats of the rich. For these belong to a false and shameful life.'[5]

---
5 Prov. 23.3.

These men hug their delicacies to themselves, yet after a while they must yield them to the privy. As for us, who seek a heavenly food, we must restrain the belly and keep it under the control of heaven, and even more that which is made for the belly which 'God will destroy,'[6] as the Apostle says, intending, no doubt, to curse gluttonous desires. 'Food is for the belly,' and the life of the body, belonging completely to this world and made for corruption, depends upon it.

If anyone dares mention the Agape with shameless tongue as he indulges in a dinner exhaling the odor of steaming meats and sauces, then he profanes the holy Agape, sublime and saving creation of the Lord, with his goblets and servings of soup; he desecrates its name by his drinking and self-indulgence and fragrant odors; he is deceiving himself completely, for he thinks he can buy off the commands of God with such a banquet. We can indulge in such gatherings for the sake of entertainment, and we would rightly call them banquets and dinners and receptions, but the Lord never called such feasts His Agape. He did say somewhere: 'When thou art invited to a wedding feast, do not recline in the first place, but when thou art invited, go and recline in the last place.'[7] And somewhere else: 'When thou givest a dinner or a supper . . .' And again: 'But when thou givest a feast, invite the poor,' for whom a supper should be given more than for anyone else. And once more: 'A certain man gave a great supper and he invited many.'[8]

(5) No, I know where the beguiling lure of dinners originated: from 'the gullets and mad frequentation of the table,'[9] in the words of the comic poet. 'There are many

---
6 1 Cor. 6.13.
7 Luke 14.8-10.
8 Luke 14.12,13,16.
9 *Adespota* 782, *CAF* III 545.

things for many people at a dinner';[10] never did they learn that God has provided food and drink for His creature, I mean man, not for his dissipation, but for his welfare. It is a natural law that the body is not benefitted by excessively rich food; quite the contrary, those who live on simpler foods are stronger and healthier and more alert, as servants are, for example, in comparision with their masters, or farmer-tenants in comparision with their landlords. It is not only that they are more robust; they are also sharper of mind than the wealthy, as the philosophers are, for they have not sated their minds with food nor seduced it with pleasure.

An Agape is in reality heavenly food, a banquet of the Word. The Agape, or charity, 'bears all things, endures all things, hopes all things; charity never fails.'[11] 'Blessed is he who eats bread in the kingdom of God.'[12] Surely, of all downfalls, the most unlikely is for charity, which faileth not,[13] to be cast down from heaven to earth among all these dainty seasonings. Do you still imagine that I refer to a meal that is to be destroyed?[14] 'If I distribute my goods to the poor and have not charity,' Scripture says, 'I am nothing.'[15] (6) On this charity depend the whole Law and the word.[16] If you love the Lord thy God and thy neighbor,[17] there will be a feast, a heavenly one, in heaven. The earthly feast, as we have proved from Scripture, is called a supper, one permeated with love, yet not identified with it, but an expression of mutual and generous good will.

---

10 *Adesp.* 432, *CAF* III 490.
11 1 Cor. 13.7.
12 Luke 14.15.
13 Cf. 1 Cor. 13.8.
14 Cf. 1 Cor. 6.13.
15 1 Cor. 13.3.
16 Cf. Matt. 22.40.
17 Cf. Mark. 12.30,31.

'Let not then our good be reviled,' the Apostle says, 'for the kingdom of God does not consist in food and drink,' meaning the daily meal, 'but justice and peace and joy in the Holy Spirit.'[18] Whoever eats of this feast is put in possession of the most wonderful[19] of all things, the kingdom of God, and takes his place in the holy assembly of love, the heavenly Church. (7) Certainly, love is pure, worthy of God, and its fruit is giving. 'The care of discipline is love,' Wisdom says, 'and love is the keeping of the laws.'[20] Festive gatherings of themselves do contain some spark of love, for from food taken at a common table we become accustomed to the food of eternity. Assuredly, the dinner itself is not an Agape, yet let the feasting be rooted in love. 'Thy children, O Lord,' it is said, 'whom Thou lovest, know that it is not the growing of fruit that nourishest men, but Thy word preserves them that believe in Thee.'[21] 'For it is not on bread that the just man will live.'[22]

Let the meal be plain and restrained, of such sort that it will quicken the spirit. Let it be free of a too rich variety, and let not even such a meal be withdrawn from the guidance of the Educator. An Agape fosters communal living very well, for it supplies ample provisions for its journey, that is, self-sufficiency.[23] Self-sufficiency, in dictating that food be limited to the proper amount, ministers to the health of the body, and, besides, can distribute some of its substance to its neighbor. But, if the diet overstep the limits of self-sufficiency, it harms man by dulling his mind and making his body susceptible to disease. Indeed, the pleasures of a luxurious table inflict untold damage:

---

18 Rom. 14.17.
19 A play on words: 'feast' is *driston;* 'most wonderful,' *dristos.*
20 Wisd. 6.19.
21 Wisd. 16.26.
22 Cf. Matt. 4.4; Hab. 2.4. For a possible explanation of the addition of 'just man' to this passage, cf. E. L. Titus, *op. cit.* 19.
23 Cf. above, p. 87 n. 2.

gluttony, squeamishness, gourmandizing, insatiability of appetite, voraciousness. Carrion flies and wheedling weasels and gladiators, as well as 'that wild tribe of parasites,'[24] are of the same type, for the first have sacrificed reason, the second friendship, and the last life itself for the pleasures of the belly, creeping upon their bellies, beasts that merely resemble man, made to the likeness of their father, the ravening beast. Those who first called such men in Greek, *asótoi*, that is, abandoned and dissolute, suggested their end, I think, meaning, instead, *asóstoi*, with elision of the *sigma*, that is, beyond salvation. Are not such men who waste their lives on dishes and frivolous elaborate preparations of highly seasoned foods, whose minds have become base, are they not hidebound to earth, living for the passing moment as though they did not live at all?

(8) The Holy Spirit complains of such men, in the words of Isaias, subtly refusing them the name of Agape, since their feast is contrary to reason: 'They made good cheer, killing calves and slaying rams, saying: Let us eat and drink, for tomorrow we die.'[25] Because He considers such revelry a sin, He adds: 'And this iniquity shall not be forgiven till you die,' meaning, not that death, which will be unfelt, will be forgiveness for their sin, but that death to salvation will be its punishment. Wisdom says: 'Take no pleasure in luxury, be it ever so small.'[26]

But let us turn our attention now to the food that is spoken of as 'idol-offered,'[27] and to the command enjoining us to avoid it. These foods I consider a sacrilege and an abomination: from the blood of them fly 'the shades from out of

---
24 Cf. *Iliad* 19.30,31.
25 Isa. 22.13.
26 Eccli. 18.32.
27 Cf. Acts 15.29; 21.25.

Erybus now dead.'[28] 'I would not have you become associates of devils,'[29] the Apostle says. There are two sorts of food, one minstering to salvation, and the other proper to those who perish. We should abstain from this last sort, not out of fear (for there is no power in them), but to keep our consciences pure and to show our contempt for the devils to whom they have been dedicated. And another reason is the impressionability of those who interpret so many things in a way that harms themselves, 'whose conscience, being weak, is defiled. Now, food does not commend us to God,'[30] 'nor does what goes into a man defile him, but what comes out of the mouth,'[31] in the words of Scripture. (9) The physical act of eating is indifferent. 'For neither do we suffer any loss if we eat,' Scripture continues, 'Nor if we do not eat shall we have any advantage.'[32] But it is not right for those judged worthy of partaking of divine and spiritual food to share 'the table of devils.'[33] 'Have we not a right,' the Apostle asks, 'to eat and drink and to take about with us a woman?'[34] But it stands to reason that we forestall passion when we keep pleasures under control: 'Still, take care lest this right of yours become a stumbling-block to the weak.'[35]

We ought not to misuse the gifts of the Father, then, acting the part of spendthrifts like the rich son[36] in the Gospel; let us, rather, make use of them with detachment, keeping them under control. Surely we have been commanded to be the

---
28 *Odysseus* 11.37.
29 1 Cor. 10.20.
30 1 Cor. 8.7.
31 Cf. Matt. 15.11.
32 1 Cor. 8.8.
33 1 Cor. 10.21.
34 1 Cor. 9.4.
35 1 Cor. 8.9.
36 Cf. Luke 15.11-14.

master and lord, not the slave, of food. It is an admirable thing indeed for a man to depend upon divine food in contemplation of the truth, and to be filled with the vision of that which really is, which is inexhaustible, tasting pleasure that is enduring and abiding and pure. Unquestionably, it is contrary to reason, utterly useless, and beneath human dignity for men to feed themselves like cattle being fattened for the slaughter, for those who come from the earth to keep looking down to the earth and ever bowed over their tables. Such men practise a life only of greed, by burying the good of this life in a way of life that will not last, and paying court only to their bellies, for whose sake they rate cooks more highly than they do those who work the soil. Not that we condemn conviviality, but we do suspect the danger lurking in banquets as unfortunate.

(10) We must shun gluttony and partake of only a few things that are necessary. And if some unbeliever invites us to a banquet and we decide to accept—although it is well not to associate with the disorderly—[the Apostle] bids us eat what is set before us, 'asking no question for conscience' sake.'[37] We do not need to abstain from rich foods completely, but we should not be anxious for them. We must partake of what is set before us, as becomes a Christian, out of respect for him who has invited us and not to lessen or destroy the sociability of the gathering. We should consider the rich variety of dishes that are served as a matter of indifference, and despise delicacies as things that after a while will cease to be. 'Let not him who eats despise him who does not eat, and let not him who does not eat judge him who eats.'[38] A little later [the Apostle] explains the reason for his com-

---
37 1 Cor. 10.27.
38 Rom. 14.3.

mand: 'He who eats,' he says, 'eats for the Lord and he gives thanks to God. And he who does not eat, abstains for the Lord and gives thanks to God.'[39] We conclude, then, that the true food is thanksgiving.[40] At any rate, he who always offers up thanks will not indulge excessively in pleasure.

But, if we would draw any of our fellow banqueters to virtue, we should refrain from these delicacies of the palate all the more, and make ourselves unmistakable examples of virtue, as Christ has done for us. 'For if any of these foods scandalize my brother, I will eat it no more for ever, lest I scandalize my brother,' that is, gaining the man by a little self-control. 'Have we not the right to eat and to drink?' 'We know the truth that there is no such thing as an idol in the world, and that there is no God but one, from whom are all things, and one Lord, Jesus Christ.' But he adds: 'through thy knowledge, the weak one will perish, the brother for whom Christ died. Now when you wound the conscience of your weak brother, you sin against Christ.'[41] Therefore, the Apostle takes great pains to reach this decision with regard to these dinners of ours: 'Not to associate with one who is called a brother if he is immoral, or an adulterer, or an idolator; with such a one not even to take food,'[42] neither the food of words nor that of meat, foreseeing the defilement of such contact, as with 'the table of devils.'

(11) 'It is good,' he says, 'not to eat meat and not to drink wine,'[43] just as the Pythagoreans say. Eating and drinking is the occupation of animals, and the fumes rising

---

39 Rom. 14.6.
40 *eucharistia*. Probably a veiled reference to the Sacrament. This term was already in use for the Body and Blood of Christ, as can be seen in Ignatius, *Ad Smyrn.* 7.1; *Ad Phil.* 4.1.
41 1 Cor. 8.13,4,6,11,12.
42 1 Cor. 5.11.
43 Rom. 14.21.

from them, heavy and earth-laden, cast a shadow over the soul. But, if anyone does partake of them, he does not sin; only let him partake temperately, without being attached to them or dependent upon them, or greedy for any delicacy. A voice will whisper to him: 'Do not for the sake of food, destroy the work of God.'[44]

Only a fool will hold his breath and gape at what is set before him at a public banquet, expressing his delight in words. But it is only a greater fool who will let his eyes become enslaved to these exotic delicacies, and allow self-control to be swept away, as it were, with the various dishes. Is it not utterly inane to keep leaning forward from one's couch, all but falling on one's nose into the dishes, as though, according to the common saying, one were leaning out from the nest of the couch to catch the escaping vapors with the nostrils? Is it not completely contrary to reason to keep dipping one's hands into these pastries or to be forever stretching them out for some dish, gorging oneself intemperately and boorishly, not like a person tasting a food, but like one taking it by storm? It is easy to consider such men swine or dogs rather than men, because of their voraciousness. They are in such a hurry to stuff themselves that both cheeks are puffed out at the same time, all the hollows of their face are filled out, and sweat even rolls down as they exert themselves to satisfy their insatiable appetite, wheezing from their intemperance, and cramming food into their stomachs with incredible energy, as though they were gathering a crop for storage rather than nourishment.

Lack of moderation, an evil wherever it is found, is particularly blameworthy in the matter of food. (12) Gourmandising, at least, is nothing more than immoderate use of de-

---
44 Rom. 14.20.

licacies; gluttony is a mania for glutting the appetite, and belly-madness, as the name itself suggests, is lack of self-control with regard to food. The Apostle, in speaking of those who offend at a banquet, exclaims: 'For at the meal, each one takes first his own supper, and one is hungry, and another drinks overmuch. Have you not houses for your eating and drinking? Or do you despise the church of God and put to shame the needy?'[45] If a person is wealthy, yet eats without restraint and shows himself insatiable, he disgraces himself in a special way and does wrong on two scores: first, he adds to the burden of those who do not have, and lays bare, before those who do have, his own lack of temperance. Little wonder, then, that the Apostle, after having taken to task those who were shamelessly lavish with their meals, and those who were voracious, never getting their fill, cried out a second time with an angry voice: 'Wherefore, my brethren, when you come together to eat, wait for one another. If anyone is hungry, let him eat at home, lest you come together unto judgment.'[46]

(13) Therefore, we must keep ourselves free of any suspicion of boorishness or of intemperance, by partaking of what is set before us politely, keeping our hands, as well as our chin and our couch, clean, and by preserving proper decorum of conduct, without twisting about or acting unmannerly while we are swallowing our food. Rather, we should put our hand out only in turn, from time to time; keep from speaking while eating, for speech is inarticulate and ill-mannered when the mouth is full, and the tongue, impeded by the food, cannot function properly but utters only indistinct sounds. It is not polite to eat and drink at the same time, either, be-

---
45 1 Cor. 11.21.
46 1 Cor. 11.23.

cause it indicates extreme intemperance to try to do two things together that need to be done separately.

'Whether you eat or drink,' the Apostle tells us, 'do all for the glory of God,'[47] cultivating the frugality of truth. It seems to me that the Lord was teaching frugality when He blessed the loaves and fishes with which He fed the disciples,[48] excellently illustrating indifference about food. (14) Then, that other fish which Peter caught at the Lord's bidding[49] is a good example of food easily gained, given by God, yet within the limits of self-restraint. In reality, Peter was commanded to rid those who rise to the bait of justice, from out the water, of all extravagance and love of money, just as he took the coin from the fish, in order to free them of vain ostentation; though he gave the stater to the tax-collector, rendering to Caesar what was Caesar's, he was commanded to keep for God what belonged to God. The stater could be explained in other ways, too, which would all be reasonable enough, but this is not the proper place to treat such explanations. It is enough to mention them in passing as we go on to ideas in keeping with our theme, ever keeping before ourselves the subject under discussion. This we have already done many times, drawing from the ever-useful fountain to irrigate the plants sown by our discussion for the main point at issue.

If it is true that 'it is lawful for me to partake of all things,' still, 'not all things are expedient.'[50] For, they who take advantage of everything that is lawful rapidly deteriorate

---
47 1 Cor. 10.31.
48 Cf. John 21.9.
49 Cf. Matt. 17.27.
50 1 Cor. 10.23.

into doing what is not lawful. Just as justice is not acquired through covetousness, or temperance through licentiousness, so, too, the Christian way of life is not achieved by self-indulgence. Far from 'lust-exciting delicacies'[51] is the table of truth. Even though all things have been created particularly for man, it is not well to make use of all things, nor to use them at all times. Surely, the occasion and the time, the manner and the motive, make some difference to one who is being educated [by Christ] to what is profitable. It is this goal that provides the strength we need to restrain ourselves from living lives centered about the table. Wealth chooses that sort of life, for its vision is blunted; it is an abundance that blinds in the matter of gluttony.

No one is destitute when it comes to the necessities of life, nor does any man need to look far for these.[52] For, He who provides for the birds and the fish, and, in a word, for unreasoning beasts, is one God.[53] They lack nothing, yet they are not anxious about their food. But we are better than they, because we are their masters, and are more akin to God, to the degree that we practise self-control. We have been created, not to eat and drink, but to come to the knowledge of God. 'The just man,' Scripture says, 'eateth and filleth his soul; but the belly of the wicked is ever in want,'[54] ever hungry with a greed that cannot be quenched.

Lavishness is not capable of being enjoyed alone; it must be bestowed upon others. (15) That is why we should shy away from foods that arouse the appetite and lead us to eat when we are not hungry. Even in moderate frugality, is there

---

51 Cf. *Adesp.* 887, *CAF* III 562.
52 Cf. Seneca, *Ep.* 17.9.
53 Cf. Matt. 6.26; Job 38.41.
54 Prov. 13.25.

not a rich and wholesome variety? Roots,[55] olives, all sorts of green vegetables, milk, cheese, fruits, and cooked vegetables of all sorts, but without the sauces. And should there be need for meat, boiled or dressed, let it be given. 'Have you anything here to eat?' the Lord asked His Apostles after His resurrection. 'And they offered Him a piece of broiled fish,' because He had taught them to practise frugality. 'And when He had finished eating, He said to them,'[56] and Luke goes on to record all that He said. We should not overlook the fact, either, that they who dine according to reason, or, rather, according to the Word,[57] are not required to leave sweetmeats and honey out of their fare. Surely, of all the foods available, the most convenient are those which can be used immediately without being cooked. Inexpensive foods come next in order, since these are so accessible, as we have already said.

As long as those other fellows stay hunched over their groaning tables, catering to their lusts, the devil of gluttony leads them by the nose. I, for one, would not hesitate to call that devil the devil of the belly, the most wicked and deadly of them all. He is very much like the so-called *engastrimythos*,[58] because he speaks, as it were, through his belly. It is far better to possess happiness than to have any daemon as a companion;[59] happiness is the practise of the virtues.

(16) Matthew the Apostle used to make his meal on

---

55 The Scholion says here: 'Father, what a word escapes the fence of thy teeth! (*Iliad* 4.350) For what food is harder to cook and more difficult to prepare than roots?'
56 Luke 24.41-44.
57 *lógos*, here used to suggest both 'reason' and the 'Word.'
58 A woman who delivered an oracle, usually by ventriloquism, throwing her voice to her stomach. Literally, the word means 'speaking through the stomach.' Cf. Aristotle, *Nic. Eth.* 3.1118B.
59 Aristotle, *op. cit.* 1.1097B-1098A. A play on the word for 'happiness' (*eu-daimōn*).

seeds and nuts and herbs, without flesh meat; John, maintaining extreme self-restraint, 'ate locusts and wild-honey';[60] and Peter abstained from pork. But, 'he fell into an ecstasy,' it is written in the Acts of the Apostles, 'and saw heaven standing open and a certain vessel let down by the four corners to the earth; and in it were all the four-footed beasts and creeping things of the earth and birds of the air. And there came a voice to him: Arise and kill and eat. But Peter said: Far be it from me, Lord, for never did I eat anything common or unclean. And there came a voice a second time to him: What God has cleansed, do not thou call common.'[61] The use of these foods is a matter of indifference for us, too, 'for not that which goes into the mouth defiles a man,'[62] but the barren pursuit of wantonness. When God formed man, He said: 'All these things will be food for you.'[63]

'Herbs with love rather than a fatted calf with deceit.'[64] This is reminiscent of what we said before, that herbs are not the Agape, but that meals should be taken with charity. A middle course is good in all things, and no less so in serving a banquet. Extremes, in fact, are dangerous, but the mean is good,[65] and all that avoids dire need is a mean. Natural desires have a limit set to them by self-sufficiency.

(17) Among the Jews, frugality was made a matter of precept by a very wise dispensation of the Law. The Educator forbade them the use of innumerable things, and He explained the reasons, the spiritual ones hidden, the material ones obvious, but all of which they trusted. Some animals [were forbidden] because they were cloven-footed; others,

---

60 Matt. 3.4.
61 Acts. 10.10-15.
62 Matt. 5.11.
63 Cf. Gen. 1.29.
64 Prov. 15.17.
65 Cf. Seneca, *Ep.* 5, *passim*.

because they did not ruminate their food; a third class, because they, alone among all the fish of the seas, had no scales;[66] until, finally, there were only a few things left fit for food. And, even of those He permitted them to touch, He placed a prohibition on the ones found dead or offered to idols or strangled.[67] They could not even touch them. He imposed upon them a contrary course of action until the inclination engendered by habits of easy living be broken, because it is difficult for one who indulges in pleasures to keep himself from returning to them.

Among men, pleasure generally gives rise to some sense of loss and of regret; overeating begets in the soul only pain and lethargy and shallow-mindedness. It is said, too, the bodies of the young in the period of their physical maturing are able to grow because they are somewhat lacking in nourishment; the life-principle which fosters growth is not encumbered—on the contrary, an excess of food would block the freedom of its course.

(18) So it is that he who of all philosophers so praised truth, Plato, gave new life to the dying ember of Hebrew philosophy by condemning a life spent in revelry: 'When I arrived,' he said, 'what is here called a life of pleasure, filled with Italian and Syracusan meals, was very repulsive to me. It is a life in which one gorges oneself twice a day, sleeps not only during the night, and engages in all the pastimes that go with this sort of life. No one upon earth could ever become wise in this way, if from his youth he had followed such pursuits as these, nor would he ever attain in that way any reputation for an excellent physique.'[68] Surely, Plato was not unacquainted with David, who, when he was settling

---
66 Cf. Lev. 11; Deut. 14.
67 Cf. Deut. 14.3-21; Acts 21.25.
68 Plato, *Ep.* 7.326BC.

the holy ark in the middle of the tabernacle of his city, made a feast for all his obedient subjects and 'before the face of the Lord, distributed to all the multitude of Israel, both men and women, to everyone, a cake of bread and baked bread and pan-cakes from the frying-pan.'[69] This food sufficed, this food of Israel; that of the Gentiles is extravagance.

'You will never be able to become wise' if you indulge in such extravagance, burying your mind deep in your belly; you will resemble the so-called ass-fish which Aristotle claims is the only living thing which has its heart in its stomach,[70] and which the comic poet Epicharmis entitles 'the huge-bellied.'[71] Such are the men who trust in their belly, 'whose god is their belly, whose glory is their shame, who mind the things of earth.'[72] For such men the Apostle makes a prediction foreboding nothing good, for he concludes: 'whose end is ruin.'

Chapter 2

(19) 'Use a little wine,' the Apostle cautions the water-drinking Timothy, 'use a little wine for thy stomach's sake.'[1] Shrewdly, he recommends a stimulating remedy for a body become ill-disposed and requiring medical attention, but he adds 'a little,' lest the remedy, taken too freely, itself come to need a cure.

Now, the natural and pure drink demanded by ordinary thirst is water. This it was that the Lord supplied for the

---

69 2 Kings 6.19.(Septuagint).
70 Aristotle, *Frag.* 326, in V. Rose, *Aristotelis Fragmenta* (Leipzig 1886).
71 Epicharmis, *Frag.* 67, in G. Kaibel *Fragmenta poetarum graecorum* VI 1 (1899).
72 Phil. 3.19.

---

1 1 Tim. 5.23.

Hebrews, causing it to gush from the split rock,² as their only drink, a drink of sobriety; it was particularly necessary that they who were still wandering should keep far from wine. Later on, a sacred vine put forth a cluster of grapes that was prophetic;³ to those who had been led by the Educator to a place of rest after their wanderings it was a sign, for the great cluster of grapes is the Word crushed on our account.⁴ The Word desired that the 'blood of the grape'⁵ be mixed with water as a symbol that His own blood is an integral element in salvation.

Now, the blood of the Lord is twofold: one is corporeal, redeeming us from corruption;⁶ the other is spiritual, and it is with that we are anointed. To drink the blood of Jesus is to participate in His incorruption.⁷ Yet, the Spirit is the strength of the Word in the same way that blood is of the body. (20) Similarly, wine is mixed with water and the Spirit is joined to man; the first, the mixture, provides feasting that faith may be increased; the other, the Spirit, leads us on to incorruption. The union of both, that is, of the potion and the Word, is called the Eucharist,⁸ a gift worthy of praise and surpassingly fair; those who partake of it are sanctified in body and soul, for it is the will of the Father that man, a composite made by God, be united to the Spirit and to the Word.⁹ In

---

2 Cf. Exod. 17.6; Num. 20.11.
3 Cf. Num. 13.24.
4 Cf. Isa. 53.5,10.
5 Cf. Gen. 49.11; Eccli. 50.16.
6 1 Pet. 1.8.
7 Cf. John 6.55.
8 Cf. above, p. 122 n. 40. De la Barre sees in this passage a clear reference to the Eucharistic Sacrament ('Clément de Alexandrie,' *DTC* III, cols. 196-197).
9 *pneûma* and *lógos*: these two words seem to refer in this context to the Third and Second Persons of the Trinity.

fact, the Spirit is closely joined to the soul depending upon Him, and the flesh to the Word, because it was for it that 'the Word was made flesh.'[10]

I have, then, only admiration for those who profess an austere life, limiting their desires to water, nourishment of sobriety, and avoiding wine as completely as they can, as they would the least threat of fire. It is conceded that boys and girls should, as a general rule, be kept from this sort of drink. It is not well for flaming youth to be filled with the most inflamable of all liquids, wine, for that would be like pouring fire upon fire. When they are under its influence, wild impulses, festering lusts, and hot-bloodedness are aroused; youths already on fire within are so much on the verge of satisfying their passions that the injury inflicted on them becomes evident by anticipation in their bodies, that is, the organs of lust mature before they should. I mean that, as the wine takes effect, the youths begin to grow heated from passion, without inhibition, and the breasts and sexual organs swell as a harbinger and an image of the act of fornication. The wound in their soul compels the body to manifest all the signs of passion, and the unrestrained throbbings aroused by temptation drive on into sin the curiosity of him who before had been sinless. (21) At that point, the freshness of youth has exceeded the bounds of modesty. Therefore, it is imperative to attempt to extinguish the beginnings of passion in the young, as far as posible: first, by excluding them from all that will inflame them—Bacchus and his threat—and second, by pouring on the antidote[11] that will restrain the smouldering soul, contain the aroused sexual movements, and calm the agitation of the storm-tossed desires.

---
10 John 1.4.
11 The Scholion says this refers to water.

As for adults, when they take their midday lunch, if that is their practise, let them take only a little bread and no liquids at all, so that the excessive moisture in their bodies may be assimilated and absorbed by the dry food. It is an indication, in fact, of disorder in the body caused by an excessive accumulation of liquids flowing through it, if we need to blow our noses constantly and experience a persistent urge to urinate. If they should become thirsty, let them relieve their thirst with water, but not too much of it. It is not good to drink water too freely, lest the food be simply washed away; the meal should be masticated to prepare it for digestion, only a little of it finally passing off as waste.

(22) Minds that bear something of the divine should not be overcome with wine for another reason, too. 'Strong wine,' in the words of the comic poet, 'keeps a man from thinking many thoughts'[12]—or, in fact, from being wise at all. But toward evening, near the time for supper, we may use wine, since we are no longer engaged in the public lectures which demand the absence of wine. At that time of day, the temperature has turned cooler than it was at midday, so that we need to stimulate the failing natural heat of the body with a little artificial warmth. But, even then, we must use only a little wine; certainly, we should not go so far as to demand whole bowls of it, because that would be sheer extravagance.

Again, those who have already passed the prime of life may be permitted more readily to enjoy their cup. They are but harmlessly making use of the medicine of wine to stimulate new warmth for the growing chill of old age as its heat dies down with the years. The passions of the aged are, for the most part, no longer storm-tossed with the threat of shipwreck from intemperance. Securely moored by the anchors of rea-

---

12 Menander, *Frag.* 779, *CAF* III 216.

son and of maturity, they easily bear the violent storm of passion aroused by drink, and they can even indulge in the merriment of feasts with composure. But, even for them, there is a limit: the point where they can still keep their minds clear, their memories active, and their bodies steady and under control, despite the wine. Those who know about these things call this the last drop before too much. (23) It is well to stop short before this point, for fear of disaster.

A certain Artorius, I recall, in a book on longevity, is of the opinion that we should drink only so much as is needed to moisten our food, if we would live a long life. It is certainly a good idea to use wine, as some do, only for the sake of health, as a tonic, or for relaxation and enjoyment, as others do. Wine makes the man who drinks more mellow toward himself, better disposed toward his servants, and more genial with his friends.[13] But, when he is overcome by wine, then he returns every offense of a drunken neighbor.

Wine is warm and gives out a sweet smell; therefore, in the proper mixture it thaws out the constipation of the intestines and with its sweetness dilutes every pungent or offensive odor. A quotation from Scripture will express it aptly: 'Wine drunken with moderation was created from the beginning as the joy of the soul and of the heart.'[14] But it is wise to dilute the wine with as much water as possible (and to avoid depending upon it as we do water), as well as to restrain our appetite for drinking bouts and to keep from drinking wine like water simply from intemperance. Both are creatures of God, and so the mixture of both, water and wine, contributes to our health. Life is made up of what is necessary, together with what is merely useful. (24) The merely useful should

---

13 Cf. Plato, *Laws* 649A.
14 Eccli. 31.36.

be combined with a very large part of what is necessary, that is, with water.

When wine is indulged in too freely, the tongue becomes thick, the jaw sags, the eyes begin to roll, for all the world as if they were swimming in pools of moisture, and the vision, forced to deceive, conceives everything as going round in a circle, and is not sure whether things are single or double. 'Indeed, I think I see two suns,' the old Theban in his cups complained.[15] Truly, the sense of sight is deranged by the heat of wine and imagines it sees many times over what is only one. But there is no difference between deranging the sense of sight and distorting the object that is seen: in either case, the vision is affected the same way in its derangement and cannot accurately perceive the object. Similarly, the gait takes on the appearance of being swept along in a stream, and then there arises, as maids-in-waiting, hiccoughing, retching, and silliness. For, 'every man overcome by wine,' says the tragedian, 'becomes subject to his passions and empty of mind, pours out idle chatter and is forced to hear against his will things he had said so willingly.'[16] Even before these words were written, Wisdom had warned: 'Wine drunken with excess raiseth quarrels and many ruins.'[17]

(25) That is why there is a common saying that we should relax over our cups and postpone serious business until dawn. But it seems to me that it is especially at that time that we should invite reason to be our companion at a feast and the controlling guide of our drinking, lest our feasting turn gradually into rioting. For, just as no one in his right mind would think of going about with his eyes shut until he

---
15 Euripides, *Bacch.* 918. The Scholion, however, says he means Pindar.
16 Sophocles, *Frag.* 843.
17 Eccli. 31.38.

was trying to sleep, so, too, no one has the right deliberately to dismiss reason from his table, or lull it to sleep on set purpose before some action. On her part, reason will never be able to separate herself from those who belong to her, even when they sleep; in fact, reason must be summoned to our beds. Wisdom, in its perfection, is the understanding of things human and divine, and includes all things; therefore, it is the art of living in that it presides over the human race. In that way, it is everywhere present wherever we live, ever accomplishing its work, which is living well.

But those pitiable people who exile temperance from their gatherings deem life the happiest when it turns into a wild drinking bout. Their life is nothing but carousing, drunken headaches, baths, undiluted wine, chamber-pots, idleness, and drinking. (26) You can see some of them, indeed, half-drunk, stumbling over themselves, with wreathes around their necks as though they were bottles,[18] spitting wine on one another in the name of good-fellowship; and others, too, suffering from the after-effects, unwashed, pallid, with flushed faces, yet, despite yesterday's spree, still gulping down one drink after the other. It is worth while, my friends, worth while indeed, to study this ridiculous yet pitiful picture, but at as great a distance as we can manage, and mend ourselves for the better, lest we ourselves some time may make a similar spectacle of ourselves, as ridiculous as they. It has been well said: 'As the kiln trieth the hard iron dipped in it, wine makes the heart arrogant' (in drunkenness).[19]

The excessive use of undiluted wine is intemperance; the

---

[18] According to the Scholion, Clement is thinking here of the cords and strings attached to amphorae.
[19] Cf. Eccli. 31.31; but in the Septuagint, from which this text is taken, 34.26.

CHRIST THE EDUCATOR 117

disorderliness resulting from it is drunkenness; and the discomfort and indisposition felt after indulgence is called the after-effect. The Greek name for this is a word that etymologically means 'to lose control of the head.'[20] (27) This sort of life—if it can be called living— is sluggish, intent only on enjoying pleasure, yet feverish in its passion for wine. Divine Wisdom, in its distrust for such a life, commands her children: 'Be not a wine-bibber, and do not reach out with your money for purchases of meat, for every drunkard and fornicator shall come to beggary, and every sleeper shall put on rags.'[21] Everyone who does not bestir himself to gain wisdom is a sleeper; he prefers to sleep deluged in drink. The drunkard, it says, will put on rags; he will become ashamed of his drunkenness because of those who see him. The rags of earthly garments are the torn [vesture] of the sinner, rent by his self-indulgences through which the shame of his soul within is exposed to view, that is, his sin because of which the garment that is so hopelessly tattered, so rotted away into countless lusts, so alien to salvation, will not easily be saved.

So it is that it adds as a stern warning: 'Who hath woe? Who hath contentions? Who falls into judgment? Who hath wounds without cause?' There you see the drunkard all in rags, neglecting reason and surrendering entirely to drink, despite all that Scripture has threatened him with. It adds more to the threat: 'Who hath redness of eyes? Are they not those that pass their time in wine? And those that seek where drink is?'[22] By the mention of redness of eyes—a sign of death—it is made clear that the wine-bibber is already dead to the Word and to reason: it declares his death to the Lord.

---

20 *kraipálē*, which Clement wrongly derives from *kára pállein*.
21 Prov. 23.20,21 (Septuagint).
22 Prov. 23.29,30.

If one forgets the motives that prompt him to seek the true life, he is dragged down to corruption. (28) With good reason, then, the Educator, in His concern for our salvation, sternly forbids us: 'Do not drink wine to drunkenness.' And do you ask why? 'Because,' He answers, 'Thy mouth will utter wicked things, and you will lie as though in the middle of the sea, and as the pilot in the great billowing.'[23]

Poetry comes to our aid, too, and warns: 'Whenever wine enters into a man with strength like fire, it tosses him on waves, as the north or south wind does the Libyan Sea,'[24] and 'Making them talk wildly, wine reveals all that has been hid; it is the ruin of those who drink; soul-deceiving wine,'[25] and so on through the rest of the passage. Do you not see the danger of shipwreck? The heart is battered by the flood of drink, and the quantity of wine drunk is like a threatening sea in which a man is swallowed like a ship in distress at sea; he sinks to the depths of disorderliness, drowned by huge waves of wine. The pilot, that is, the human mind, is tossed about by the billows of the overabundant wine, and in the middle of the whirlpool of a hurricane with its darkness fails to discover the harbor of truth, until, dashed against the hidden reefs, it is hurled upon the rocks of pleasure and destroyed.

(29) The Apostle commands, therefore, with good reason: 'Do not be drunk with wine, for in that is much debauchery,'[26] by debauchery meaning the hopeless state of the drunkard. Christ turned water into wine at the marriage feast,[27] but He did not encourage them to become drunk. He

---
23 Prov. 23.31,33,34 (Septuagint).
24 Eratosthenes, *Frag.* 34 (Hiller).
25 From an unknown poet.
26 Eph. 5.18
27 John 2.7,8.

was infusing life into the water of a [lukewarm] heart, pouring the blood of the vine into the whole world that was expected to fulfill the law born of Adam;[28] that is, He was supplying piety with a drink of truth, a mixture of the Old Law and the New Word, until the fulfillment of the time already decided upon. Scripture, then, always uses wine in a mystical sense, as a symbol of the holy Blood, and always repudiates any intemperate use made of it: 'Wine is licentious, and drunkenness is wanton.'[29]

It is in conformity with right reason that those who are very susceptible to cold use wine during the winter to keep from shivering and at other seasons of the year to take proper care of their stomach. Just as food is permitted to relieve hunger, so drink is to ease thirst, provided the greatest caution is taken against any abuse, for tasting wine is fraught with danger. If such a policy is followed, our souls should become clean and dry and lightsome: 'a soul that is dry is a light very wise and very noble.'[30] So, too, it will be initiated into the mysteries; its substance will not become oversaturated with water, from the mists rising like a cloud from wine.

(30) There should never be any wild search for Chian wine when it is not available, nor for Ariousian when that

---

28 This is a difficult passage, with the syntax almost unintelligible. Another possible translation, that of E. Molland, *The Conception of the Gospel in the Alexandrian Theology* (Oslo 1938) 25-26: 'He gave life to the watery element of the meaning of the Law, filling with the blood of the Vine, the true drink, him who was the doer of the Law ever since Adam, i.e., the whole world, holding out to the [sic] piety the mixture of the Old Law and the New Word as a fulfillment of the time which had been foreordained in the preaching [of the Old Testament].'
29 Prov. 20.1.
30 Heraclitus, *Frag.* 74, in H. Diels, *Die Fragmente der Vorsakratiker, griechisch und deutsch* (Berlin 1903).

fails. Thirst is simply the awareness of a need and requires only a relief corresponding to the need, one that will satisfy it, not deluge the mind. Importing wines from across the seas indicates cupidity grown soft from self-indulgence and a soul deranged by passion before it took to drink. There is the Thasian wine, which is sweet-smelling; Lesbian wine, which is fragrant; the Crean sweet wine; Syracusan pleasant-tasting wine; Mendesian wine from Egypt; insular Nazian wine; and Italian wine that is redolent of flowers. There exist all these various brands of wine, but for the temperate drinker it is only wine cultivated by the one only God. Why in the world is native wine insufficient to satisfy the taste? They even import water, as those foolish kings imported Choaspian water (from the so-called Choaspis river where the purest drinking water is found), cherishing this water as they would their dearest friends.[31] The Holy Spirit declares the rich wretched in their self-indulgence, exclaiming through the mouth of Amos: 'Those who drink purified wine, and sleep upon beds of ivory,'[32] and He adds other remarks to manifest His displeasure.

(31) We ought also to give special thought here to proper decorum. (Legend has it that even Athena, whoever she is, prudently renounced the pleasure of her flute because it made her look undignified.) We should drink without turning our head about, without swallowing all we can hold, without feeling compelled to roll our eyes around in the presence of the drink, and without draining the cup in one gulp with utter lack of self-control; thus we will not wet our chin or our clothes as we tip the cup all at once, practically washing or bathing our face in it. It is certainly a disgusting and

---
[31] Modern Karhkeh in Iran and Iraq.
[32] Cf. Amos 6.6,4.

undignified spectacle of self-indulgence to see a person greedily swallowing a drink with noisy intake of air, with a noise like a liquid being poured into an earthen jar, and making sounds with his throat from the forced swallowing. Besides, hasty drinking is a harmful practise to one who does it. If you are such a one, do not by excessive haste hurt yourself; your drink will not be snatched away; it was but just now given you, it will wait. Do not hurry to burst with such hasty drinking. Your thirst will be relieved just as well if you drink slowly, maintaining proper dignity and sipping the drink bit by bit in becoming manner. Time will not rob self-indulgence of that which it is in such hurry to grasp. 'Do not be foolhardy in wine,' Scripture says, 'for wine has destroyed very many.'[33]

(32) 'The Scythians and the Celts and the Iberians and the Thracians engage in drunkenness freely, for all of them are warrior nations, and they think they are following a noble and pleasant occupation.'[34] Let us who are a peaceful people give our feasts and drink our cup of friendship without wine, just to enjoy ourselves, not to commit sin; then, indeed, in keeping with its name, that cup will be recognized as proving friendship. How do you think the Lord drank when He had become man for our sake? As shamelessly as we do? Was it not rather with good manners, with dignity, and leisurely? You are aware, of course, that He, too, took wine; He, too, was man. In fact, He blessed wine, saying: 'Take, drink, this is My blood.'[35] He used the 'blood of the vine'[36] as a figure of the Word who 'was shed for us unto the remission of sins,'[37] a

---
33 Cf. Eccli. 31.30; in the Septuagint, from which this reading is taken, 34.24.
34 Plato, *Laws* I 637DE.
35 Cf. Mark 14.25.
36 Cf. Gen. 49.11; Eccli. 50.16.
37 Matt. 26.28.

stream of gladness. From the things He taught about banquets, He plainly insisted that one who drinks must keep self-control. He set the example by not drinking freely Himself. Yet, He proved that what He blessed was really wine when He said to His disciples: 'I will not drink of this fruit of the vine, until that day when I shall drink it with you in the kingdom of My Father.'[38] And that it was really wine which He drank, He said on another occasion when He reproached the Jews with their hardness of heart: 'The Son of Man came, and they say: Behold a glutton and a wine-drinker, a friend of publicans.'[39] (33) This is a quotation we can use to make the Encratites[40] look ridiculous.

As for women, who are especially trained in good manners, if only they would not keep their lips wide open as they drink from big cups, with their mouths distorted out of shape! And if only they would not lean their heads back when they drain vessels narrow of neck, thereby exposing their throats with—or so it seems to me—such immodesty! They hold their chins high as they pour the drink down, as if they were trying to reveal as much of themselves as they can to their companions at table; then they belch like men, or, rather, like slaves, and at their carousals begin to play the coquet. There is no fault that can be excused in a man of reason, and much less so in a woman to whom notoriety, whoever she is, brings only disgrace. 'A drunken woman,' in the words of Scripture, 'is a great wrath,'[41] as if to say that a woman become dissolute from wine is the wrath of God. Why? Because 'her shameless conduct shall not be hid.' A woman is quickly

---

38 Matt. 26.29.
39 Matt. 11.19.
40 An heretical sect which practised austere asceticism in a Gnostic distrust of matter.
41 Eccli. 26.11.

drawn into immorality even by only giving consent to pleasure.

Now, we have not proscribed drinking from precious alabaster cups, but we do condemn as overostentatious the practise of drinking from them alone. We recommend indifference in using whatever is at hand, and a desire to restrain desires, for desires always and repeatedly betray a person into sin. The emission of the breath in a belch should be made noiselessly. Women are not at all to be allowed to expose or lay bare any part of their bodies, lest both men and women fall: the one by being aroused to steal glances, the other by attracting the eyes of men to themselves. We must always behave with good manners, realizing that the Lord is present, so that He may never say to us reproachfully what the Apostle said to the Corinthians: 'When you meet together, it is no longer to eat the Lord's Supper.'[42]

(34) It strikes me that the constellation called by astronomers 'the Headless', enumerated just before the Wandering Star, its head sunk upon its breast, is a figure of those who are so indulgent in their foods, so given over to pleasure, and of those who are so fond of wine. Certainly, the reasoning power of such men is not located in their head, but in their stomach, for it is the slave of passion and lust and gluttony. Truly, just as Elpenor fell down in a drunken stupor and broke his neck,[43] their mind, become dizzy from excessive drink, falls down to the liver and the heart, that is, to love of pleasure and to passion. This is a greater fall than that which the tribe of poets tell us Hephaestus took when cast down by Zeus from heaven to earth.[44]

'The pain of sleeplessness and cholera and cramp are with

---

42 1 Cor. 11.20.
43 *Odysseus* 10.560.
44 Cf. *Iliad* 1.590-593.

the intemperate man,'[45] it is written. That is why the drunkenness of Noe also has been described,[46] so that we may guard against drunkenness as much as possible, with the picture of such a fall clearly described before our eyes in Scripture. That is why, too, the Lord blessed those who covered the shame of his drunkenness.

Scripture, summing everything up in one succint verse, has said: 'Wine that is sufficient for a man well taught, and upon his bed, he shall rest.'[47]

Chapter 3

(35) The use of drinking cups made of gold or silver, and of those set with precious stones, is without any purpose at all, a fraudulent display merely for the eyes. Either someone pours a hot drink into such a cup, and it becomes too hot to be handled with comfort; or something cold, and then the drink is spoiled, no matter how costly it was, because it changes its nature and even becomes poisonous. Away, then, with all Thericleian and Antigonidan chalices, with scarab- and greed- and limpet-cups and the thousand and one other varieties, and along with them, wine-coolers and wine-pourers as well![1]

'Gold and silver, in general, are a possession that corrupts both the individual and the community,'[2] for they exceed the

---

45 Eccli. 31.23.
46 Cf. Gen. 9.21.
47 Eccli. 31.22.

---

1 According to the Scholion, these cups were of all different shapes, adapted to the convenience of the drinkers. The first two were named from their inventors; the next three, from their shapes.
2 Cf. Plato, *Laws* XII 955E.

demands of real need, are possessed too rarely, are difficult to retain, and are not suited for ordinary use. Surely, the elaborate ostentatiousness of glass-workers should find no place in a well-regulated way of life, because the overdelicate artistry of the glass makes it more easily broken, and us everfearful as we drink. Besides that, couches made of silver, dishes and saucers, the smaller dishes and bowls of silver, and other gold and silver utensils, some for serving food, others for needs I blush to name, 'three-legged stools worked of soft cedar, of thyme, ebony and ivory,'[3] couches with silver legs and inlaid with ivory, folding-doors speckled with gold and embellished with tortoise-shell, blankets dyed in purple and other fast dyes, all these things are manifestations of vulgar self-indulgence, of the treacherous and selfish devices of envy and sloth and must be absolutely forbidden, for they do not serve one single worth-while purpose. 'For the time is short,' the Apostle says.[4]

This is to say that we should not make ourselves ridiculous, like the women who can be seen in processions, painted up outlandishly exteriorly, but interiorly wretched. (36) To leave no doubt, [the Apostle] adds in greater detail: 'It remains that those who have wives be as if they had none, and those who buy as though not possessing.'[5] Now, if that is said of wedlock, of which God commands: 'Increase and multiply,'[6] can you doubt that such vulgar display is to be banished, on the authority of the Lord Himself? Indeed, the Lord also said: 'Sell what thou hast, and give to the poor and come follow Me.'[7] Follow God, rid of false pretenses, rid of

---
3 *Odysseus* 5.60.
4 1 Cor. 7.29. The text is defective here.
5 1 Cor. 7.29,30.
6 Gen. 1.28.
7 Matt. 19.21.

pomp that perishes, possessing only what is really yours, the good that cannot be taken from you: faith in God, belief in Him who suffered, good works toward men, your most valuable possessions.

As for me, I heartily approve of Plato's forthright legislation: 'one ought not to labor to possess wealth of gold or silver,'[8] or superfluous utensils, either, because they exceed the limits of moderation if they do not serve some practical purpose. A utensil should be adaptable to many varied services, so that we can eliminate excessive possessions. Divine Scripture says aptly somewhere: 'Where are the princes of the nations, and they that rule over the beasts that are upon the earth? That take their diversion with the birds of the air? That hoard up silver and gold wherein men trust, and there is no end of their getting? Who work in silver and gold and are solicitous? And their works are unsearchable. They are cut off and gone down to hell.'[9] (37) That is the reward for their cheap ostentatiousness. Certainly, if we need a hoe or a plough for farm work, we would never fashion a one-pronged silver pickaxe to serve as a two-pronged hoe, or a golden harrow for our plough. We would look not for a precious metal, but for one suitable for tilling the soil. When it comes to household utensils, what prevents those who have a similar useful purpose in mind from manifesting the same sense of values? Expensiveness should not be the goal in objects whose purpose is usefulness. Why? Tell me, does a table knife refuse to cut if it be not studded with silver or have a handle of ivory? Must it be made of Indian steel to cut a piece of meat, like a man in search of an ally? What difference does it make if the wash basin be only of clay?

---

8 Plato, *Laws* VII 801B.
9 Bar. 3.16-19.

Will it not hold water anyway to wash the hands? And the foot basin, water to wash the feet? Will a table with legs carved of ivory take it ill that it supports only bread worth one obol, or will a lamp refuse to shed light because it came from the hands not of a goldsmith, but of the potter? A lowly cot affords no worse repose than an ivory bed, and the goat-hair cloak can so easily be thrown over one as covering that there is no need of special purple and crimson-dyed blankets.[10] Yet, for my part, I still say that I am accused of frugality because of the stupidity engendered by self-indulgence, the mother of all evil.

(38) See how great an error this is, and what a false sense of beauty. The Lord ate His meal from an inexpensive bowl;[11] made His disciples recline on the ground, upon grass;[12] washed their feet, girding Himself with a linen towel; He, the humble God, Lord of the universe, carried a foot basin made, be it noted, of no precious silver brought from heaven.[13] He asked the Samaritan woman, who had drawn water from the well with a bucket made only of clay, to give Him to drink;[14] He did not seek the gold of kings, but taught us to rest content with what will quench thirst. Beyond question, He confined Himself to the useful, not the ostentatious, good. When He ate and drank at banquets, He did not require metals dug out of the earth, or dishes that tasted of gold or silver, that is, poison, as if exuding from steaming matter.

I maintain, then, that food and clothing and dishes, and, in a word, all the items of the household, ought to be, as a gene-

---
10 Cf. Musonius, in Stobaeus, *Florilegium* 85.20.
11 Cf. Matt. 26.23.
12 Cf. Matt. 14.19.
13 John 13.4,5.
14 John 4.7.

ral rule, in keeping with a Christian way of life and in conformity with what is fitting, adapted to person, age, occupation, and occasion. For we are servants of the one God, and so ought to insure that our belongings and the equipment needed for them manifest the one noble way of life. Every individual, in unquestioning faith and in his own individual way of life, should openly perform the duties that naturally follow from, and are consonant with, this one mentality. We easily praise what we acquire by using them with contentment of mind, by preserving them readily, and by sharing them readily. Certainly, things that have a practical utility are better; therefore, inexpensive things are obviously better than costly.

Generally speaking, riches that are not under complete control are the citadel of evil. If the ordinary people look on them covetously, they will never enter the kingdom of heaven,[15] because they are letting themselves become contaminated by the things of this world and are living above themselves in self-indulgence. (39) Those concerned for their salvation should take this as their first principle, that, although the whole of creation is ours to use, the universe is made for the sake of self-sufficiency, which anyone can acquire by a few things. They who rejoice in the holdings in their storehouses are foolish in their greed. 'He that hath earned wages,' Scripture reminds us, 'put them into a bag with holes.'[16] Such is the man who gathers and stores up his harvest,[17] for by not sharing his wealth with anyone he becomes worse off.

It is farcical and downright ridiculous for men to bring out urinals of silver and chamber-pots of transparent alabaster, as if grandly ushering in their advisers, and for rich women in

---
15 Cf. Matt. 19.23.
16 Ag. 1.6.
17 Cf. Luke 12.16-21.

their silliness to have privies made of gold. It is as if the wealthy were not able even to relieve nature except in a grandiose style. Yet I would wish that for the rest of their lives they considered gold worthy only of dung.[18]

But, as it is, love of money is proved to be the citadel of evil, and, as the Apostle says, 'the root of all evil.' 'Some in their eagerness to get rich have strayed from the faith, and have involved themselves in many troubles.'[19] Poverty of heart is the true wealth,[20] and the true nobility is not that founded on riches, but that which comes from a contempt for it.[21] It is disgraceful to boast about one's possessions; not to be concerned about them any longer very clearly proves the just man. Anyone who wishes can buy such things from the market; but wisdom is bought, not with any earthly coin, nor in any market, but is acquired in heaven, at a good price: the incorruptible Word, the gold of kings.

Chapter 4

(40) In the feasts of reason that we have, let the wild celebrations of the holiday season have no part, or the senseless night-long parties that delight in wine-drinking. The wild celebration ends up as a drunken stupor, with everyone freely confiding the troubles of his love affairs. But love affairs and drunkenness are both contrary to reason, and therefore do not belong to our sort of celebrations. And as for all-night drinking parties, they go hand-in-hand with the holiday celebration

---
18 Cf. Phil. 3.8.
19 Cf. 1 Tim. 6.10.
20 Cf. Matt. 5.3.
21 A play on words: 'true nobility' he calls *megalo-phronein*, ('to think great things'), identifying it with *kata-phronein* ('to think down upon').

and, in their wine-drinking, promote drunkenness and promiscuity. They are brazen celebrations that work deeds of shame. The exciting rhythm of flutes and harps, choruses and dances, Egyptian castanets and other entertaiments get out of control and become indecent and burlesque, especially when they are re-enforced by cymbals and drums and accompanied by the noise of all these instruments of deception. It seems to me that a banquet easily turns into a mere exhibition of drunkenness. The Apostle warned: 'Laying aside the works of darkness, put on the armor of light. Let us walk becomingly as in the day, not occupying ourselves in revelry and drunkenness, not in debauchery and wantonness.'[1]

(41) Leave the pipe to the shepherd, the flute to the men who are in fear of gods and are intent on their idol-worshiping. Such musical instruments must be excluded from our wineless feasts, for they are more suited for beasts and for the class of men that is least capable of reason than for men. We are told that deer are called by horns and hunted by huntsmen to traps, there to be captured by the playing of some melody; that, when mares are being foaled, a tune is played on a flute as a sort of hymeneal which musicians call a *hippothorus*.[2] In general, we must completely eliminate every such base sight or sound—in a word, everything immodest that strikes the senses (for this is an abuse of the senses)—if we would avoid pleasures that merely fascinate the eye or ear, and emasculate. Truly, the devious spells of syncopated tunes and of the plaintive rhythm of Carian music[3] corrupt morals by their sensual and affected style, and insidiously inflame the passions.

---

1 Rom. 13.12.
2 Literally, 'horse's mating-song.'
3 Carian melodies were a sort of funeral dirge.

The Spirit, to purify the divine liturgy from any such unrestrained revelry, chants: 'Praise Him with sound of trumpet,'[4] for, in fact, at the sound of the trumpet the dead will rise again; 'praise Him with harp,' for the tongue is a harp of the Lord; 'and with the lute, praise Him,' understanding the mouth as a lute moved by the Spirit as the lute is by the plectrum; 'praise Him with timbal and choir,' that is, the Church awaiting the resurrection of the body in the flesh which is its echo; 'praise Him with strings and organ,' calling our bodies an organ and its sinews strings, for from them the body derives its co-ordinated movement, and when touched by the Spirit, gives forth human sounds; 'praise Him on high-sounding[5] cymbals,' which mean the tongue of the mouth, which, with the movement of the lips, produces words. (42) Then, to all mankind He calls out: 'Let every spirit praise the Lord,' because He rules over every spirit He has made. In reality, man is an instrument made for peace, but these other things, if anyone concerns himself overmuch with them, become instruments of conflict, for they either enkindle desires or inflame the passions. The Etruscans, for example, use the trumpet for war; the Arcadians, the horn; the Sicels, the flute; the Cretans, the lyre; the Lacedemonians, the pipe; the Thracians, the bugle; the Egyptians, the drum; and the Arabs, the cymbal. But as for us, we make use of one instrument alone: only the Word of peace, by whom we pay homage to God, no longer with ancient harp or trumpet or drum or flute which those trained for war employ. They give little thought to fear of God in their festive

---

4 Cf. Ps. 150.3-6.
5 The Scholion says: 'This word (*alalagmoú*) means a shout of victory. To those who have conquered sensual uncleanness, a shout of victory is very appropriately assigned.'

dances, but seek to arouse their failing courage by such rhythmic measures.

(43) But make sure that the sociability arising from our drinking is twofold, in keeping with the direction of the Law. For, if 'Thou shalt love the Lord thy God,' and after that, 'thy neighbor,'[6] then intimacy with God must come first, and be expressed in thanksgiving and chanting of psalms. Only then are we free to show sociability toward our neighbor in a respectful comradeship. 'Let the word of the Lord dwell in you abundantly,' the Apostle says. But this Word adapts Himself and adjusts Himself to the occasion, person, and place; in our present discussion, He is the congenial companion of our drinking. The Apostle adds further: 'In all wisdom teach and admonish one another by psalms, hymns and spiritual songs, singing in your hearts to God by His grace. Whatever you do in word or in work, do all in the name of the Lord Jesus, giving thanks to God His Father.'[7] This Eucharistic feast of ours is completely innocent, even if we desire to sing at it, or to chant psalms to the lyre or lute. Imitate the holy Hebrew king in his thanksgiving to God: 'Rejoice in the Lord, O ye just; praise becometh the upright,' as the inspired psalm says: 'Give praise to the Lord on the harp, sing to Him with the lyre'—an instrument with ten strings—'Sing to Him a new canticle.'[8] There can be little doubt that the lyre with its ten strings is a figure of Jesus the Word, for that is the significance of the number ten.[9]

(44) It is fitting to bless the Maker of all things before we partake of food; so, too, at a feast, when we enjoy His created gifts, it is only right that we sing psalms to Him. In

---
6 Cf. Matt. 22.37-39.
7 Col. 3.16,17.
8 Ps. 32.1-3.
9 The Greek 'I' (iota) of *Iesoús* represents the numeral ten.

fact, a psalm sung in unison is a blessing, and it is an act of self-restraint. The Apostle calls the psalm 'a spiritual song.'[10] Again, it is a holy duty to give thanks to God for the favors and the love we have received from Him, before we fall asleep. 'Give praise to Him with canticles of your lips,' Scripture says, 'because at His command, every favor is shown, and there is no diminishing of His salvation.'[11] Even among the ancient Greeks, there was a song called the skolion which they used to sing after the manner of the Hebrew psalm at drinking parties[12] and over their after-dinner cups. All sang together with one voice, and sometimes they passed these toasts of song along in turn; those more musical than the rest sang to the accompaniment of the lyre.

Yet, let no passionate love songs be permitted there; let our songs be hymns to God. 'Let them praise His name in choir,' we read, 'let them sing to Him with the drum and the harp.' And the Holy Spirit explains what this choir is which sings: 'Let His praise be in the church of the saints: let them be joyful to their king.' And He adds: 'For the Lord is well-pleased with His people.'[13] We may indeed retain chaste harmonies, but not so those tearful songs which are too florid in the overdelicate modulation of the voice they require. These last must be proscribed and repudiated by those who would retain virility of mind, for their sentimentality and ribaldry degenerate the soul. There is nothing in common between restrained, chaste tunes and the licentiousness of intemperance. Therefore, overcolorful melodies are to be left to shameless[14] carousals, and to the honeyed and garish music of the courtesan.

---

10 Cf. Col. 3.16; Eph. 5.19.
11 Eccli. 39.20-23.
12 *Sympósia*, as described by Plato or Xenophon.
13 Ps. 149.3,1,4.
14 Literally, 'colorless'; thus a play on words.

Chapter 5

(45) Men who imitate laughable or ridiculous behavior are to be excluded from our city.[1] All exterior words have their source in the temperament and in the character; therefore, no foolish words can be spoken without betraying a foolish temperament. The old saying holds good here, that 'there is no good tree that bears bad fruit, neither again is there a bad tree that bears good fruit.'[2] The fruit of the temperament is words.

But, if we feel that clowns are to be excluded from our city, we should be the first to give over playing the clown. It is inconsistent for us to be found performing the very role to which we have forbidden ourselves to listen. It is even more inconsistent for us to make ourselves a laughing-stock deliberately, that is, the butt of insults and of jokes. If we cannot bear cutting a ridiculous figure such as some are seen to do in the processions, how can we possibly tolerate a man in his right senses cutting an even more ridiculous figure? And if we would not deliberately turn to watch some absurd clowning, how can we make a practise of being and appearing clownish in our conversation, turning the most respectable possession man has, his speech, into a joke? It is a sorry sight to see anyone make an habitual practise of such a thing, because a conversation consisting of nothing but jests is certainly not worth listening to; by the repetition of unbecoming words we lose all fear of unbecoming deeds. We should be pleasantly witty, but not clowns.

(46) As for laughter itself, it, too, should be kept under restraint. Of course, when it rings out as it should, it proves

---
1 Cf. Plato, *Republic* X 606C.
2 Luke 6.4,3.

the presence of discipline, but if it gets out of hand, it is a sure index of lack of self-control. We need not take away from man any of the things that are natural to him, but only set a limit and due proportion to them. It is true that man is an animal who can laugh;[3] but it is not true that he therefore should laugh at everything. The horse is an animal that neighs, yet it does not neigh at everything. As rational animals, we must ever maintain proper balance, gently relaxing the rigor of seriousness and intensity without dissipating it out of all bounds.

Now, the proper relaxation of the features within due limits—as though the face were a musical instrument—is called a smile (that is the way joy is reflected on the face); it is the good humor of the self-contained. But the sudden loss of control over one's composure, in the case of women, is called a giggle, the laugh of harlots, and in the case of men, a guffaw, the laughter of idle suitors,[4] offensive to the ear. 'A fool lifteth up his voice in laughter,' Scripture says, 'but a cunning man will scarce laugh low to himself.'[5] The one called cunning here is really the prudent man, just the opposite of a fool. (47) On the other hand, we should not become gloomy, either; only serious-minded. I certainly welcome the smiling fellow who showed up 'with a smile on his grim face,'[6] for 'then his laughter would be less disdainful.'[7]

It is well that even the smile be kept under the influence of the Educator. If it is a question of indecencies, we should make it plain that we are blushing in shame, rather than smiling, lest we be thought to give consent and agreement. If it is some misfortune, we should not manifest a light-

---
3 Cf. Aristotle, *De partibus animalium* III 10.673A.
4 That is, Penelope's suitors. Cf. *Odysseus* 23.100.
5 Eccli. 21.23.
6 *Iliad* 7.212.
7 Plato, *Republic* VII 518B.

hearted appearance, but look sorrowfully sober. That indicates human tact; the other would be cruelty. But, we should not be always laughing—that would be lack of judgment—nor should we laugh in the presence of older persons or of those who deserve respect, unless, perhaps, they themselves make some witticism to put us at our ease. Nor should we give way to laughter with every chance companion, nor in every place, nor at everything, nor with everyone. Laughter can easily give rise to misunderstandings, particularly among boys and women.

(48) Then, too, it takes nothing more than a serious expression to keep at arm's length those who would tempt us. There is some quality in seriousness to strike fear into those who approach with immoral intent, and at that, simply by its bearing. But wine causes those who have become, so to speak, without sense 'to laugh gently and to dance,'[8] transforming an already weak character into a completely unmanly one. We should never lose sight of the fact, too, that excessive garrulousness quickly leads indelicacy into downright indecency: 'And he spoke a word which it were better left unsaid.'[9] At any rate, it is especially under the influence of drink that the characters of those who are interiorly festering become exposed to view stripped of all hypocrisy, for drunkenness gives free rein to loquaciousness. It lulls reason to sleep, for it lays heavy hands upon the soul itself, arouses passions, and oppresses the weakness of the mind.

---
8 *Odysseus* 7.212; 5.463.
9 *Ibid.* 5.465.

Chapter 6

(49) We ourselves must steer completely clear of all indecent talk, and those who resort to it we must silence by a sharp look, or by turning our face away, or by what is called a grunt of disgust, or by some pointed remark. 'For the things that come out of the mouth,' Scripture says, 'defile a man,'[1] and reveal him as uncouth, barbaric, undisciplined, and unrestrained, and as completely without self-possession, decorum, or modesty.

As for listening to or gazing upon indecent things, the divine Educator, in an effort to keep our hearing from being offended against, has proposed words on self-restraint for those of His children engaged in the fight with such things, as mufflers for the ears. Thus, talk about indecent things will not be able to penetrate into the soul and injure it. The eyes, too, He directs to the vision of good things, saying that it is better to stumble with the feet than with the eyes.[2]

(50) Then, the Apostle, lashing out at this indecent talk, cautions us: 'Let no ill speech proceed from your mouth, but whatever is good,'[3] and another time: 'As becomes saints, let obscenity or foolish talk or scurrility not even be named among you; which are out of place, but rather thanksgiving.'[4] If he who merely calls his brother a fool is liable to judgment,[5] what sentence should be passed upon obscene conversation? 'Whoever speaks an idle word shall give an account to the Lord on the day of judgment,' and again: 'By thy words

---
1 Matt. 15.18.
2 Cf. Matt. 18.9.
3 Eph. 4.29.
4 Eph. 5.3.
5 Cf. Matt. 5.22.

thou wilt be justified, and by thy words thou wilt be condemned.'⁶

Now, what are these protecting mufflers for the ears? And what the directions He gives for eyes so prone to stumble? The precaution of cultivating the friendship of good people, and of turning deaf ear to those who would lead us away from the truth. 'Evil associations corrupt good manners,' the poet says.⁷ But a quotation from the Apostle is more to the point: 'Hate what is evil, hold to what is good.'⁸ He who associates with the holy will become holy.

(51) It is imperative, then, that we neither listen to nor look at nor talk about obscene things. And it is even more imperative that we keep free of every immodest action, exposing or laying bare any parts of our body improperly, or looking at its private parts. The chaste son could not endure looking upon the immodest nakedness of a good man; chastity covered over what drunkenness had exposed in a transgression committed in ignorance but manifest to all.⁹ It is no less urgent that we keep ourselves pure in our choice of words, avoiding those which should be alien to the ears of one who believes in Christ. That is why, I believe, the Educator has forbidden us to utter the least thing that is unbecoming, to keep us far from immorality. He is ever skillful in cutting to the very roots of sin, commanding: 'Thou shalt not lust,'¹⁰ to safeguard the other command: 'Thou shalt not commit adultery.'¹¹ Adultery is only the fruit of lust, and lust is its evil root.

---

6 Matt. 12.36.
7 Menander, *Thais Frag.* 218 *CAF* III 62.
8 Rom. 12.9.
9 Cf. Gen. 9.21-23.
10 Cf. Matt. 5.27,28.
11 *Ibid.;* Exod. 20.14; Deut. 5.18.

(52) For the same reason, our Educator has proscribed the too free use of certain terms, meaning to eliminate too free contact with immorality. Lack of restraint in the words we use gives rise to habitual disorderliness in actions, while to take pains to be discreet in our language is to control licentiousness. In a more profound discussion,[12] we have shown that it is not the terms, or the sexual organs, or the marriage act, to which names not in common use describing intercourse are affixed, that we should consider obscene. It is not the knee, or the thigh, or the names given to them, or even the use made of them, that is obscene. (In fact, even the private parts of a man's body deserve to be treated not with prudery but with privacy.) It is only the unlawful use of these organs that is improper and that is to be considered shameful, and therefore deserving of punishment. Evil alone is truly shameful, and deeds marked with evil.

In the same way, writings that treat of evil deeds must be considered indecent talk, such as the description of adultery or pederasty or similar things. Nonsensical chatter, too, should be silenced. 'In the multitude of words,' it is written, 'there shall not want sin.'[13] Talkativeness will draw down upon itself some kind of penalty. 'There is one that holds his peace, that is found wise.' But the chatterer has already made himself a bore to himself: 'He that useth many words shall abominate his own soul.'[14]

---
12 It is uncertain whether this is a special work, not extant, or *Strōmateis* II 23 and III. Cf. J. Patrick, *op. cit.* 301-308.
13 Prov. 10.19.
14 Eccli. 20.5,8.

Chapter 7

(53) Let us keep far, very far, from raillery, the starting-point of insults; from it, great quarrels and feuds and enmities develop. We are of the opinion that insolence is the attendant of drunkenness. It is not only by his deeds, but also by his words, that a man is judged.[1] 'Rebuke not thy neighbor,' Scripture says, 'in a banquet of wine; and speak not to him a word of reproach.'[2] Certainly, if we have been strongly advised to associate with the holy,[3] then to make fun of a holy man is a sin. 'In the mouth of a fool,' it is said, 'is the rod of pride,'[4] meaning by 'rod' that which supports insolent pride, that on which it leans and rests. So, I admire the wisdom of the Apostle when he advises us for this reason not to use words that are coarse or out of place.[5]

If we meet at banquets for charity's sake, and if the purpose of such feasts is the goodfellowship created among the guests, with the food and drink merely accessories of charity, then should we not maintain a behavior that bespeaks the control of reason? (Incidentally, we need not impoverish ourselves to practise charity.) And if we gather with the intention of showing good-will toward one another, then why do we stir up ill-will by railing at others? It is better to keep silent than to engage in bickering, adding the fault of deed to that of boorishness. Surely, 'blessed is the man that hath not slipped by a word out of his mouth, and is not pricked with the remorse of sin,'[6] or at least has repented of the sins committed in speech, or has conversed without inflicting pain on anyone.

---

1 Cf. Matt. 12.37.
2 Eccli. 31.41,42.
3 Cf. Eccli. 37.15.
4 Prov. 14.3.
5 Cf. Eph. 5.4.
6 Eccli. 14.1.

(54) Let young men and women be kept from banquets of this sort, as a general rule, so that they may not fall into any improper misconduct. There can be no doubt that the indecent things heard, and the unbecoming things seen, unsettle their faith, set their imagination afire, and add fuel to the natural fickleness of their youth to make them ready victims of their passions. At times, too, they are to blame for the fall of others, proving how dangerous an occasion such a banquet can be. It is a good command that Wisdom gives: 'Sit not at all with another man's wife, nor repose upon a couch with her,' that is, do not dine or eat with her too often. Then it adds: 'Do not have a meal with her in wine, lest perhaps thy heart decline toward her, and by thy blood, thou fall into destruction.'[7] Drinking unrestrainedly is dangerous because it can so easily degenerate into licentiousness. Scripture speaks of 'another man's wife,' because there is a greater danger in such a case of destroying the wedding bond.

But, if there arise any need for women to be present, let them be amply clothed: exteriorly with a cloak, interiorly with modesty. The worst accusation that can be brought against any woman not subject to a husband is that she was present at a party for men, and, at that, for men in their cups. And as for young men, let them keep their eyes fixed on their own couch, lean on their elbow without too much fidgeting, and be present only with their ears. If they should be sitting down, let them not put their feet one on top of the other, nor cross their legs, nor rest their chin on their hands. It is lack of good breeding to fail to support oneself, yet a fault common in the young. (55) To be forever restlessly shifting one's position argues for levity of character.

It is the mark of a temperate man to take only a small

---
7 Eccli. 9.12.

amount while eating or drinking, yet a good amount of time in doing it; not rushing as fast as he can in the way he begins to eat, and pausing now and then; to be the first to finish and to cultivate an attitude of indifference. 'Eat,' Scripture says, 'as a man, what is set before thee, leave off first, for discipline's sake, and if thou sittest among many, reach not thy hand out first of all.'[8] Needless to say, we should not lean forward to get our helping first, under the impulse of gluttony, nor should we eagerly reach out too far, confessing lack of self-control by our fault. Neither should we, in the meantime, stand guard over our food like animals over their meat, nor indulge in too many dainties. (56) It is a mark of a temperate man, too, to rise before the rest and modestly withdraw from the table. 'And at the time of rising,' it is said, 'be not slack: and run home to thy house.'[9] Again: 'The Twelve called together the multitude of the disciples and said: It is not desirable that we should forsake the word of God and serve at Tables.'[10] Certainly, if they avoided such service, they avoided serving their own belly much more.

The same Apostles, writing 'to the brothers in Antioch, and Syria and Cilicia,' said: 'The Holy Spirit and we have decided to lay no further burden upon you but this indispensable one, that you abstain from things sacrificed to idols, and from blood, and from what is strangled, and from immorality: keep yourselves from these things and you will get on well.'[11] We are to shun drinking parties, then, as we would the poison of the hemlock, for both drag us down to death.

'We must also restrain ourselves from undue laughter and

---

8 Eccli. 31.19.
9 Eccli. 32.15.
10 Acts 6.2.
11 Acts 15.23-28.

tears,'[12] beyond due measure. In fact, those who just now were guffawing over almost everything under the influence of wine often become overcome, I know not how, by some drunken stupor and give way to depression to the point of tears. Both womanish and insolent conduct are discordant with reason. (57) Old men who look on young men as children may, perhaps, although only infrequently, jest with them, teasing them in a way that will teach them good manners. With a shy and taciturn youth, for example, they may make this pleasantry: 'My son,'—indicating the youth who is so quiet—'never stops talking.' Such teasing encourages the young man in his modesty, for, by accusing him of a fault he does not have, it jestingly calls attention to his good qualities. This is, indeed, a sort of instruction, securing what one has by reference to what one does not have. He who says that a man who confines himself to water and is self-controlled is always attending parties and getting drunk accomplishes the same sort of thing. If there should be present any of those who take delight in ridiculing others, we must still hold our tongue and dismiss their flow of words as a cup filled to overflowing. Such sport is dangerous. 'The mouth of the fool-hardy comes near to a fall.'[13] 'Thou shalt not welcome a foolish report, nor consent with an unjust man to be an unjust witness,'[14] whether to accuse someone or to speak ill of him or to show ill-will toward him.

(58) It is my opinion that a limit should be imposed upon the speech, if a person would practise self-control; that limit should be merely to reply to questions, even when we can speak. Silence is a virtue in a woman, an ornament free of

---
12 Plato, *Laws* V 732C.
13 Prov. 10.14.
14 Cf. Exod. 23.1.

danger in the young; only for old age held in honor is speech good. 'Speak, thou that art elder, at a banquet, for it becometh thee. Speak without embarrassment and in carefulness of knowledge. Young man,'—it is Wisdom giving this advice—'scarcely speak if there is need of you; if you be asked twice, let your answer be short, in few words.'[15] Both should keep their voices moderately subdued while they speak. Loud talking is annoying, yet speaking inaudibly to one close by suggests ineptitude, inability to make oneself heard. The one is a sign of timidity, the other of brashness.

Do not let quarrelsomeness with its love of empty victory creep into our midst, for our aim is the elimination of all discord. Surely, this is the meaning of the expression: 'Peace be to you.'[16] 'Before thou hear, answer not a word.'[17] (59) A muffled voice is the voice of an effeminate man; however, the speech of a temperate man is moderate in tone, not too loud nor too long, not too quick nor too verbose. We should not be long-winded in our conversations, nor wordy, nor engage in idle chatter, nor rattle on rapidly without drawing a breath. Surely, even the voice ought to have its share, so to speak, of moderation, and those who talk out of turn and those who shout should be silenced. The self-restrained Odysseus struck Thersites a blow because he alone 'kept chattering on, of measureless speech, whose mind was full of a great store of disorderly words, idly and in no orderly wise.'[18] 'A man full of tongue is terrible in his destruction.'[19] The rest of the body of a chatterer is worn away like an old shoe by evil, with only the tongue left to inflict harm.

---
15 Eccli. 32.4.
16 John 20.19,21; 3 John 1.15.
17 Eccli. 11.8.
18 *Iliad*, 2.212-214.
19 Eccli. 9.18.

Therefore, Wisdom advises us well: 'Be not full of idle words in a multitude of ancients.'[20] Again, He seeks to eliminate idle chatter even in our relations with God by imposing restraint with this command: 'Repeat not the word in your prayer.'

(60) Then, too, whistling and hissing and snapping the fingers—all sounds made to summon servants—should not be used by men who have the ability to speak, since these are wordless signals. At banquets, we should not be forever spitting or violently coughing or blowing our nose. We must consider the feelings of our companions at table, and avoid disgusting or nauseating them by our crude conduct, testifying to our own lack of self-control. Not even cattle or asses relieve nature at their feeding troughs, yet many people blow their nose and keep spitting while engaged at table. Again, if a sneeze take us by surprise, or, even more so, a belch, we need not deafen our neighbor with the noise and in so doing exhibit our lack of manners. A belch should be released silently, as we exhale, with our mouths shut, not wide open and gaping like the masks of the tragedy. The irritation that causes a sneeze may be relieved by quietly holding the breath; therefore, we should suppress the accumulated force of the breath politely by controlling our exhaling, so as to try to pass unnoticed if some of the excessive air, under pressure, escapes.

It is a sign of boorishness and of lack of discipline to want to add to the noises, rather than lessen them. And those who scrape their teeth so much that they draw blood from their gums, besides injuring themselves, also annoy their companions. And beyond a doubt, scratching the ear and irritations to prompt sneezing are gestures proper to swine, suggestive of the search for immoral pleasures. Unbecoming

---
20 Eccli. 7.15.

glances and indecent conversations about such things must be renounced. Let the gaze be composed, and the movement of the head and the gestures be steady, as well as the motion of the hands in conversation. In general, the Christian is, by nature, a man of gentleness and quiet, of serenity and peace.

Chapter 8

(61) The use of wreathes and of perfumes is not a necessity for us. Rather, it shipwrecks us upon pleasure and frivolity even as night draws near.[1] I know that a woman brought perfume in an alabaster box and anointed the feet of the Lord with it at that holy supper,[2] and that the Lord was pleased with it. I know too, that the ancient kings of the Jews used to wear precious gold and jewels.[3] But that woman had not yet entered into communion with the Word (for she was still a sinner), and so she paid the Master honor with what she considered the most precious thing she had, her perfume, and then, wiping off the remainder of the perfume with the garland of her head, her hair, she poured out upon the Lord her tears of repentance. So her sins were forgiven her.

This may be used as a symbol of the Lord's teachings and of His sufferings. The anointing of His feet with sweet-smelling myrrh suggests the divine teaching whose good odor and fame has spread to the ends of the earth: 'Their sound has gone forth to the ends of the earth.'[4] And those anointed feet of

---
1 Cf. John 9.4; 1 Thess. 5.2.
2 Cf. Luke. 7.37.
3 Cf. 2 Kings 12.30; Eccli. 45.14.
4 Ps. 18.5; Rom. 10.18.

the Lord—not to be too subtle—are the Apostles, the sweet odor of the myrrh prefiguring their reception of the Holy Spirit. (62) I mean that the figure of the Lord's feet is to be understood of the Apostles who journeyed about the whole world preaching the Gospel. In another place, in a psalm, the Spirit speaks of those feet: 'We will adore in the place where His feet stood,'[5] that is, where His Apostles, His feet, have already been, through whose preaching He has come to the ends of the earth. The tears are repentance and the unloosed hair means conversion from love of finery and suffering borne patiently for the Lord when they preached, unloosing the old vanity by the new faith.

Considering this deed in another way, mystically, this figure also symbolizes the suffering of the Master. The oil is the Lord Himself, from whom we receive mercy;[6] the myrrh, which is diluted oil, is the traitor Judas, because, when the Lord was departing from life in this world, He was anointed with myrrh, as the dead are anointed with it. The tears are sinners who have repented, who have come to believe in Him, whose sins have been forgiven. And the unloosed hair is desolate Jerusalem in mourning, over whom the lamentations of the Prophets were sung. The Lord Himself said that Judas would prove false: 'He who dips with Me in the dish, he it is who will betray Me.'[7] Do you not recognize in him the disloyal table companion?[8] This same Judas betrayed the Master with a kiss; he became a hypocrite, imitating with his teacherous kiss the hypocrite of old,[9]

---
5 Ps. 131.7.
6 In Greek, 'oil' (*élaion*), akin to *eleéō* ('to have mercy'), is a symbol of mercy.
7 Matt. 26.23.
8 Cf. Eccli. 6.10.
9 Cf. 2 Kings 20.9.

and becoming an example of the people spoken of: 'This people honoreth Me with their lips, but their hearts are far from Me.'[10] (63) It is not far-fetched, then, to suppose that He intended the oil to mean the Apostle who received mercy, and the treated, diluted oil the deceitful betrayer. This it is that the anointing of the feet with perfume prefigured.

By washing the feet of His disciples with His own hands as He sent them forth to noble deeds, the Saviour manifested in an excellent way their journeying to bestow graces upon the nations, and He purified that journeying in anticipation by His own power. The perfume left its odor after it, and suggests the sweet-smelling accomplishments that reach everyone. The suffering of the Lord, indeed, has filled us with its fragrance, but the Hebrews with sin. The Apostle states this clearly: 'Thanks be to God who always leads us in triumph in Christ, manifesting through us the odor of His knowledge in every place. For we are the fragrance of the Lord for God, alike as regards those who are saved, and those who are lost; to these an odor that leads from death to death, but to those an odor that leads from life to life.'[11]

And as for the Jewish kings who wore crowns of gold, set with precious jewels and richly ornamented, they were the anointed ones,[12] symbolically carrying Christ on their heads without knowing it, in the sense that their heads were adorned with an ornament representing Christ. The precious stone, whether pearl or emerald, beyond a doubt is the Word Himself; the gold is the incorruptibility of the Word, since gold is impervious to the rust of corrosion. At His birth, the

---
10 Isa. 29.13.
11 2 Cor. 2.14-16.
12 That is, *christoi*.

Magi brought Him gold as a sign of His kingship.[13] A crown such as that, being an image of the Lord, endures without decaying, and does not fade like one of flowers.

(64) The words of Aristippus the Cyrenian, who loved ease and comfort, come to mind. He devised this sophistical argument: 'A horse, when it is anointed with perfume, does not lose any of its excellence as a horse, nor does a dog, when it is anointed, lose any of its excellence as a dog.' Then he went on to draw the conclusion: 'neither, then, does man.'[14] But the horse and the dog do not have any understanding of what perfume is; those whose perception is intellectual are more to be blamed for their indulgence when they make use of such effeminate sweet odors.

There is an unlimited variety of these perfumes: Brenthian and Metallian and Royal and Plangonian, and there is an Egyptian ointment. Simonides, in his iambics, is not ashamed even to declare: 'I was anointed with myrrhs and ointments and baccar nard. For there was an importer close at hand.'[15] Habitually, some people use both the oil of lilies and that of cypress; they prize the oil of roses highly, and so many other kinds which women still use, some liquid, others dry, some in the form of salves, others only for scenting. Day after day they plan ways of procuring them, with an insatiable desire for this sweet fragrance. There are women who always exude extreme vulgarity; they keep scenting and sprinkling their bed covers and their houses, and, in their daintiness, stop short only of making their chamber-pots fragrant with myrrh. (65) Some complain so feelingly

13 Cf. Matt. 2.11.
14 Cf. Diogenes Laertes II 76.
15 Simonides of Amorgos, *Frag.* 16, in T. Bergk, *Poetae lyrici graeci* II 4 (1882).

about this extreme and seem to me so dead set against these ointments that undermine virility that they would exclude from a well-regulated city both perfumers and those who manufacture the perfumes, as well as the dyers of gay-colored wools.[16] For it is not right that garments and cosmetics that betray artificiality be allowed entry into a city of truth. Men of our way of life should be redolent, not of perfume, but of perfection, and women should be fragrant with the odor of Christ, the royal chrism, not that of powders and perfumes. Let her be ever anointed with the heavenly oil of chastity, taking her delight in holy myrrh, that is, the Spirit. Christ provides this oil of good odor for His followers, compounding His myrrh from sweet heavenly herbs. With this myrrh the Lord anoints Himself, as David says: 'Therefore, O God, thy God hath anointed thee with the oil of gladness above thy fellows. Myrrh and stacte and cassia from thy garments.'[17]

(66) Yet, let us not develop a fear of perfume, like vultures and scarabs who are said to die if anointed with the oil of roses. Let the women make use of a little of these perfumes, but not so much as to nauseate their husbands, for too much fragrance suggests a funeral, not married life. In fact, oil itself is harmful to bees and insects, but with men, some it strengthens, others it prepares for battle, for when timid men are rubbed down with oil they become ready for any sort of contest in the stadium.

Do you not realise that myrrth, a soft oil, is able to emasculate noble characters? Certainly it is. Just as we have already forbidden pampering the sense of taste, so, too, we proscribe indulgence of the sense of sight and of smell. Other-

---

16 Cf. Plato, Republic, II 373A.
17 Ps. 44.8.

wise, we may reopen the doors of the soul without being aware of it, through the senses as through unfortified doors, to the very dissipation we had put to flight. (67) If anyone object that the great High Priest, the Lord, offers up to God incense of sweet odor,[18] let this not be understood as the sacrifice and good odor of incense, but as the acceptable gift of love, a spiritual fragrance on the altar, that the Lord offers up.

By its nature, oil is useful for softening the skin and for relaxing the muscles and removing the offensive odors of the body. For such purposes we may need oil, but the constant use of sweet odors bespeaks pampering, and pampering arouses lustful desires. The man without self-control is easily led about by anything: eating, sleeping, social gatherings, as well as by his eyes and ears and stomach, and particularly to the point, by his sense of smell. Just as cattle are led by rings through their noses and by ropes, so, too, the self-indulgent are led by odors and perfumes and sweet scents rising from their wreathes. (68) Since we make no allowance for pleasure not connected with a necessity of life, surely let us also make distinctions here and choose only what is useful. There are perfumes that are neither soporific nor erotic, suggestive neither of sexual relations nor of immodest harlotry, but wholesome and chaste and refreshing to the mind that is tired and invigorating to the appetite. We must not completely turn away from such things, but take advantage of myrrh as an aid and remedy to stimulate our failing powers, for catarrh and chills and indispositions. The comic poet says somewhere: 'The nostrils are to be anointed with myrrh; the greatest secret of good health is to keep pleasant odors in the head.'[19] There is even a practise of rubbing the feet with a

---
18 Cf. Eph. 5.2.
19 Alexis, *Frag.* 190, *CAF II* 368.

salve made of either warming or of cooling oil, for its effects; when the head is congested, such a salve will draw the congestion off and away to a less important part of the body.

But a luxury without any useful purpose gives grounds for the charge of being sensual in character, and is a drug to excite the passions. There is all the difference in the world between rubbing oil on oneself and scenting oneself with it. The one makes a man effeminate, whereas the anointing with oil is very beneficial. (69) That is why Aristippus the philosopher used to say, when he was being anointed with oil, that the debauched ought to have an evil end in their wickedness, because they change the benefit that should be derived from oil into a reproach.

'Honor thy physician for the need thou hast of him,' Scripture says, 'for the most High has created him; for all healing is from God.'[20] But it adds: 'And the apothecary shall make sweet confections,' that is, ointments given us for our use, not for our pleasure. We should not desire myrrhs that only stimulate, but choose those which are of real benefit, for God has permitted men to produce oil as a relief from their labors. Silly women dye their gray hair, and by continually anointing it make it even grayer, and gray sooner than it should be, because the sweet perfume absorbs so much moisture. Similarly, men who anoint themselves look more and more dry; dryness makes them gray (whether grayness comes from the drying up of the hair or from lack of warmth), since the dryness absorbs the moisture the hair needs for nourishment and turns it gray. If they would escape gray hairs, how can they reasonably seek ointments that actually cause them? Just as hounds track down wild animals by following their scent, so, too, temperate men

---
20 Eccli. 38.1.

can detect the sensual by their elaborate sweet-smelling myrrhs.

(70) The same thing must be said of wreaths which are proper to revelries and drinking parties. 'Away, do not place a crown upon my head!'[21] In springtime, it is indeed pleasant to while away the time in soft grassy meadows, moist with dew, where flowers of every color are in bloom, amid natural and pure odors, like a bee gathering nectar. But to wear indoors 'a garland gathered from the meadow in full-bloom'[22] is not done by men of good sense. It is not right to appropriate to oneself the first green shoots of spring, and to encircle the head at banquets with rosebuds or violets or lilies or any other similar flower. A wreathe cools the head, both because of its moisture and because of its coolness. Physicians, considering the head cool by nature, believe that the chest and the tip of the nostrils should be anointed with oil, so that a warm vapor may fill the head and warm what is cold. But to chill it by the use of flowers is to use the wrong method if one wants to warm the membranes.[23] Besides, those who wear wreathes lose the pleasure the flower affords. They put it up on their heads, out of sight, and cannot enjoy the pleasure of seeing it or even of smelling it, since they keep the flower out of range of their sense of smell. The fragrance is emitted over their heads, and rises upward by a natural law, depriving the nostrils of all delight in the scent being wafted away. Like everything that is beautiful, the flower gives pleasure by being seen, and we should give glory to the Creator by looking at and enjoying its beauty. The other use, however, is harmful, and causes the flower to

---
21 Cf. *Adesp.* 1258, *CAF* III 617.
22 Euripides, *Hipp.* 73.
23 The Scholion strangely suggests that *pollóu deî* should be translated as 'should particularly be done.'

wilt and to take revenge in the sense of remorse it leaves behind. Surely, this is the proof of its ephemeral nature in that both the flower and its beauty quickly fades away. (71) The flower has cooled those who used it and its beauty has inflamed them. Simply put, it is a sin to enjoy either in any way other than by looking at them; any other way is not true enjoyment. As was done in Paradise, we should enjoy things in moderation, in true obedience to the Scripture.[24]

The crown of the woman must be considered the husband,[25] and the crown of the husband is his marriage; for both, the flower of their union is the child who is indeed the flower that the divine Cultivator culls from the meadow of the flesh. 'The crown of old men is their children's children and the glory of children is their father,'[26] it is said. Our glory is the Father of all, and the crown of the whole Church is Christ.

Like herbs and plants, flowers have their own properties, some beneficial, some harmful, and others even dangerous. For example, ivy cools, the walnut tree relieves drowsiness, as even the etymology of its Greek name shows.[27] There is the narcissus, a flower with heavy perfume, whose name itself suggests that it acts as a narcotic on the nerves.[28] The perfume of roses or of violets, being more on the cooling side, relieves and alleviates headaches, but this does not mean that we may get intoxicated in any degree, either with other people or by ourselves. Then, the crocus and the flower of

---

24 Cf. Gen. 2.15-17.
25 Cf. Prov. 12.4.
26 Prov. 17.6.
27 Clement is deriving *karúa* ('walnut tree') from *karóō* ('plunge into a heavy sleep').
28 *nárkissos*, according to Plutarch II 647B, is derived from *nárkē* ('numbness') because of its narcotic properties.

the cypress, which bring freedom from pain by inducing sleep, must be shunned. Yet, many of these flowers do warm the head, cold by nature, by clearing it out with their perfume. That is how the rose gets its name, because, in a general way, it sends forth a flow of odors, and that is also why it quickly fades.[29]

(72) The ancient Greeks never made use of wreathes. Neither the suitors[30] nor the Phaeacians, with all their luxurious living, adopted them. But, with the games, they began to give prizes, then to hold triumphal processions, after that, to deck out [the victor] with leaves, and finally, when Greece had degenerated into licentiousness after the Medean war, to use the wreathe of flowers. Therefore, those who are educated by the Word will reject wreathes, not only because they lie heavy upon the reason which has its seat in the head, nor only because the garland might serve as a symbol of arrogance at a pagan festival,[31] but because it has been dedicated to the service of idols. Sophocles, at any rate, calls the narcissus 'the ancient garland-flower of the great gods,'[32] meaning the gods of Hades. And Sappho crowns the Muses with roses, saying: 'For there were no roses for you in Pieria in the beginning.'[33] The story goes that Hera delights in the lily and Artemis in the myrtle. If flowers have been created for the sake of men, yet foolish men have taken them, not for their own use and benefit, but have turned them

---

29 *Rhódon* ('rose') is derived by Clement from *rhéō* ('flow').
30 Cf. *Odysseus* 1.144-155.
31 This might possibly be translated 'as a symbol of the noble accomplishments [of an Olynthic victor] in the festival honoring him,' as Pindar uses these words in such a sense.
32 Sophocles. *Oed. Col.* 683.
33 *Frag.* 68, in S. Elter, *De gnomologiorum graecorum historia atque origine commetatio* (Bonner Universitätsprogramme, Bonn 1893-1896) 12.

into the evil service of idols, then we should reject them 'for conscience' sake.'[34]

(73) The garland is a symbol of calm[35] freedom from care; that is why wreathes are placed on the brow of the dead. It is for that reason, too, that they are placed upon idols, giving witness that they, too, are dead. Those who celebrate the festivals of Bacchus never think of performing their orgies without garlands and, once the flowers encircle their brow, they work themselves into a frenzy over the mystic rite. We should have no communication with demons nor should we, the living image of God, crown ourselves like dead idols. A beautiful crown of flowers that never fade awaits those who live well;[36] earth has never been capable of bearing such a crown, for only heaven holds the secret of bringing it to blossom.

Besides, it is inconsistent for us who celebrate the holy suffering of the Lord, who know that He was crowned with thorns, to crown ourselves with flowers. The crown the Lord wore is a figure of ourselves who were once barren, but now encircle Him as a garland through His Church, of which He is the head. That crown is also a type of our faith: it is a type of life, through the substance of wood; of joy, because it is a crown; of trial, because it is a crown of thorns, and no one can approach the Word without shedding blood. But the other crown, the one interwined [with flowers], withers away; a wreathe of wickedness, it falls apart and its flowers fade, just as the beauty of those who do not believe in the Lord withers away.

Jesus [the Jews] crowned and raised aloft, giving clear

---
34 Cf. 1 Cor. 10.25.
35 *aóchlētos*, a Stoic term suggestive of *apatheia*.
36 Cf. 1 Pet. 4.5.

proof of their lack of understanding. In their fallacious reasoning they did not see that that very deed was a prophecy; they meant it as dishonor to the Lord. They were people gone astray, who did not know their Lord; they were uncircumcised in mind;[37] not recognizing God, they rejected their Lord and so lost the promise implied in their name Israel,[38] for they persecuted God and tried to bring disgrace to the Word. Still, Him whom they crucified as an evil-doer they crowned as a king. (74) For that reason, they will recognize the loving God, in whom they did not believe when He was man, as just and as the Lord. They showed that they were provoking Him to manifest Himself as Lord when they raised Him on high, for they placed upon the brow of Him who is exalted above every name[39] a diadem of holiness, in the never-fading thorns. Certainly, such a diadem is painful to those who plot against it, and it restrains them, but it is consoling for those who remain in communion with the Church, and is their protection. Such a crown is like a flower for those who believe in Him who has been glorified, but those who do not believe it wounds and punishes.

It is, in fact, a symbol also of the Master's victory, for at that time He was carrying upon His head, the principal part of the body, all our sins by which we are pierced. Saving us from temptations and sins and all such things by His sufferings, rendering the work of the Devil ineffective, well did He cry out in triumph: 'Death, where is thy victory?'[40] We gather grapes even from thorns, and figs from thistles;[41] but those others, to whom He stretched forth His hands as

---
37 Cf. Ezech. 44.7; Acts 7.51.
38 That is, 'people of God,'; cf. Gen. 35.10.
39 Cf. Phil. 2.9.
40 1 Cor. 15.55.
41 Cf. Matt. 7.16.

to an unbelieving and barren people,[42] are ever lacerated into shreds.

(75) I can speak of another mystery in these things. When the almighty Lord of the universe began to legislate through the Word and decided to make His power visible to Moses, He sent Moses a divine vision with the appearance of light, in the burning bush. Now, a bramble-bush is full of thorns.[43] So, too, when the Word was concluding His legislation and His stay among men as their Lord, again He permitted Himself to be crowned with thorns as a mystic symbol; returning to the place from which He had descended, the Word renewed that by which He had first come, appearing first in the bush of thorns, and later being surrounded with thorns that He might show that all was the work of the same one power. He is one and His Father is one, the eternal beginning and end.

(76) But I have departed from the manner of the moralist and encroached upon the field of the teacher. Let me once more return to my own subject. We have already proved that even from a medical point of view we should not entirely renounce the pleasures that flowers afford, and the benefit there is in ointments and vapors, for the sake of our health, as well as, at times, by way of moderate relaxation. If anyone should ask, in the name of those who turn away from flowers, what good there is in them, let him know that myrrhs are prepared from flowers, and myrrh has many uses. Lily oil, made from white lilies and other kinds, imparts warmth, stimulates the appetite, draws [infections] to a head, moistens, purges, has the excellent quality of being composed of fine particles, flushes the bile, and softens the skin. The

---
42 Cf. Isa. 65.2.
43 Cf. Exod. 3.2 This passage is taken from Philo, *De vit. Mos.* 1.63.

oil of the narcissus is just as beneficial as that of the lily. That from the leaf of the myrtle, and from its berry, is an astringent and checks the flow [of blood] from the body. Oil of roses invigorates. In a word, all these myrrhs have been created for our good. 'Hear me,' Scripture says, 'and bud forth as the rose planted by the brooks of water. Give ye a sweet-odor as frankincense, and bless the Lord in His works.'[44]

This discussion could go on indefinitely, dwelling on the fact that these flowers and herbs have been created for our needs, not to be misused as luxuries. We concede room for some little indulgence, but it is sufficient if we enjoy their fragrance; we need not be decked out with them. The Father treats man with great care, putting at our disposal all His handiwork for this one purpose. Scripture says well: 'Water and fire and iron and milk, bread of flour and honey, the blood of the cluster of grape and oil and clothing. All these things shall be for good to the holy.'[45]

Chapter 9

(77) Now we must discuss the way we are to sleep, still mindful of the precepts of temperance. After our dinner, once we have given thanks to God for having granted us such pleasures and for the completion of the day, then we should dispose our minds for sleep. We must forbid ourselves the use of expensive bedding, gold-sprinkled rugs and plain carpets embroidered in gold, rich purple bed robes or precious thick cloaks, purple blankets of elaborate art, with

---
44 Cf. Eccli. 39.17-19.
45 Eccli. 39.31,32.

fleecy cloaks thrown over them,¹ and beds 'too soft to be slept in.'² The habit of sleeping in soft down is injurious, apart from the danger of pampering the body, because those who sleep in it sink deep into the softness of the bed; it is not healthy for the sleeper who cannot move about in it because of the high elevation on either side of his body. Sleep is the time for digesting food, but such a bed causes the food simply to burn up and be destroyed, while those who can toss about on their beds, level as though a natural place of exercise during sleep, digest their food more easily and prepare themselves the better to face any contingencies.

Again, a bed with silver legs stands as an accusation of extreme ostentatiousness, and couches made of 'ivory, the product of a body separated from its living spirit, is not free from defilement,'³ and is for holy men only a resting place that encourages sloth. (78) We should not be too anxious for such things. Not that they who have them need to leave them unused, but they are forbidden to desire them excessively. Happiness does not lie in that sort of thing. On the other hand, it is Cynic vanity to make a practise of sleeping like Diomedes, under whom 'was spread the hide of an ox of the field.'⁴ Odysseus supported the weak part of his marriage couch with a wooden post.⁵ That is the degree of frugality and industry practised, not by a private citizen, but by a leader of the ancient Greeks. But, what further example do I need, when Jacob slept on the ground with a stone for his pillow?⁶ It was then that he was accounted worthy of beholding a vision beyond the power of man.

---

1 Cf. *Odysseus* 7.335.
2 Theocritus 5.51; 15.125.
3 Plato, *Laws* XII 956A.
4 *Iliad* 10.155.
5 Cf. *Odysseus* 23.195.
6 Cf. Gen. 28.11.

Following the dictates of reason, then, we should make use of a bed that is level and unadorned, yet affording some minimum of convenience: of protection, if it be summer; of warmth, if it be winter. Let the couch, too, be unadorned and its posts plain, for ornamented and molded wood readily and frequently becomes an easy path for creeping animals, providing them sure footing in the grooves carved by the craftsmen. But we must specially keep the softness of the bed within limits, for sleep is meant to relax the body, not to debilitate it. For that reason, I say that sleep should be taken not as self-indulgence, but as rest from activity.

(79) We should sleep half-awake. 'Let your loins be girt,' Scripture says, 'and your lamps burning; and you like men awaiting their master when he returns from the wedding; that when he does come and knock, they may open straighway to him. Blessed are those servants whom the Master, when He comes, shall find awake.'[7] A man who is asleep is not good for anything, any more than a man who is dead. Therefore, even during the night we should arouse ourselves from sleep often and give praise to God. Blessed are they who have kept watch for Him, for they make themselves like the angels whom we speak of as ever wakeful. 'No man who is asleep is good for anything, any more than if he were dead.'[8] He who has the light stays awake, and the darkness does not overcome him, and if darkness does not, much less does sleep. Therefore, he who has been enlightened stays awake, and such a one lives. 'For what was in Him, was life.'[9] 'Blessed is the man,' Wisdom adds, 'who hears me, and the man who watches at my ways, and lies awake daily at my gates, observing the posts of my entrance.'[10] (80) 'There-

---
7 Luke 12.35-37.
8 Plato, *Laws* VII 808D.
9 Cf. John 1.5,4.
10 Prov. 8.34 (Septuagint).

fore, let us not sleep as do the rest,' Scripture tells us, 'but let us be wakeful and sober. For they who sleep, sleep at night, and they who are drunk, are drunk at night,' that is, in the night of ignorance, 'but let us, who are of day, be sober. For you are all children of the light and of the day. We are not of night nor of darkness.'[11] 'He who has the most respect for life and for reason will stay awake as long as he can, reserving only as much time for sleep as his health demands; much sleep is not required, if the habit of moderation be once rightly formed.'[12]

The care of discipline begets a constant alertness in our labors. Therefore, food ought not to make us heavy but enliven us so that sleep will harm us as little as possible. Incidentally, how capable a wineless meal is of lifting one from the very depths to the peak of wakefulness! Falling asleep, indeed, is like dying, because it renders our minds and our senses inactive, and, when we close our eyes, shuts out the light of day. So, let us who are the sons of the true light not shut out that light, but, turning within into ourselves, casting light upon the vision of the inner man, let us contemplate truth itself, welcome its rays and discover with clarity and insight what is the truth of dreams.

(81) But the belchings of the drunk, the wheezing of those who are stuffed with food, the snoring smothered by bed clothes, the rumblings of cramped stomachs, all these things obscure the clear-sightedness needed by the eye of the soul and fill the mind with a thousand imaginations. The blame must be placed on overindulgence in food, for it reduces reason to silliness. 'Much sleep is not helpful, either for our souls or

---

11 1 Thess. 5.6,7,8,5.
12 Plato, *Laws* VII 808BC.

bodies, nor is it adapted to the actions it performs in its search for the truth, even if it is according to nature.'[13]

Lot the just (for the present, I am going to pass over an explanation of the way of life demanded by the new birth) would not have been betrayed into unlawful intercourse if his daughters had not first made him drunk and overcome by sleep.[14] Therefore, if we remove the cause for an excessive tendency to drowsiness, we shall sleep more soundly. Those who cultivate an alert mind ought not 'to sleep all night long.'[15] We must keep vigil by night, especially when the days are short: one person, that he might study; another, that he might practise his trade; women, to devote themselves to their wool-spining. In general, all of us must struggle against sleep, accustoming ourselves gently and gradually to utilize a greater proportion of our lives and not waste them in sleep. (Sleep, indeed, like a tax-collector, claims half the portion of our lives.) When we do manage to keep awake the greater part of the night, we should not allow ourselves, for any consideration, to take a nap during the day. Listlessness and drowsiness, stretching and yawning, are all distressing in a soul that is inconstant.

(82) There is another general principle that we should recognize, too, and it is this: it is not the soul that needs sleep (for it is ever-active); the body becomes relaxed when it takes its rest, and the soul ceases to operate in any bodily way, but continues to operate mentally in keeping with its nature. Then, if we consider the matter carefully, the truth that lies in dreams is the thinking of the soul, not drugged [by sleep], nor distracted here and there in sympathy for the body, but

---
13 *Ibid.*
14 Cf. Gen 19.32-38.
15 Cf. *Iliad* 24.1159; Plato, *Laws* VII 808B.

making its own judgment for itself. To keep itself inactive would be for it to cease to exist. The soul, then, ever keeping its thoughts on God and attributing those thoughts to the body by its constant association with it, makes man equal to the angels in their loveliness. So, from its practise of wakefulness, it obtains eternal life.

Chapter 10

(83) It remains for us now to consider the restriction of sexual intercourse to those who are joined in wedlock. Begetting children is the goal of those who wed, and the fulfillment of that goal is a large family, just as hope of a crop drives the farmer to sow his seed, while the fulfillment of his hope is the actual harvesting of the crop. But he who sows in a living soil is far superior, for the one tills the land to provide food only for a season, the other to secure the preservation of the whole human race; the one tends his crop for himself, the other, for God. We have received the command: 'Be fruitful,'[1] and we must obey. In this role man becomes like God, because he co-coperates, in his human way, in the birth of another man.

Now, not every land is suited to the reception of seed, and, even if it were, not at the hands of the same farmer. Seed should not be sown on rocky ground nor scattered everywhere,[2] for it is the primary substance of generation and contains imbedded in itself the principle of nature. It is undeniably godless, then, to dishonor principles of nature by wasting them on unnatural resting places. In fact, you recall how Moses, in his wisdom, once denounced seed that

---
1 Cf. Gen. 1.28.
2 Cf. Matt. 13.3-24; Plato, *Laws* VIII 838E.

bears no fruit, saying symbolically: 'Do not eat the hare nor the hyena.'[3] He does not want man to be contaminated by their traits nor even to taste of their wantonness, for these animals have an insatiable appetite for coition. As regards the hare, legend claims that it needs to void excrement only once a year, and possesses as many anuses as the years it has lived.[4] Therefore, the prohibition against eating the hare is nothing else than a condemnation of pederasty. And with regard to the hyena, it is said that the male changes every year successively into a female, so that Moses means that he who abstains from the hyena is commanded not to lust after adultery.

(84) While I agree that the all-wise Moses means, by this prohibition just mentioned, that we should not become like these beasts, I do not entirely agree with the explantion given these symbolic prohibitions. A nature can never be made to change; what has been once formed in it cannot be re-formed by any sort of change. Change does not involve the nature itself; it necessarily modifies, but does not transform the structure. For instance, although many birds are said to change their color and their voice according to the season (like the blackbird which changes its black feathers to yellow, and its melodious voice to a harsh one, or the nightingale which changes its plumage and song at the same time), even so, their nature itself is not so affected that a male becomes female. Rather, a new growth of feathers, like a new garment, is bright with one color, but a little later, as winter threatens, it fades away, like a flower when its color goes. In the same way, the voice, affected unfavorably by the cold, loses its vibrancy: the surface of the whole body contracts with the climate, and the bronchial tubes, narrowly constricted

---
3 Cf. Deut. 14.7; *Epistle of Barnabas* 10.6.
4 *Ibid.*

in the throat, restrict the breath to the point that it is made quite muffled and capable of producing only harsh sounds. (85) Later on, in the spring, responding to the weather and relaxing, the breath is once again freed of all constraint and is carried through passages that were tightly closed but are now wide open. No longer does the voice croak in dying tones, but bursts forth clear, pouring out in full-throated voice, and now in springtime there arises melodious song from the throats of the birds.[5]

Therefore, we should not believe at all that the hyena changes its sex. Neither does it possess both the male and the female sexual organs at the same time, as some claim, conjuring up some freakish hermaphrodite and creating this female-male, a third new category halfway in between the male and the female. Erroneously they misconstrue the strategy of nature, mother of all and author of all existence. Because the hyena is of all animals the most sensual, there is a knob of flesh underneath its tail, in front of the anus, closely resembling the female sex organ in shape. It is not a passage, I mean it serves no useful purpose, opening neither into the womb nor into the intestines. It has only a good-sized opening to permit an ineffective sexual act when the vagina is preparing for childbirth and is impenetrable. (86) This is characteristic of both male and female hyena, because of hyperactive abnormal sexuality; the male lies with the male so that it rarely approaches the female. For that reason, births are infrequent among hyenas, because they so freely sow their seed contrary to nature.

This is the reason, I believe, that Plato, in excoriating pederasty in *Phaedrus,* terms it bestiality and says that these libertines who have so surrendered to pleasure, 'taking the

---
5 Cf. Aristotle, *Hist. Animal.* 11.49 632B.

bit in their own mouths, like brutish beasts rush on to enjoy and beget.'⁶ Such godless people 'God has given over,' the Apostle says, 'to shameful lusts. For the women change their natural use to that which is against nature, and in like manner the men, also, having abandoned the natural use of the women, have burned in their lusts one towards another, men with men doing shameful things, and receiving in themselves the fitting recompense of their perversity.'⁷ (87) Yet, nature has not allowed even the most sensual of beasts to sexually misuse the passage made for excrement. Urine she gathers into the bladder; undigested food in the intestines; tears in the eyes; blood in the veins; wax in the ear, and mucous in the nose; so, too, there is a passage connected to the end of the intestines by means of which excrement is passed off. In the case of hyenas, nature, in her diversity, has added this additional organ to accomodate their excessive sexual activity. Therefore, it is large enough for the service of the lusting organs, but its opening is obstructed within. In short, it is not made to serve any purpose in generation. The clear conclusion that we must draw, then, is that we must condemn sodomy, all fruitless sowing of seed, any unnatural methods of holding intercourse and the reversal of the sexual role in intercourse. We must rather follow the guidance of nature, which obviously disapproves of such practises from the very way she has fashioned the male organ, adapted not for receiving the seed, but for implanting it. When Jeremias, or, rather, the Spirit through him, said: 'The cave of the hyena is my home,'⁸ He was resorting to an expressive figure to

---

6 Cf. Plato, Phaed. 254, 250E.
7 Rom. 1.26,27.
8 Cf. Jer. 12.9 (Septuagint). The word for 'cave' (*spélaion*) also means 'privy.'

excoriate idolatry and to manifest His scorn for the nourishment provided for dead bodies. The house of the living God surely ought to be free of idols.

(88) Again, Moses issued a prohibition against eating the hare. The hare is forever mounting the female, leaping upon her crouching form from behind. In fact, this manner of having intercourse is a characteristic of the hare. The female conceives every month, and, even before the first offspring is born, she become pregnant again. She conceives and begets, and as soon as she gives birth is fertilized again by the first hare she meets. Not satisfied with one mate, she conceives again, although she is still nursing. The explanation is that the female hare has a double womb, and therefore her desire for intercourse is stimulated not only by the emptiness of the womb, in that every empty space seeks to be filled, but also, when she is with young, her other womb begins to feel lustful desires. That is why hares have one birth after the other. So the mysterious prohibition [of Moses] in reality is but counsel to restrain violent sexual impulses, and intercourse in too frequent succession, relations with a pregnant woman, pederasty, adultery, and lewdness.

(89) Moses forbade, too, in clear language and with his head uncovered, no longer under a figure: 'Thou shalt not fornicate, nor commit adultery, nor corrupt children.'[9] This is the command of the Word; it must be obeyed with all our strength and not transgressed in any way; His commandments may not be set aside. Evil lust bears the name wantonness; Plato, for example, calls the horse representing lust 'wanton' when he writes: 'You have become in my eyes horses mad for the female.'[10] The angels who visited Sodom reveal the

---

9 Cf. Exod. 20.14; *Ep. of Barn.* 19.4.
10 Cf. Plato, *Phaed.* 238A.

punishment reserved for wantonness. They struck down with fire those who attempted to dishonor them, and their city along with them.[11] Such a deed demonstrates clearly that fire is the reward of wantonness. As we have already said, the calamities that befell the ancients are described for our instruction that we may not imitate their example and merit the same punishment.

(90) We should consider boys as our sons, and the wives of other men as our daughters. We must keep a firm control over the pleasures of the stomach, and an absolutely uncompromising control over the organs beneath the stomach. If, as the Stoics teach, we should not move even a finger on mere impulse,[12] how much more necessary is it that they who seek wisdom control the organ of intercourse? I feel that the reason this organ is also called the private part[13] is that we are to treat it with privacy and modesty more than we do any other member. In lawful wedlock, as with eating, nature permits whatever is conformable to nature and helpful and decent; it allows us to desire the act of procreation. However, whoever is guilty of excess sins against nature and, by violating the laws regulating intercourse, harms himself. First of all, it is decidedly wrong ever to touch youths in any sexual way as though they were girls. The philosopher who learned from Moses taught: 'Do not sow seeds on rocks and stones, on which they will never take root.'[14] (91) The Word, too, commands emphatically, through Moses: 'Thou shalt not lie with mankind as with womankind, for it is an abomination.'[15] Again, further on, noble Plato advises:

---

11 Cf. Gen. 19.1-25.
12 Cf. Chrysippus, *Frag. moral.* 730 (Arnim).
13 That is, *aidoion*, derived from *aidomai* ('reverence').
14 Plato, *Laws* VIII 828E.
15 Lev. 18.22.

'Abstain from every female field of increase,'[16] because it does not belong to you. (He had read this in the holy Scripture and from it had taken the Law: 'Thou shalt not give the coition of thy seed to thy neighbor's wife, to be defiled because of her.'[17]) Then he goes on to say: 'Do not sow the unconsecrated and bastard seed with concubines, where you would not want what is sown to grow.'[18] In fact, he says: 'Do not touch anyone, except your wedded wife,'[19] because she is the only one with whom it is lawful to enjoy the pleasures of the flesh for the purpose of begetting lawful heirs. This is to share in God's own work of creation, and in such a work the seed ought not be wasted nor scattered thoughtlessly nor sown in a way it cannot grow.[20] (92) As an illustration of this last restriction, the same Moses forbade the Jews to approach even their own wives if they happened to be in the period of menstruation.[21] The reason is that it is wrong to contaminate fertile seed, destined to become a human being, with corrupt matter of the body, or to allow it be diverted from the furrow of the womb and swept away in a fetid flow of matter and excrement.

He discouraged the ancient Jews, also, from having relations with a wife already with child.[22] Pleasure sought for its own sake, even within the marriage bonds, is a sin and contrary both to law and to reason. Moses cautioned them, then, to keep away from their pregnant wives until they be

---

16 Plato, *Laws* VIII 828E.
17 Lev. 18.20.
18 Plato, *Laws* VIII 839A
19 *Ibid.* 841D.
20 Literally, 'do not scatter seeds too hard to be cooked.'
21 Cf. Lev. 15.19.
22 In *Stromateis* III 11.71, Clement explains: 'You can produce no one of the ancients in the Scriptures who had relations with a pregnant woman.'

delivered. In fact, the womb, situated just below the bladder and above the part of the intestine known as the rectum, extends its neck in between the edges of the bladder, and the outlet of this neck, by which the sperm enters, closes tight when the womb is full, opening again only when delivered of the fetus. It is only when it has become empty of its fruit that it can receive the sperm again. (It is not wrong for us to name the organs of generation, when God is not ashamed of their function.) (93) The womb welcomes the seed when it yearns for procreation, but it refuses the seed when intercourse is contrary to nature; that is, once impregnated, it makes immoral relations impossible by drawing its neck tight together. All its instincts, up to now aroused by loving intercourse, begin to be directed differently, absorbed in the development of the child within, co-operating with the Creator. It is wrong, indeed, to interfere with the workings of nature by indulging in the extravagances of wantonness.

Wantonness has many names and is of many kinds. When it centers about sexual pleasure in a disorientated way, it is called lewdness, something vulgar and common and very impure, and, as its name suggests, preoccupied with coition. As this vice increases, a great swarm of diseases flows from it: gourmandizing, drunkenness, lust, and particularly dissipation and every sort of craze for pleasure in which lust plays the tyrant. A thousand-and-one like vices join the company and aid in effecting a thoroughly dissolute character. 'Whips are prepared for the unbridled,' Scripture says, 'and punishment for the shoulders of the intemperate,'[23] meaning by 'shoulders of the intemperate' both the strength of the intemperance and the length of its duration. So, Scripture also advises: 'Keep empty hopes, O Lord, from thy servants, and

---
23 Prov. 19.29.

avert unbecoming desires from me, and let not the greediness of the belly and lusts of the flesh take hold of me.'[24] We must hold off at a great distance any excessive evil-doing, for it is not only the wallet of Crates, but also our own city, that 'no parasite, nor elegant bawd given over to unnatural vices nor immoral prostitute may enter,'[25] nor, for that matter, any other hedonist of the same sort. Unmistakably good behavior should permeate our whole life.

(94) In my treatise on continence,[26] I have discussed in a general way the question whether we should marry or not (and this is the point of our investigation). Now, if we have to consider whether we may marry at all, then how can we possibly permit ourselves to indulge in intercourse each time without restraint, as we would food, as if it were a necessity? Certainly, we can see at a glance that the nerves are strained by it as on a loom and, in the intense feeling aroused by intercourse, are stretched to the breaking point. It spreads a mist over the senses and tires the muscles. This is obvious in irrational animals and in men in training. Of these last, those who practise abstinence while engaging in contests get the best of their opponents; while animals are easily captured if they are caught at and all but torn from coition, because then they are entirely emptied of strength and energy.

The sophist of Abdera called intercouse 'a minor epilepsy,' and considered it an incurable disease. Indeed, does not lassitude succeed intercourse because of the quantity of seed lost? 'For a man is formed and torn out of a man.'[27] See

---

24 Cf. Eccli. 23.5.
25 Crates, *Frag.* 4, in H. Diels, *Poetarum philosophicorum fragmenta* 218.
26 Cf. above, p. 139 n. 12.
27 Cf. Democritus, *Frag.* 86, n. 32, in H. Diels, *Die Fragmente der Vorsokratiker* 416.

how much harm is done. A whole man is torn out when the seed is lost in intercourse. 'This is bone of my bone, and flesh of my flesh,'[28] Scripture says. Man is emptied of as much seed as is needed for a body that can be seen. After all, that which is separated from him is the beginning of a new birth. Besides that, the very agitation of matter upsets and disturbs the harmony of his whole body. (95) Wise indeed was he who replied to someone asking him his attitude toward the pleasures of sex: 'O man, quiet! I have been supremely happy in avoiding them as a fierce and wild tyrant.'[29]

Yet, marriage in itself merits esteem and the highest approval, for the Lord wished men to 'be fruitful and multiply.'[30] He did not tell them, however, to act like libertines, nor did He intend them to surrender themselves to pleasure as though born only to indulge in sexual relations. Let the Educator put us to shame with the word of Ezechiel: 'Put away your fornications.'[31] Why, even unreasoning beasts know enough not to mate at certain times. To indulge in intercourse without intending children is to outrage nature, whom we should take as our instructor. Her wise directions concerning the periods of life are meant to be obeyed; I mean that she allows us to marry at any time but after the advent of old age and during childhood (for she does not permit the one to marry yet, the other, any more). The attempt to procreate children is marriage, but the promiscuous scattering of seed contrary to law and to reason definitely is not. (96) If we should but control our lusts at the start and if we would not kill off the human race born and developing ac-

---
28 Cf. Gen. 2.23.
29 Sophocles. Cf. Plato, *Republic* I 329BC
30 Gen. 1.28.
31 Ezech. 43.9.

cording to the divine plan, then our whole lives would be lived according to nature. But women who resort to some sort of deadly abortion drug kill not only the embryo but, along with it, all human kindness.

Those whom nature has joined in wedlock need the Educator that they might learn not to celebrate the mystic rites of nature during the day, nor like the rooster copulate at dawn, or after they have come from church, or even from the market, when they should be praying or reading or performing the good works that are best done by day. In the evening, after dinner, it is proper to retire after giving thanks for the good things that have been received. (97) Sometimes, nature denies them the opportunity to accomplish the marriage act so that it may be all the more desirable because it is delayed. Yet, they must not forget modesty at night time under the pretext of the cover of darkness; like the light of reason, modesty must ever dwell in their souls. If we weave the ideals of chastity by day and then unravel them in the marriage bed at night, we do not better than Penelope at her loom.[32] Certainly, if we are required to practise self-control—as we are—we ought to manifest it even more with our wives, in the way we avoid every indecency in intimate embraces. Let the reliability and trustworthiness of the husband's purity in his dealings with his neighbor be present also in his home. He cannot possibly enjoy a reputation for self-control with his wife if she can see no signs of self-control in such intense acts of pleasure. Love, which tends toward sexual relations by its very nature, is in full bloom only for a time, then grows old with the body; but sometimes, if immoral pleasure mars the chastity of the marriage bed, desire becomes insipid and love ages before the body does. The hearts of lovers have

---

32 Cf. *Odysseus* 2.104; 19.149.

wings; affection can be quenched by a change of heart, and love can turn into hate if there creep in too many grounds for loss of respect.

(98) We should not even mention the names of impurity: ribald speech, indecent behavior, sensuous love affairs and all such immoralities. Rather, let us obey the Apostle, who tells us explicitly: 'But all fornication and uncleanness and covetousness, let it not so much as be named among you, as becometh saints.'[33] Someone has well said: 'Sexual intercourse does no one any good, except that it harms the beloved.'[34] Intercourse performed licitly is an occasion of sin, unless done purely to beget children, while Scripture says of that done illicitly: 'A hired wife shall be accounted as a sow, but one already married to a husband shall be a tower of death to those who use her.'[35] Impure passion makes a man resemble a boar or pig, and, according to Scripture, fornication with a kept prostitute is seeking death. (99) Even the poetry circulating among you condemns the city and house in which immorality reigns, saying: 'Wicked city, all unclean, adulteries and lawless lying with men and illicit effeminacy dwells in you.'[36] On the other hand, it admires the chaste 'who have neither base lust for lying with other's wives, nor passion for the loathesome and abominable sin committed with men,'[37] because it is contrary to nature. The greater number consider these sins of theirs simply as pleasure, while others, more virtuous, recognize that they are sins, even though they are overcome by the pleasure. For such as these, darkness is a veil to conceal their passion. Yet, he who seeks only sexual plea-

---

33 Eph. 5.3.
34 Epicurus, *Frag.* 62, in H. Usener, *Epicurea* (Leipzig 1887) 118.
35 Gloss on Eccli. 26.22.
36 *Orac. Syb.* 5.166-168.
37 *Ibid.* 4.33.

sure turns his marriage into fornication. He forgets the words of the Educator: 'Every man that passeth beyond his own bed, who says in his soul: Who seeth me? Darkness compasseth me about, and the walls cover me, and no man seeth my sins: whom do I fear? The Most High will not remember.'[38] Such a man is most wretched, for he fears only the eyes of men, and thinks to hide from God. 'He knows not,' Scripture continues, 'that the eyes of the Most High Lord are far brighter than the sun, beholding all the ways of men and looking into the most hidden parts.'[39] Another time, the Educator gives warning through Isaias: 'Woe to you who made your counsel in secret and say: Who seeth us?'[40]

A light that can be seen by the senses may pass unnoticed, but that which illumines the mind cannot be ignored. Heraclitus remarks: 'How can anyone fail to notice that which never sets?'[41] Let us not, then, allow ourselves to be swallowed up in any way by darkness, for light dwells in us: 'And the darkness,' Scripture says, 'did not overcome it.'[42] Night is turned into day by chaste reasoning. Scripture calls the reason of a good man a lamp which cannot be extinguished.[43]

(100) In fact, the very attempt to cover over what one is doing is a sign that the man is knowingly committing sin.

Anyone who does sin, for example by fornication, wrongs not so much his neighbor as himself by the very act of fornicating; he decidedly becomes more immoral and loses the right to respect. The sinner becomes more immoral and loses the right to respect which he had before, to the extent that

---

38 Eccli. 23.25-26.
39 Eccli. 23.28.
40 Isa. 29.15 (Septuagint).
41 Heraclitus, *Frag.* 16, in H. Diels, *op. cit.*
42 John 1.5.
43 Cf. Wisd. 7.10.

he sins; yet, Lord knows, immorality is already present when a man gives in to base pleasure. Therefore, he who sins dies to God entirely, and is abandoned by the Word, as well as by the Spirit, and is without life. What is holy shrinks from being defiled, and rightly so; the pure are always the only ones who may handle what is pure. Let us, therefore, never divest ourselves of our modesty when we take off our clothes,[44] for a just man should never strip himself of chastity. 'Behold, this corruption shall put on incorruption,'[45] when the intensity of desire that degenerates into sensuality is educated to self-control and, losing its love for corruption, allows man to practise constant chastity. 'The children of this world marry and are given in marriage,'[46] but if we renounce the deeds of the flesh and clothe this pure flesh with incorruption, we are living a life like that of the angels.

Plato, who was so well versed in pagan philosophy, in his *Philebus* called those men atheists, in a mystical sense, who corrupt reason, the god dwelling with them, and defile it according to their ability by surrendering to their passions.[47] (101) We ought not to live only for this mortal life, for we are consecrated to God, nor should we, as Paul tells us, turn the members of Christ into members of a harlot,[48] nor make the temple of God into a temple of base passion.[49] Remember the four and twenty thousand who were rejected because of their fornication.[50] The punishment of those who fornicated is an example, as I have already said, to restrain our passions. Our Educator clearly warns us: 'Go not after

---
44 Cf. Herodotus 1.8.
45 1 Cor. 15.53.
46 Cf. Matt. 24.38.
47 Not in *Philebus;* probably *Republic* IX 589E.
48 1 Cor. 6.15.
49 Cf. 1 Cor. 3.16,17.
50 Cf. Num. 25.9.

thy lusts and abstain from thy desires. Wine and women make wise men fall, and he that joins himself to harlots shall become more foolhardy; rottenness and the worm shall inherit him, and he shall be lifted up for a great example.'[51] And in another place (for He never tires of helping us): 'He who defies pleasure crowns his life.'[52] (102) It is unmistakably sinful to give in to sexual pleasure or to become inflamed by our lusts or to be excessively aroused by our unreasonable desires or to desire to dishonor oneself. Sowing seed is permissible only for the husband, as the farmer of the occasion, and even for him only when the season is favorable for sowing. Against every other sort of self-indulgence the best remedy is reason. It will be helpful, too, to avoid satiety, for in satiety desires wax strong and become unruly in their search for pleasures.

We should not seek for expensive clothes, either, any more than for elaborate dishes. In fact, the Lord Himself set Himself to give special counsel for the soul, for the body and for a third class, external things, all separately. He advised that external things were to be provided for the body, the body to be governed by the soul, and then instructed the soul: 'Be not solicitous for your life, what you shall eat nor for your body, what you shall put on. The life is more than the meat, and the body is more than the raiment.' Then He went on to illustrate His teaching: 'Consider the ravens, for they sow not, neither do they reap, neither have they storehouse or barn, and God feedeth them. Are not you more valuable than birds?' This is what He says about food, and He has much the same thing to say about clothing, which belongs to the third class of external things, too: 'Consider the lilies,'

---

51 Cf. Eccli. 18.30; 19.2,3.
52 Gloss on Eccli. 19.5.

He says, 'how they neither spin nor weave, but I say to you that not even Solomon was clothed as one of these.' Solomon took extravagant pride in his wealth; but what is more beautiful or of richer hue than a flower? (103) And what gives greater pleasure than a lily or myrrh or rose? 'Now if God clothe in this manner the grass that is today in the field, and tomorrow is cast into the oven, how much more you, O ye of little faith! And seek not what you shall eat or what you shall drink.'[53]

In that last sentence, the pronoun 'what' excludes elaborateness of menu, and the meaning intended by Scripture is this: 'Be not solicitous for what sort of things you eat, or what sort of things you drink.'[54] To be solicitous about such things is gluttony and gourmandizing. In itself, eating should be understood simply as implying a necessity; but repletion suggests only desire, as we have said. But the 'what' indicates superfluity and superfluity comes from the Devil, according to the Scriptures. The phrase he adds explains what he means: 'Seek not what you shall eat or what you shall drink, and do not exalt yourselves.' It is ostentatiousness, a false imitation of the truth and extravagance that exalts us above and away from the truth; concentration on needless comforts also turns us away from the truth. Therefore, He shrewdly adds: 'After all these things, the heathens seek.' The heathen are they who are without discipline and without understanding. What does He mean by 'these things'? Needless comforts, self-pampering, highly spiced and rich foods, gourmandizing, gluttony. These are the things that correspond to the 'what.' But, when He speaks of plain fare, food and drink, that is a necessity, He says: 'Your Father knoweth that you need these.' If we have become sincere

---
53 Luke 12.22-24,27-29.
54 That is, *poia* ('what sort of things') instead of *ti* ('what thing').

seekers, let us not waste our efforts in a search for pleasure, but let us enliven them by the discovery of the truth. 'Seek the kingdom of God,' He insists, 'and these things'—food—'shall be given you besides.'[55]

(104) Now, if Christ forbids solicitude once and for all about clothing and food and luxuries, as things that are unnecessary, do we need to ask Him about finery and dyed wools and multicolored robes, about exotic ornaments of jewels and artistic handiwork of gold, about wigs and artificial locks of hair and of curls, and about eye-shadowings and hair-plucking and rouges and powders and hair-dyes and all the other disreputable trades that practise these deceptions? Are we not reasonable in concluding that what He says about the grass is to be applied also to this disgraceful ostentation? The world is a field and we are the harvest watered by the grace of God; although we shall be cut down, we shall rise again, as I shall discuss in a treatise on the Resurrection.[56] But, grass is a figure of the ordinary multitude, who by nature indulge in feasting for a day and flourish for a short while, who love pretentiousness and grand show and everything but the truth, but who are fit, finally, only to be fuel for the fire.

(105) 'Now there was a certain rich man,' the Lord declared, 'who was clothed in purple and fine linen, and feasted sumptuously every day,'—he was grass—'and there was a certain beggar, named Lazarus, who lay at his gate full of sores, desiring to be filled with the crumbs that fell from the rich man's table.'[57] He was the good harvest. The one, the rich man, was punished in hell and had his share of its fire, while the other gained new life in the bosom of his father.

---
55 Cf. Luke 12.30,31.
56 Not extant.
57 Luke 16.19-20.

I admire the ancient city of the Lacedemonians for allowing only courtesans to wear brightly colored garments and gold ornaments; in this way, restricting such showy finery to that type of woman, they bred into their good women a reluctance to adorn themselves. On the other hand, in Athens, even the archons utterly forgot their manhood in their lust for the finer delicacies of life; they used to put on flowing tunics and load themselves with gold. The fashion was to wear their hair in a crobulus, a special kind of braid, set off by a brooch in the form of a golden cicada. Such esoteric extravagances, indicative of unnatural lust, simply put on public view their earthiness. The practise of the archons spread to other Ionians, for Homer speaks of them as 'robe-trailing,'[58] to imply their effeminacy. (106) Such men turn rather to imitation beauty, artificial ornamentation, than to Beauty itself, and are, therefore, image-worshipers in the true sense of the word. They must be considered strangers to the truth, who do no more than day-dream about the nature of truth, fashioning it more to their own fancy than according to knowledge. For them, this life is only a deep sleep of ignorance. But, as for ourselves, we must awaken from that sort of sleep and sincerely seek true beauty and the true adornment; we must long to possess that alone, and, ridding ourselves of the ornaments of this world, detach ourselves from it before we slip off into our final sleep.

I maintain that man needs clothing only for bodily covering, as a protection against excessive cold or intense heat, so that the inclemency of the weather may not harm him in any way. If that is the purpose of clothes, then one kind of garment surely should not be provided for men and another for women. The need for clothing, like the need for food and drink, is common to both, (107) and where the need is

---
58 *Iliad* 6.442; 7.297.

common, our minds should turn to the same kind of means to fulfill it. Both have the same need of being protected; therefore, what they use as protection should be very similar, except, perhaps, that women ought to use a type of garment that will cover their eyes.[59] If the female sex is rightly allowed more clothing out of deference to its weakness, then the practise of a degenerate way of life must be censured which accustoms men to unworthy customs that so often make them more womanish than the women.

But we do not feel free to relax our strictness in any way. If we need to make any concessions, we might allow women to use softer garments, provided they give up fancy weaves, symptoms of vanity, and fabrics too elaborate in weave, or with gold thread, Indian silks and all products of the silk-worm. The silkworm is a worm only at its first stage; it turns into a hairy caterpillar, and then, in its third stage, into a larva (although some call it the nymph of the silk-worm); it is by this larva that the thread is spun, just as the spider spins its web. These flimsy and luxurious things are proof of a shallow character, for, with the scanty protection they afford, they do nothing more than disgrace the body, inviting prostitution. An overly soft garment is no longer covering, since it cannot conceal the bare outline of the figure; the folds of such a garment clinging to the body and following its contours very flexibly take its shape and outline the woman's form so that even one not trying to stare can see plainly the woman's entire figure.

(108) We disapprove also of dyed garments. They do not satisfy the demands either of necessity or of truth; besides, they give cause for defamation of character. They serve no useful purpose, for they do nothing to protect against

---

59 The text is defective here.

the cold, nor do they add any advantage to that given by any other garment, save criticism alone. The enjoyment of these colors is injurious to the luxury-loving people who use them, to the point of provoking a strange eye-affliction. It is much more fitting that they who are pure and upright interiorly be clothed in pure white and plain garments. Daniel the Prophet, for instance, makes this observation clearly and simply: 'Thrones were placed, and there sat on them, as if an Ancient of days, and his garment was white as snow.'[60] The Lord, too, was seen in a vision clothed in the same color of vesture.[61] The Apocalypse also says: 'I saw under the altar the souls of them who had given testimony. And a white robe was given to every one of them.'[62]

If there is need for some other color, the natural color of real life is sufficient; garments colored like flowers should be left for the farces of the Bacchanals and of the pagan mystery rites. To this must be added what the comic poet says: 'Purple and silver plates are good enough for tragedies, but not for life.'[63] Our lives ought to be different from a play. But Sardinian dye and those other violet and green dyes, that compounded from the rose, and scarlet dye, and the thousand-and-one others have all been invented with so much eagerness the more to gratify demoralizing love of luxury. (109) These kinds of garments are not for clothing's sake, but for appearance. They must all be renounced, together with the art that produces them: gold embroideries, purple-dyed robes, those embroidered with figurines (all such vanity is but a puff of wind), as well as the saffron-hued

---
60 Cf. Dan. 7.9.
61 Cf. Matt. 17.2.
62 Apoc. 6.9-11.
63 Philemon, *Frag.* 105, *CAF* II 512.

Bacchic mantle dipped in myrrh, and the expensive multicolored mantle of costly skins with figures dyed in purple. 'For what sensible or outstanding thing do these women accomplish,' the comic poet asks, 'who sit sparkling with colors, wearing their saffron dresses and so highly ornamented?'[64] Our Educator distinctly advises: 'Glory not in apparel, and be not lifted up in glory, since it does not endure.'[65] More explicitly, He speaks ironically of those who wear soft garments, saying in the Gospel: 'Behold, they who live in costly apparel and in luxury, are in the houses of kings.'[66] He means the palaces of earth, those which crumble away, where vanity and vainglory and sycophancy and error dwell. Those who serve the heavenly court, that of the King of all, sanctify their bodies, the untainted garment of their souls, and clothe it with incorruption.

Now, a woman who is not wed is concerned with God alone, and her mind is not distracted every which way; the chaste woman who is wed divides her life between God and her husband;[67] but one of a different mind gives herself wholly to her married life, that is, to her passion. In the same way, I believe, the chaste wife practises true, unfeigned love of God by busying herself for her husband, but, if she turns to vanities, she proves false both to God and to the chastity of her married life; she values finery more than her husband, just like the Argive harlot, Eriphyle, 'who took precious gold as the price of the life of her own dear husband.'[68]

(110) I like the description that the Ceian Sophist gave

---

64 Aristophanes, *Lys.* 42-44.
65 Eccli. 11.4.
66 Luke 7.25.
67 Cf. 1 Cor 7.32-34.
68 *Odysseus* 11.327.

of the similar and corresponding figure of good and of evil.[69] The one he pictured standing simply, clothed in white, pure: this is virtue, adorned only with her modesty (that is the way fidelity ought to be, virtuous and modest); the other he describes as just the contrary: wrapped in many robes, decked out in outlandish colors, with a movement and posture best calculated to insure her own enjoyment in company with other shameless women. Now, one who obeys reason will not associate in any way with base pleasure; therefore, he ought to prefer the sort of garment that is useful. Even the Word says about the Lord, in David's psalm: 'The daughters of the king have delighted thee in thy glory; the queen stood on thy right hand, clothed in a garment interwoven with gold and in a golden-fringed tunic,'[70] referring not to a garment of luxury, but to the ornament the Church wears, woven out of faith, undefiled, composed of those who have obtained mercy. In that Church, the sinless Jesus 'shines out as gold,' and the elect as golden fringes.[71]

(111) But we must moderate our severity for the sake of the women. We say, then, that their garment may be woven smooth and soft to the touch, but not adorned with gaudy colors, like a painting, just to dazzle the eye. For, just like a picture which fades with time, so the constant rinsing and steeping of these woolen robes in plant juices serving as dyes deteriorates the garments, wears them out, weakens the weave, and is definitely opposed to economy. It is the height of vanity to let oneself be fascinated by the flowing robes and gowns and cloaks and mantles and tunics 'that cover nakedness,'[72] as Homer says. I am really ashamed to see so much

---
69 Prodicus the Sophist; cf. Xenophon, *Mem.* II 21-34.
70 Cf. Ps. 44.9,10,14.
71 Cf. 1 Pet. 2.22.
72 *Iliad* 2.262.

money squandered just to cover the private parts. Of old, man fashioned a covering for his shame out of branches and leaves from the garden,[73] but, now that we have sheep for our use, let us not imitate the sheep in their stupidity, but follow the guidance of reason and refuse to have anything to do with expensive clothing, insisting: 'Wool, you belong to the sheep.' Even if Miletus does boast, even if Italy prides itself, and even if the wool is fortified by hides, and the people go madly after them, let us at least not covet them.

(112) The blessed John disdained sheep's wool because it savored of luxury; he preferred camel's hair and clothed himself in it, giving us an example of simple, frugal living.[74] Incidentally, he also ate only honey and locusts, food that is sweet and with a spiritual significance. So it was that he prepared the way of the Lord, and kept it humble and chaste. He fled from the false pretenses of the city and led a peaceful life in the desert with God,[75] away from all vanity and vainglory and servitude. How could he possibly have worn a purple mantle? Elias used a sheepskin for his garment, and girded it tight with a belt made of hair.[76] Isaias, another historic Prophet, went 'naked and without sandals,'[77] and often put on sack-cloth as a garment of humility. (113) If you protest and make mention of Jeremias, he wore only a girdle made of linen.[78] Just as the bare framework of the body is revealed once the accumulated tissue is stripped away, so magnificent beauty of character will become manifest if only it be not shrouded in the nonsense of vanity.

---

73 Cf. Gen. 3.7.
74 Cf. Matt. 3.4.
75 The text is defective here.
76 Cf. 1 Kings 19.13,19.
77 Isa. 20.2.
78 Cf. Jer. 13.1.

But to trail around garments that reach down even to the feet is nothing more than ostentatiousness. Besides, it is actually a hindrance in walking, for such a garment sweeps up piles of dirt after it on the ground, like a broom. Not even dancers, with all their elegance, permit themselves such flowing robes as they engage in their silent and unnaturally lewd performance on the stage, although the meticulous arrangement of their costumes, the folds of their dresses, as well as the studied rhythm of their every gesture, manifest the unspeakable languidness with which they drag themselves around, so to speak. If someone should remind us of the full-length robe of the Lord, [we reply that] His multicolored tunic really represents the brillance of wisdom, the manifold and unfading value of Scripture, words of the Lord that glow with rays of truth. For this reason, the Spirit clothed the Lord with another similar garment when it said in the psalm of David: 'I will put on praise and beauty, clothed with light as with a garment.'[79]

(114) Therefore, we must avoid any irregularity in the type of garment we choose. We must also guard against all waywardness in our use of them. For instance, it is not right for a woman to wear her dress up over her knees, as the Laconian maidens are said to do, because a woman should not expose any part of her body. Of course, when someone tells her: 'Your arm is shapely,'[80] she can always cleverly make the witty reply: 'But it is not public property'; to 'Your legs are beautiful,' this reply: 'But they belong to my husband'; or if he says: 'Your face is lovely,' she can answer: 'But only for him to whom I am married'; still, I am unwill-

---
79 Ps. 103.1.
80 The Scholion remarks this was said of a Spartan woman, because of the sleeveless dress worn there.

ing that a chaste woman even give occasion for such praise from men with sinful intent. I should like, too, not only that it be forbidden them to expose their ankle, but also that it be made obligatory for them to wear a veil over their face and a covering on their head. It is not becoming, either, for a woman to make a show of herself by wearing a purple veil. If I could but wring the purple out of all the veils, that passersby might not turn to catch a glimpse of the face behind it! Yet, such women, who weave almost the whole ensemble of their wardrobe, make everything purple to inflame lusts. Indeed, through their fatuous and elegant purples, 'dark death'—in the words of the old poem—'has seized upon them.'[81] (115) For the sake of this purple, Tyre and Sidon and the shores of the Laconian Sea are sedulously cultivated, and the dyers and purple-shell fishers and the shell fish themselves of these localities are highly prized because purple dye is procured from the blood of the shell fish. Affected women and men who are effeminate in their self indulgence have become insanely covetous of these artificial dyes to color their fine woven robes. They import linen no longer from Egypt alone, but also from Palestine and Cilicia; as for Amorgian and Byssian flax, I have nothing to say, for their luxuriousness surpasses all that words can convey.

A covering, it seems to me, should make what it covers more conspicuous than itself, as the temple does the statue, the body the soul, and the clothing the body. Now, everything is just the opposite. If these women sold their bodies, they would get scarcely a thousand Attic pieces, yet they pay ten thousand talents for one garment, proving that that they are less valuable and profitable than their clothes. Why do you seek things that are rare and expensive, rather than ordinary

---

81 *Iliad* 5.83.

and cheaper articles? You do not know what is truly beautiful and good. The foolish eagerly seek what seems to be good, rather than what is really good, like the insane who believe that black is white.

Chapter 11

(116) There are women who manifest a very similar vanity in their footwear, thereby revealing considerable shallowness of character. It is a matter for shame to have sandals plated with the costliest gold, and even worse to decide, as some do, to have nails hammered into the soles in a circular pattern. Many even engrave love messages on them so that they mark the earth in recurring pattern as they walk, and stamp the eroticism of their own hearts upon it with their footprints. We must give up such foolish artistries of golden and gem-studded sandals, of Attic and Sicyonian boots, and buskins, and Persian and Tyrrhenian slippers as well. We must first set before our eyes what our true goal is, according to the truth, and then choose what conforms to nature. Sandals are used for two things: one, as a covering for the feet, and the other, as a precaution against stumbling and against the roughness of climbing uphill, to protect the soles of the feet.

(117) We permit women the use of white sandals, unless they are traveling, when they should use sandals anointed with oil. They also need footwear that has soles nailed on, for their traveling. Otherwise, they should always use sandals, because it is unbecoming for women to expose their bare foot, and also because they are more easily hurt. But it is certainly permissible for a man to go about without sandals, unless he

is on some military expedition. Being sandaled, in fact, is much like being bound. It is very frequent among athletes to go barefooted, both for the sake of their health and for greater freedom of movement; so, no necessity should prevent us from doing the same.

But, if we are not traveling and are wearing shoes, we should wear the slipper or the white shoe. Athenians call them dust shoes because, I believe, they keep the feet close to the dust. When we put them on, the prayer that should be said is drawn from the witness given by John, who confessed that he was not worthy to loose the latch of the sandals of the Lord. For, He who suggested the model of true philosophy to the Hebrews did not wear anything elaborate on His feet. This means something here, but it will be explained more fully in another place.

Chapter 12

(118) It is pure childishness to let ourselves become fascinated by gems, whether they are green or dark red, and by the stones disgorged by the sea, and by metals dug up out of the earth. To set one's heart on shining pebbles and peculiar colors and irridescent glass is simply to play the part of a man without intelligence, easily spell-bound by gaudy appearances. Just so, little children are attracted by the brillance of a fire they see, not realizing, in their immaturity, the danger of touching it. That holds true, too, of the stones that silly women hang about their necks on chains, and the amethysts and ceraunites that they string together on necklaces, as well as the jasper and topaz and 'the Milesian emeralds, the most valuable of all wares.'[1]

---
1 *Adesp.* 109, *TGF.*

The precious pearl has become an all too common item in the apparel of our women. This stone is formed in the oyster, a bivalve very similar to the pinna, in size about the shape of the eye of a large fish. These bewitched women are not ashamed to center all their interests on this small oyster. Yet they could adorn themselves instead with that holy stone, the Word of God, called somewhere in Scripture 'a pearl,'[2] that is, Jesus in all His splendor and purity, the mysterious eye of the divine vision in human form,[3] the glorious Word through whom human nature is born again and receives a great new value. The pearl is formed by the oyster after it has covered its flesh about to protect itself from the water that is in it. (119) Tradition assures us that the heavenly Jerusalem that is above is built up of holy gems and we know that the twelve gates of the heavenly city, which signify the wonderful beauty of the apostolic teaching, are compared to precious jewels.[4] These priceless stones are described as possessing certain colors which are themselves precious, while the rest is left of an earthy substance. To say that the city of the saints is built of such jewels, even though it is a spiritual edifice, is a cogent symbol indeed. By the incomparable brillance of the gems is understood the spotless and holy brillance of the substance of the spirit.

But these women, not understanding that the Scriptures speak only metaphorically, totally blinded by their passion for jewels, offer this remarkable excuse: 'Why may we not make use of what God has manifested? I already possess them, so why may I not enjoy them? For whom have they been made if not for us?' Such words can come only from those who

---

2 Cf. Matt. 13.46.
3 Literally, 'the contemplating eye in the flesh.' But the word *epóptēs*, savoring of the pagan mysteries, suggests the higher vision of divine things granted to the initiate.
4 Cf. Apoc. 21.18-21.

are completely ignorant of the will of God. He supplies us, first of all, with the necessities such as water and the open air, but other things that are not necessary He has hidden in the earth and sea. (120) That is why there are lions to dig for gold, and griffins to guard it,[5] and why the sea conceals the stone we call the pearl. You trouble yourselves about things you do not need. Behold, the whole heavens have opened up, and you do not see God. Only those who have been condemned to death in our courts are made to mine buried gold and stones. Make answer to the Scripture when it calls out so explicitly: 'Seek first the kingdom of heaven, and all these things shall be given you besides.'[6] Even if all things have been given you, and if all things have been permitted you, and if all things are possible for you, yet, as the Apostle says, 'not all things are expedient.'[7]

It is God Himself who has brought our race to possession in common, by sharing Himself, first of all, and by sending His Word to all men alike, and by making all things for all. Therefore, everything is common, and the rich should not grasp a greater share. The expression, then, 'I own something, and have more than enough; why should I not enjoy it?' is not worthy of man nor does it indicate any community feeling. The other expression does, however: 'I have something, why should I not share it with those in need?' Such a one is perfect, and fulfills the command: 'Thou shalt love thy neighbor as thyself.'[8]

This is true extravagance, the lavishness that lays up treasure, but to spend money on foolish desires comes more under the heading of destruction that of expenditure. God

---
5 Cf. Herodotus IV 13.27.
6 Matt. 6.33.
7 1 Cor. 10.23.
8 Matt. 19.19.

has given us the power to use our possessions, I admit, but only to the extent it is necessary: He wishes them to be in common. It is unbecoming that one man live in luxury when there are so many who labor in poverty. How much more honorable it is to serve many than to live in wealth! How much more reasonable it is to spend money on men than on stones and gold! How much more useful to have friends as our ornamentation than lifeless decorations! Who can derive more benefit from lands than from practising kindness?

(121) The only problem left to answer, then, is this: for whom do precious things exist, if everyone is going to choose what is less costly? For us men, I should reply, but provided we use them without attachment or distinction. And if it should be impossible for all to practise the virtue of temperance, then at least in our use of the necessities we should confine ourselves to what is more easily obtainable and forget about exotic articles. As a general rule, ornaments should not be desired, as they are mere childish toys, and women should eschew the very thought of embellishment. A woman should be adorned, assuredly, but interiorly; there she should be beautiful indeed. Beauty or ugliness is found only in the soul. Only he who is sincere is truly noble and virtuous, and only the noble can be considered good. 'Virtue alone is noteworthy even in a beautiful body,'[9] and comes to full maturity afterwards in the flesh. The attractiveness of temperance is made manifest when the character glows with a brilliant appearance, as though with light. The beauty of anything, whether plant or animal, is admittedly in its perfection.[10] But man's perfection is justice and temperance and

---
9 *Adesp.* 412, *CAF* III 486
10 That is, *areté*, which means 'excellence' or 'virtue.'

courage and piety.[11] Therefore, it is the just and temperate, or, in a word, the good man who is noble, and not the wealthy one. But now, even soldiers want to be decorated with gold; they have never read the line of the poet: 'And he came to the war, all decked out with gold, like a foolish girl.'[12]

(122) Surely we should uproot all love for ornamentation, for it contributes nothing to the growth of virtue, but, instead, pampers the body. Nor should we yield to any ostentatious pursuit of vanity. Women who deck themselves out with things not made for the body as though they were fall into a habit of deception and pretense, and display, not gravity and simplicity and humility, but pompousness and light-mindedness and self-indulgence. They conceal natural beauty by overshadowing it with gold; they do not realize the serious mistake they make in hanging countless chains about themselves, as 'criminals,' it is said, 'are bound with gold by the barbarians.'[13] These women, it seems to me, are actually envious of those richly laden prisoners of war. Is not their golden necklace still only a collar-band? And are their neck-pieces anything more? In fact, the so-called collar, shaped like a chain, is really called 'chain' by the Athenians. Besides, the ugly little trinket women wear about their ankle, Philemon calls 'fetters' in his *Synephebos,* speaking of 'an article of dress that is very conspicuous, and a golden fetter.'[14]

(123) Why these much-desired decorations, O women, except that you want yourselves to appear bound in fetters? If the material used lessens the shame, the effect is still no different. I mean to say that they seem to me, as they carry about these willing bonds, to be boasting of the state of their

---
11 Cf. Epictetus III 1.6.
12 Cf. *Iliad* 2.873.
13 Cf. Herodotus III 23.
14 Philemon, *Frag.* 81, *CAF* II 501.

wealth. Similarly, the myth told by the poet describing the bonds cast about Aphrodite as she was committing adultery[15] implies that these ornaments are nothing but a symbol of adultery. Even though they were made of gold, Homer still calls them bonds. Yet, these women do not blush when they wear such conspicuous symbols of wickedness. Just as the serpent deceived Eve, so, too, the enticing golden ornament in the shape of a serpent enkindles a mad frenzy in the hearts of the rest of womankind, leading them to have images made of lampreys and snakes as decorations.

The comic poet Nikostratos has words about 'chains, collars, rings, bracelets, serpents, anklets and earrings.'[16] (124) Aristophanes, too, in his *Thesmoforiaszousai,* lists a whole catalogue of feminine ornamentation, obviously in a disapproving tone. I shall quote these words of the comic poet, because they describe in such detail the wearying lengths of your vulgar display:

'*A*. Turbans, hair-bands, soap, pumice-stone, breast-band, sling-band, veil, rouge, necklace, undershading for the eyes, soft tasseled robes, golden hellebore, hairnets, girdle, shawl, trinkets, bordered tunics, the expensive xystis, cloaks, the ornament called barathron, the outer- and the underdress. Yet, the greater part of these I still have not mentioned.

'*B*. What else?

'*A*. Ear pendants, jewel-studded trinkets, earrings, mallow-colored dresses, grape-shaped earrings, bracelets, brooches, clasps, neck-bands, anklets, signet rings, chains, rings, poultices, head ornaments, bands, leather phalli, Sardian stones, neckpieces, twisted earrings.'[17]

For my part, I grow weary and find it burdensome to speak

---
15 Cf. *Odysseus* 8.296-333.
16 *Frag.* 33, *CAF* II 228.
17 *Frag.* 320, *CAF* I 474.

of all these luxuries; as for the women, I have to marvel that they can carry such a heavy load and not grow faint. (125) Oh, the senseless industry! The vain ostentation! To their shame, they pour out their money like harlots, and caricature, with their vulgar extravagance, the gifts of God and rival the skill of the Evil One. In the Gospel, the Lord called the rich man a fool, in plain language, because he was laying up treasures in his storehouse and saying to himself: 'You have many good things stored away for many years. Eat, drink, and be merry.' For, as the Lord said: 'This night they are demanding your soul of you. The things, then, that you have prepared, shall belong to another.'[18]

Apelles the painter, seing one of his pupils painting a picture of Helen with liberal applications of gold, remarked: 'Boy, you cannot make her beautiful, therefore you are making her rich.' Nowadays, women have become so many Helens, not beautiful by nature, but covered over with wealth. (126) Of such the Spirit announced through Sophonias: 'Neither shall their silver and their gold be able to deliver them in the day of the wrath of the Lord.'[19] It is not right that they who are being educated by Christ should be adorned with gold; they should be adorned only with the Word, by whom gold has been made. How fortunate the Hebrews of old would have been if they had taken hold of the ornaments of their women and thrown them away, or had simply put them in a melting pot! As it was, they fashioned them into a golden calf and made an idol of the calf,[20] and so derived no benefit either from their art or from their plan, but only provided our women a striking lesson

---
18 Cf. Luke 12.18-20.
19 Soph. 1.10.
20 Cf. Exod. 32.1-6.

on the advantage of laying ornaments aside. To be sure, the prostitution of desire before a golden image is punished with fire, for it is only in fire that pleasure is discovered to be not the truth but only an image.

As a consequence, the Word reproaches the Hebrews through the Prophet: 'They made silver and gold [trinkets] for Baal,' that is, ornaments. Then He adds, as a forceful threat: 'And I will visit upon her the days of [the destruction of the] Baalim in which she burnt incense for herself, and decked herself out with her ear-rings and her necklaces,' adding the reason for all these ornaments: 'She went after her lovers and forgot Me, saith the Lord.'[21]

(127) Therefore, let them leave these playthings for the sophists who trifle with the truth; let them not take part in such gawdy embellishment nor worship images under a fair veil. The blessed Peter says eloquently: 'In like manner, women adorning themselves not with plaited hair or gold, or pearls or costly attire, but as it becometh women professing godliness, with good works.'[22] As a matter of fact, there is sound reasoning in his command that such adornments be left alone, for either a woman is already beautiful, and then nature is sufficient (and let art not contend with nature, that is, let deception not vie with the truth), or else she is naturally ugly, and then she proves what she does not have by attiring herself with all these things. (128) Those who worship Christ ought to accept plainness. Indeed, plainness promotes the growth of holiness because it moderates avarice and ministers to real need from what is ready at hand. The plain, as its name suggests, is not excessive or distended in any way, or inflated, but is uniform, level and equal, never excessive. For this reason it is effective, for effectiveness is a

---

21 Osee 2.8,13 (Septuagint).
22 Not Peter; cf. 1 Tim. 2.9,10.

quality that reaches its goal without deviations or extravagances.

The mother of such as these is justice, and their nurse is self-sufficiency. This last virtue rests content with what is necessary, and provides from its own resources the things that conduce to a happy life. (129) Wear, then, as a holy ornament of good fruits on your arms, the generous giving of your possessions and the faithful fulfillment of your household duties. 'He who gives to a beggar gives to God,'[23] and 'The hands of the industrious begetteth riches,'[24] meaning the industrious who despise money and are quick to give alms. Let there appear upon your feet the ornament of unhesitating readiness for good deeds and steadiness in the path of justice. Modesty and temperance are the true neck-bands and necklaces, for they are chains God forges out of gold. 'Blessed is the man who has found wisdom, and the mortal who has seen understanding,'[25] the Spirit says in the words of Solomon, 'for to buy her is better than treasures of gold and silver, and she is more precious than costly stones.'[25] She it is who is the true adornment.

The ears of women should not be pierced, either, to enable them to suspend earrings and ear pendants from them. It is contrary to nature. It is wrong to do violence to nature in a way nature does not intend. Surely, there is no better ornament for the ears than learning the truth, nor is there any that enters the ears in as natural a way. Eyes anointed by the Word and ears pierced to hear are ready to contemplate holy things and to hear divine things. It is only the Word who reveals true beauty 'which eye has never seen before, nor has ear heard.'[26]

---
23 Prov. 19.17.
24 Prov. 10.4.
25 Prov. 3.13-15.
26 1 Cor. 2.9.

BOOK THREE

Chapter 1

TO KNOW ONESELF has always been, so it seems, the greatest of all lessons. For, if anyone knows himself, he will know God; and, in knowing God, he will become like Him,[1] not by wearing golden ornaments or by trailing long flowing robes, but by performing good deeds and cultivating an independence of as many things as possible. God alone has no needs, and He rejoices in a particular way when He sees us pure in the adornment of our minds and our bodies clothed with the adornment of the holy garment of self-control.

The soul consists of three parts.[2] The intelligence, which is also called the reason, is the inner man, the ruler of the external man. But it is led by someone else, that is, by God. The part in which anger resides is akin to the beasts and lives close to madness. The third part, desire, takes many forms and is more changeable than Proteus the sea god, assuming a different form for every different occasion, seeking

---
1 Cf. 1 John 3.2.
2 Cf. Plato, *Republic* IV *passim*, esp. 435-441.

satisfaction in adultery, promiscuity, and seduction. 'At first, he [Proteus] turned into a bearded lion,' retaining only his adornment, the hair of his chin which proved his manhood. 'Then into a serpent and a leopard and a huge boar.' Vanity degenerated into immorality. Finally, his human nature is evident no longer, not even in the appearance of a lordly beast, but 'he turned into flowing water, and into a tree high and leafy.'[3] The passions are poured out, pleasures sprout forth, and beauty withers and falls to the ground—more quickly than the leaf—when the violent storms of lust blow upon it; before late autumn can come, it has withered in decay.

In fact, desire becomes everything, turns itself into a counterfeit of everything, and seeks to play the impostor to conceal man's true nature. But the man in whom reason dwells does not keep shifting, makes no false pretenses, retains the form dictated by reason, is like God and possesses true beauty with no need of artificial beauty. Beauty is what is true, for it is in fact God. Such a man becomes God because God wills it.[4] (2) Heraclitus said well: 'Men are gods and gods are men, for reason is the same'[5]—manifestly a mystery. God is in man and a man is God, as the Mediator, fulfilling the will of His Father. For the reason common to both is the mediator: that is, the Word, Son of God, Saviour of man, the servant of God, our Educator.

If the flesh is a slave,[6] as even Paul claims, is it at all reasonable to adorn such a handmaid, as the bawd does? To prove that the flesh has the form of a slave, the Apostle says of the

---
3 *Odysseus* 4.456-457.
4 Cf. Ps. 81.6; John 10.34.
5 Heraclitus, *Frag.* 62, in H. Diels, *op. cit.*
6 Cf. Rom. 6.16; 7.14; Phil. 2.7.

Lord: 'He emptied Himself, taking the form of a slave,'[7] calling the exterior man a slave even before the Lord assumed flesh and became a slave. In His compassion, God has freed the flesh from corruption and, delivering it from its bitter slavery to death, has clothed it with incorruption, clothing the flesh with the holy ornament of eternity, immortality.[8]

(3) But there is another sort of beauty for men: charity. 'Charity,' according to the Apostle, 'is patient, is kind, does not envy, is not pretentious, is not puffed up.'[9] But artificial beauty is pretentiousness, because it presents the appearance of extravagance and superfluity. That is why he adds: 'It does not behave unbecomingly.'[10] An appearance that is borrowed and not natural is surely unbecoming. Every sort of application is artificial, which is what he has in mind when he continues: 'It does not seek the things that are not its own.'[11] Truth calls what is proper to itself its own, while vanity seeks what is artificial, putting itself in opposition to God, to reason and to charity. The Spirit gives witness through Isaias that even the Lord became an unsightly spectacle: 'And we saw Him, and there was no beauty or comeliness in Him, but His form was despised, and abject among men.'[12] Yet, who is better than the Lord? He displayed not beauty of the flesh, which is only outward appearance, but the true beauty of body and soul: for the soul, the beauty of good deeds; for the body, that of immortality.

---
7 Phil. 2.7.
8 Cf. 1 Cor. 15.53.
9 1·Cor. 13.4.
10 Cf. 1 Cor. 13.5. The Greek is *aschēmoneî*, which Clement understands in a more literal sense than most translators do.
11 *Ibid.*, but Clement's text obviously has a second negative.
12 Isa. 53.2 (Septuagint).

Chapter 2

(4) It is not the appearance of the outer man that should be made beautiful, but his soul, with the ornament of true virtue. It should be possible, too, to speak of an ornament for his body, the ornament of self-control.

But women, busy in making their appearances beautiful, allowing the interior to lie uncultivated, are in reality decorating themselves, without realizing it, like Egyptian temples. The entrances and vestibules of these temples are elaborately ornamented, the sacred groves and meadows are cultivated, the halls are adorned with huge columns, and the walls, each covered with some highly finished painting, glitter with rare jewels. The temples themselves are studded over with gold and silver and electrum, and sparkle with gems from India and Ethiopia which cover them, while the inner sanctuary is curtained off by an overhanging gold-embroidered veil. But if, anxious to see the lord of such a temple, you pass beyond into the interior of the sacred precincts, seeking the god that dwells in the temple, a pastophore or some other hierophant will look sharply about the sacred shrine, chant a hymn in the Egyptian tongue, and then draw back a bit of the veil that you might see his god, but he reveals an object of veneration that is utterly absurd. There is no god within, whom we were so anxiously looking for; there is only a cat, or a crocodile, or a snake native to the land, or some other similar animal suited for life in a cave or den or in the mud, but certainly not in a temple. The god of the Egyptians, then, turns out to be only a beast curled up on a rich purple pillow.

(5) Women who are loaded down with gold seem to me much like that temple. They carefully curl their locks, paint

their cheeks, stencil under their eyes, anxiously dye their hair, and practise perversely all the other senseless arts; true imitators of the Egyptians, they adorn the enclosure of the flesh to lure lovers who stand in superstitious dread of the goddess. But, if anyone draw back the veil of this temple, I mean the hairnet and the dye and the garments and gold and rouge and cosmetics[1]—or the cloth woven of all these things, which is a veil—if he draws back this veil to discover the true beauty that is within, I am sure he will be disgusted. He will not find dwelling within any worthy image of God, but, instead, a harlot and adulteress who has usurped the inner sanctuary of the soul. The beauty within will turn out to be nothing more than a beast, 'an ape painted up with powder';[2] as a deceitful serpent, it will devour man's intellect with love of ornaments and make the soul its den. Filling the whole soul with its deadly drug and vomiting out the poison of its deception, this serpent-seducer has transformed women into harlots (for gaudy vanity bespeaks not the woman, but the harlot).

Such women have little care for managing household expenses for their husbands. Rather, they unloose the strings of their husbands' purses and waste their fortunes on their own desires, that they might win for themselves a host of admirers charmed by their cultivated appearances. They spend the entire day with their slaves—who, incidentally, were bought at a handsome sum—engaged in their toilet. (6) They labor to make their body attractive, as though it were an unappetizing morsel. By day, they stay closeted up, devoting themselves to their toilet, lest they be caught dyeing their hair blonde; then at night, this artificial beauty comes creeping out

---

1 The Scholion says this is a scarlet sea weed.
2 *Adesp.* 517, *CAF* III 503; cf. Aristophanes, *Eccles.* 1072.

into candle light, as if from her lair, and both the dimness of the light and the bleary-eyed vision of drunkenness aid her in her deception. Yet, the comic poet Menander forbade his house to a woman who had bleached her hair: 'Creep out of this house, for a chaste woman should never make her hair blonde,'[3] or for that matter paint her cheeks or shade under her eyes.

These deluded souls are actually destroying their natural beauty, without being aware of it, when they add all this artificial beauty. As soon as day breaks, they massage their skin and rub it down, then coat it with lotions—but this only dries the skin; while the many preparations make the flesh flabby, and excessive use of soaps robs it of its natural healthy bloom. Women acquire a paleness of face from all these lotions, and their bodies, made delicate from all their beautifying cosmetics, become very susceptible to diseases. Besides, they insult the Creator of mankind, implying that He has not given them the beauty they deserve. Of course, they do none of their household duties, but stay sitting to be looked at, as if they were in a painting, not required to work. (7) That is why the comic poet has his prudent woman say in the comedy: 'What sensible or worthwhile thing would we women accomplish, if we sat idle with our hair blonde-dyed?'[4] This is the way they undermine their own reputation as noble women, break up homes, destroy marriages, and bring into the world illegitimate children.

Even Antiphanes, the comic poet, ridiculed this same thing in his comedy *Malthake*, as a sign of looseness of character in a woman; he used words that may be applied commonly to all women in their constant toiletry: 'She comes, she goes

---

3 Menander, *Frag.* 610, *CAF* III 184.
4 Aristophanes, *Lys.* 42,43.

back, she comes again, she goes away, she comes, she stays, she washes; she comes back, she dries herself, she combs, she puts in her appearance, she rubs herself, she washes, she looks in, she dresses, she uses perfumes, she puts on her ornaments, she rubs herself with oil; and if she were to have one thing more, she chokes.'[5] Certainly, such a woman deserves to perish not once, but three times over, using as she does the droppings of crocodiles, anointing herself with the scrapings of decayed wood, and rubbing charcoal into her eyebrows and white lead on her cheeks. (8) When such a person palls even upon a pagan dramatist, should she not be condemned unhesitatingly by the truth?

Alexis, another comic dramatist, also condemns this type of woman. In fact, I am going to quote the lines of this poet, too, because he satirizes in such minute detail their headstrong shamelessness. Not that he is overdetailed, but I blush to see womankind made the subject of such satire. She was created as a helpmate for her husband,[6] yet brought only ruin upon him. Alexis says: 'Her first deeds look to her own gain and the plunder of her neighbor; all her other actions are but incidental. One woman may by chance be small; she stitches cork in the soles of her shoes. Another is tall; she wears slippers with thin soles and walks with her head hunched down on her shoulders to take off some of her height. Another has no hips; she wears padding underneath, sewed on so that those who look at her may remark on her fine shape. She has a protruding stomach; or her breasts are of the sort that comic dramatists describe; she dons some kind of tight garment that holds in her stomach as if by wooden sticks. She has red eyebrows, so she paints them with charcoal. She hap-

---
5 Antiphanes, *Frag.* 148, *CAF* II 71.
6 Cf. Gen. 2.18.

pens to be dark-complexioned, so she powders herself with white lead. She is too pale, so she rubs on rouge. She has a part of her body that is particularly comely; she must leave it exposed. She has nice teeth; then she must laugh, to let those around her see what a pretty mouth she has. And if she does not feel like laughing, she passes the day with a small sprig of myrtle between her lips so that she will keep on grinning whether she wish to or not.'[7]

(9) I quote all these passages to turn you from vanity with all its ill-devised schemes sprung from worldly wisdom. But, since the Word is ever ready and willing to save us, I will in a few moments also suggest the remedy sacred Scripture proposes. It may possibly happen that the fact that such women do not go unnoticed will draw them from sin, in fear of the shame of being corrected. Just as a hand swathed in a poultice or an eye bathed in oil gives rise, by its very appearance, to the suspicion of disease, so, too, cosmetics and dyes indicate that the soul is sick to its core. The divine Educator exhorts us to pass by 'another's river,' a figure of speech meaning another man's wife, dissolute, ready to flow out to anyone, giving herself over to pleasure with anyone in impure lust. 'Keep away from another's water,' He says, 'and do not drink from another's stream,' meaning that we should be wary of the stream of loose living, 'that you may live long and that years of life may be added to us,'[8] whether because we do not seek the pleasure that belongs to someone else or because we avoid attachments.

(10) Although gluttony and intemperance are strong passions, they are not as strong as vanity. A full table or cups in quick succession can satisfy gluttony, but those who love

---

7 Alexis, *Frag.* 98.1,2,7-22,24-26, *CAF* II 329.
8 Prov. 9.18a (Septuagint).

gold and purple and jewels would not be content with all that is upon the earth or under it, nor the whole of the Tyrrhenian sea, nor the cargo of ships from India and Ethiopia, nor even with the Pactolus overflowing with riches.[9] Even if one of them become a Midas, he is not satisfied, but remains restive, eager for more wealth, ready to cling to the gold he has, even to death. If Plutus is blind, as he is indeed, are not these women, who have such an admiration for him and are on such intimate terms with him, also blind? Their passion, in fact, knows no limits, but drives them shipwrecked upon the shoals of complete loss of shame. They feel a need of theater, and of processions, and of hosts of people to see them, and of visits to sacred places and of loitering on the streets that they may give everyone ample opportunity to look at them. They deck themselves out to attract the attention of others, priding themselves more on their appearance than on the state of their hearts. But, just as the brand remains to mark a runaway slave, so their bright colors mark them off as adulteresses. 'Though thou clothest thyself in scarlet,' the Word says through Jeremias, 'though thou deckest thee with ornaments of gold and paintest thy eyes with stibic stone, thou shall dress thyself in vain.'[10]

(11) Is it not odd that horses and other animals roaming about the fields and meadows, and birds soaring above them, pride themselves on their natural beauty—the horse on his mane, and the others on their particular color or rich plumage —yet women, as if they are less perfect than animals, consider themselves so lacking beauty that they need artificial beauty that is bought and painted on? Hairnets of all different

---

9 That is, the Lydian river in which Midas is supposed to have washed off his gift of turning everything into gold.
10 Jer. 4.30.

sorts, elaborate styles of hair-do, numberless arrangements of their locks, costly mirrors to keep adjusting their looks— all that they may ensnare men dazzled by appearances like senseless children. Such practises unquestionably stigmatize a woman as without sense of shame, or as one whom we rightly call a harlot, turning her face into a mask. The Word, however, exhorts us: 'Look not at the things that are seen, but at those that are not seen. For the things that are seen are temporal, while those that are not seen are eternal.'[11]

They have gone beyond the limits of impropriety. They have invented mirrors to reflect all this artificial beautification of theirs, as if it were nobility of character or self-improvement. They should, rather, conceal such deception with a veil. It did the handsome Narcissus no good to gaze on his own image, as the Greek myth tells us. (12) If Moses forbade his people to fashion any image to take the place of God,[12] is it right for these women to study their reflected images for no other reason that to distort the natural features of their faces?

In much the same way, when Samuel the Prophet was sent to anoint one of the sons of Jesse as king, and when he brought out his chrism as soon as he saw the oldest son, admiring his handsomeness and height, Scripture tells us: 'The Lord said to him: Look not on his countenance, nor on the height of his stature, because I have rejected him. For man seeth those things that appear, but the Lord beholdeth the heart.'[13] He finally anointed not the one who was fair in body, but the one who was fair of soul. If the Lord places more importance on beauty of soul than on that of the

---
11 2 Cor. 4.18.
12 Cf. Exod. 20.4; Deut. 5.8.
13 1 Kings 16.7.

body, what must He think of artificial beautification when He abhors so thoroughly every sort of lie? 'We walk by faith, not by sight.'[14]

As a matter of fact, it is the Lord who plainly teaches by the example of Abraham that one who obeys God will make small account of even father and relations and possessions, and of his entire fortune. He made Abraham an exile, and then, because of that, gave him the name 'friend,' because he was so little attached to the things of his own home.[15] Yet, Abraham was of a noble family and had possessed a large fortune. A proof of this is that he overcame the four kings who had captured Lot, with 318 servants belonging to him.[16] As for women, the only one we know of who used ornaments without blame is Esther. Her action in making herself beautiful had a mystical significance, however, for, as the wife of her king, she obtained deliverance for her people by her beauty when they were being slaughtered.[17]

(13) One of the tragic poets also lends his authority to prove that artificial beauty turns women into harlots, and makes men effeminate and adulterous. He says this: 'The man who judged goddesses, after he came from Phrygia, as the Argive tale relates, splendid in his finery of clothes and shining with gold, in ornaments that were barbaric, fell in love with the Spartan Helen who loved him in return; he went away carrying her off to the ox-stalls of Ida, with Menelaus away from home.'[18] O perverse beauty! The vanity of a barbarian and his effeminate luxury turned Greece upside down. Although the Spartan had been chaste, clothes and

---
14 2 Cor. 5.7.
15 Cf. Gen. 12.1.
16 Cf. Gen. 14.14.
17 Cf. Esth. 5.
18 Euripides, *Iphig. in Aul.* 71-77.

finery and a handsome appearance corrupted her. The vanity of the barbarian led the daughter of Zeus to become guilty of harlotry. They did not have the Educator to uproot their cupidities, nor anyone to command them: 'Thou shalt not commit adultery,' or 'Thou shalt not lust,'[19] that is, 'thou shalt not approach adultery by thy desires, nor inflame thy desires by love of ornaments!' What an end came upon them because of all these things, and what evils they reaped who were unwilling to restrain their self-indulgence! Two continents were aroused because of their uncontrolled passion, and everything was thrown into disorder because of one foreign youth. All Greece put out in ships, and the sea bristled under the burden of continents. A long war broke out, mighty battles were fought, and the plains were filled with the dead. A foreigner hurls insult upon ships at anchor, injustice prevails, and Zeus the creator looks down with favor upon the Thracians. Foreign soil drinks noble blood and rivers are halted in their course by the bodies of the slain, breasts are struck in lamentation, and grief grips the whole earth, while 'the roots of many-fountained Ida were shaken, and all her peaks, and the cities of the Trojans and the ships of the Achaeans.'[20] (14) Where shall we flee, O Homer, and find a resting place? Show us a land that is not convulsed.[21]

'Do not touch the reins, boy, for you are inexperienced, and do not mount the war chariot, for you have not learnt how to drive.'[22] Yet the heavens were gratified with two charioteers, for those two are the only ones who have ever driven the sun. The mind, however, is led astray by pleasure, and the

---
19 Cf. Exod. 20.14,17.
20 *Iliad* 20.59,60.
21 There is a lacuna in the text here which makes the thought difficult.
22 Possibly from the lost play of Euripides, *Phaethon*.

virgin center of the mind, if not disciplined by the Word, degenerates into licentiousness, and reaps disintegration as reward for its transgressions. An example of this for you is the angels who forsook the beauty of God for perishable beauty and fell as far as heaven is from the earth,[23] or, again, the Sichemites, who were punished for desecrating the holy virgin and cut down.[24] Their punishment was the grave; the monument that testifies to their lust is a discipline for us on the way to salvation.

Chapter 3

(15) Garishness has, in fact, gone so far that not only women are sick from this disease of attachment to frippery, but men, too, have become strongly infected by it. Unless they rid themselves of artificial beautification, they will never become well again, but, ever tending toward the softer things, they will become ever more effeminate, begin to wear their hair in a disreputable fashion that savors of the brothrel, and go about 'clad in brightly-colored mantles, chewing mastich and smelling of sweet perfume.'[1]

What must one think when he sees them? Undoubtedly, like the man who reads people's character from their foreheads, he must conclude that such men are adulterers and women, that they indulge in both kinds of immoral sexual pleasure, since they abhor hair and are themselves hairless, and are not interested in the vigor of true manhood, preferring to groom their locks like women. Unreliable in

---
23 Cf. Gen. 6.2.
24 Cf. Gen. 34.

---
1 *Adesp*. 338, *CAF* III 470. The mastich is a kind of gum.

manliness, they live, as the Sibyl says of them, 'only for unholy deeds of shame, committing evil and wicked deeds.'[2]

Indeed, because of them the towns are full of pitch-plasterers, barbers who pluck the hair of these effeminate creatures. Shops are set up and opened for business everywhere, and the craftsmen of this shameful trade akin to harlotry obviously amass a substantial income of money. They present themselves to these craftsmen, who then proceed to cover them with pitch and pluck out their hair every sort of way; yet they are not in the least embarrassed either by the onlookers, or by the passersby, or even by their own manhood. This is the sort these hunters of base pleasure are, getting their whole bodies made smooth by the painful plucking of the pitch. (16) I have not the least intention of passing over all this display of shamelessness, for, if they leave nothing undone, I shall not leave anything unsaid. Once, Diogenes tried to embarrass one of these depraved fellows, for his instruction, by remarking roughly and ironically when he was making a purchase: 'Come, boy, buy a man for yourself!' By this sarcastic quip he meant to humiliate the man for his immorality. For, is it not disgraceful that, although they are men, they have themselves shaved and their bodies rid of hair?

Further, they ought to avoid dyeing their hair, anointing and bleaching their gray locks—practises of complete reprobates—as well as ladylike combings of their hair. They think they can slip their old age off over their heads, like the snake, and change themselves back to being young again. Even if they succeed in keeping their hair dark by artificial means, they will not be rid of wrinkles, nor will they escape death, no matter how they conceal their age. Surely, it is not a

---

2 *Orac. Syb.* 4.154.

thing to be frightened at that we should begin to look old; anyway, we cannot help it. In fact, the closer a man comes to his end, the more venerable he becomes in the light of truth, for, then only God is more ancient than himself. God, the most ancient of all beings, is the eternal old man. 'Ancient of days,' Scripture calls Him, 'and the locks of His head are as pure wool.'[3] 'No one else,' the Lord says, 'is able to make hair white or black.'[4] (17) How can these godless men undo God's work, or, rather, make every effort to keep the hair He has made gray from becoming gray, thereby distorting the color of their locks? 'The crown of old men,' Scripture says, 'is much experience,'[5] and their gray hairs are the wreaths testifying to that experience. Yet, some are ashamed of their advanced years and of their gray head. Nevertheless, it is completely impossible to show that the soul adheres to the truth when a man maintains an untruthful appearance of countenance. 'But you have not so learned Christ,' it is said, 'if at least you have heard Him and been taught by Him, as the truth is in Jesus, that you put aside'— not gray hairs, but—'the old man according to your former way of living, what was corrupted according to the desires of deceit. But be renewed,' not with dyes and cosmetics, but 'in the spirit of your mind, and put on the new man made according to God in justice and holiness of truth.'[6]

Is it not womanish for a man to have his hair combed slick, putting each lock in place before a mirror, and to have himself shaved with a razor, for appearance' sake, to have his chin shaved and the hair plucked out and made com-

3 Dan. 7.9.
4 Matt. 5.36.
5 Eccli. 25.6.
6 Eph. 4.20-24.

pletely smooth? Indeed, unless one were to see such a person naked, one would think he was a woman. They may be commanded not to wear gold, yet, in their effeminate desires, they at least wrap shreds of gold about their straps and hems, or make it into a little ball and clasp it on their ankle or hang it about their neck. (18) Such trinkets prove the emasculated man who has debased himself to a woman's mentality and leads the life of both man and woman, like the most lustful of the animals. This is a sort of double life that has much in common with harlotry and is godless. God planned that woman be smooth-skinned, taking pride in her natural tresses, the only hair she has, as the horse in its mane. But man He adorned like the lion, with a beard, and gave him a hairy chest as proof of his manhood and a sign of his strength and primacy. (So, too, God put combs as helmets on roosters who fight for their hens.) He places such importance on these growths of hair that He causes them to come to maturity in a man at the same time as his intelligence. It is worth adding, too, that because He delights in majestic appearances He has surrounded gravity of bearing with honor by gracing it with venerable gray hair. Prudence and accurate reasoning, venerable in understanding, come to their full bloom together with age and impart strength to old age by the force of much experience; so, gray hairs, the attractive wreath of revered prudence, is the badge of attractive trustworthiness.

(19) His beard, then, is the badge of a man and shows him unmistakably to be a man. It is older than Eve and is the symbol of the stronger nature. By God's decree, hairiness is one of man's conspicuous qualities, and, at that, hairness distributed over his whole body. Whatever smoothness or softness there was in him God took from him when He fashioned the delicate Eve from his side to be the receptacle of

his seed, his helpmate both in procreation and in the management of the home. What was left (remember, he had lost all traces of hairlessness) was manhood and reveals that manhood. His characteristic is action; hers, passivity. For, what is hairy is by nature drier and warmer than what is bare; therefore, the male is hairier and more warm-blooded than the female; the uncastrated, than the castrated; the mature, than the immature. Thus, it is a sacrilege to trifle with the symbol of manhood.

But to seek beauty in hairlessness—and here my words grow warm—is sheer effeminacy, if done by men; adulterousness, if by women. Both of these vices are to be eliminated from our way of life as far as possible. 'But all the hairs of your head are numbered,'[7] the Lord says. The hairs of the beard have been numbered, too, and for that matter those of the whole body. (20) They should not be plucked out at all, contrary to the decision made by the free will of God numbering them one by one. 'Otherwise, you do not know yourselves,' the Apostle says, 'that Christ Jesus is in you.'[8] But, if we knew it is He who dwells in us, I do not understand how we could have dared to dishonor Him.

The practise of using pitch (I dislike even speaking of the indecency accompanying this performance), requiring the client to bend backward and forwards, to strip bare to public view the unmentionable parts of nature, to hop about, to bend backward toward the ground, and not to feel any shame in such shameful postures right in the middle of a group of youths and of the gymnasium where manly excellence is trained, to act so indecently and practise things so contrary to nature—is not all this an indication of the lowest

---
7 Matt. 10.30.
8 Cf. 2 Cor. 13.5.

form of immorality? Those who carry on in such a way out in the open could scarcely have respect for anyone behind closed doors. Their utter shamelessness in public is a sure proof of their wilful depravity in private. He who disowns his manhood by light of day will, beyond the least shadow of doubt, prove himself a woman at night. 'There shall be no whores among the daughters of Israel,' the Word says through Moses, 'and there shall be no whore-monger among the sons of Israel.'[9]

But, they object, pitch is beneficial. I say it disfigures. No one in his right mind would want to look like a catamite, unless he were actually infected with the disease; nor could anyone want to deliberately and habitually defame a beautiful image. Now, if 'those who are called according to His purpose, whom He has foreknown, He has also predestined to become conformed to the image of His Son,' according to the holy Apostle, 'that He should be the firstborn among many brethren,'[10] then are not they who dishonor what is conformed to the Lord, their body, guilty of godlessness? If a man desires to become beautiful, he should embellish what is the most beautiful part of human nature: his mind. Let him pluck out, not his hair, but his desires. (21) I pity the young boys belonging to the slave-dealers, dressed up so as best to excite lust. But these unfortunate boys are put to shame not at their own doings; they are beautified under duress for the sake of some miserable gain. If they were men, they would draw down on themselves the death penalty for doing these things, even under duress. Then, are not these others utterly

---
9 Deut. 23.17
10 Rom. 8.28-30.

contemptible for doing the same things willingly and by their own free choice?

But, now, debauched living and indulgence in illicit pleasures have gone to such a limit, and every sort of libertinism has become so rife in the cities, that they have become the norm. Women live in brothels, there offering their own bodies for sale to satisfy lustful pleasure, and boys are taught to renounce their own natures and play the role of women. Self-indulgence has turned everything upside down. Over-refinement in comfortable living has put humanity to shame. It seeks everything, it attempts everything, it forces everything, it violates even nature. Men have become the passive mate in sexual relations and women act as men; contrary to nature, women now are both wives and husbands. No opening is impenetrable to impurity. Sexual pleasure is made public property common to all the people, and self-indulgence their boon companion. What a pitiful spectacle! What unspeakable practises! They are the monuments to your widespread lack of self-control, and whores are the proof of your deeds. Alas, such disregard for law! These wretched men do not realize that furtive indulgence in intercourse often creates tragedy; a father, not recognizing the child he had exiled by exposure, may have frequent relations with a son turned catamite, or with a daughter become a harlot, and the freedom with which license is indulged may lead fathers into becoming husbands [of their children].

(22) Those who are skilled in the law actually permit these things. It is possible for them to sin legally; they call forbidden pleasure obligingness. They who debase their sex think to be free of the charge of adultery, but justice pursues them and avenges their brazenness; inevitably they draw down upon themselves some calamity and purchase death at

only small cost. Merchants of such cargo, these bedeviled fools, set sail, carrying their gross immoralities as wares like grain or wine, while others, far more pitiable, buy these pleasures as they would bread or meat. They do not take to heart the command of Moses: 'Do not defile thy daughter, to commit fornication with her, and the earth shall not commit fornication, and be filled with lawlessness.'[11] Those words were said long ago under divine inspiration; but their effect can be seen clearly: the whole earth has become filled with fornication and lawlessness. (23) I admire the ancient lawgivers of Rome; they abhorred homosexuality, and in the justice of their laws condemned to the mines anyone guilty of allowing his body to be used in a feminine role contrary to the law of nature.

It is never permissible to pluck out the beard, for it is a natural adornment, and one that is genuine;[12] 'with the first down upon his lip, in whom the charm of youth is the fairest.'[13] When the lad has become older, he anoints it with oil, proud of his beard, upon which descended the prophetic myrrh of the venerable Aaron.[14] One who has been properly educated, with whom peace has made its abode, ought to keep peace with his hair, also. Indeed, when the wives are only too anxious to lower the barriers of modesty, what would they not get into the habit of doing, since they but mirror the outrageous practises of their husbands? We should call them, not men, but pederasts and effeminate creatures; their voices are unmanly and their clothes are the clothes of women both in texture and in color. Men of this sort advertise openly the

---

11 Lev. 19.29.
12 A play on words: 'chin' is *géneion;* 'genuine' is *gennaíon.*
13 *Iliad* 24.348.
14 Cf. Ps. 132.2. E. Molland (*op. cit.* 14 n. 4) sees in the use of 'prophetic' here, only the sense that it is mentioned in the prophetic psalm.

sort of character they possess, for they stand self-condemned by their fine robe, their sandals, their bearing, their way of walking, the cut of their hair, and their glances. 'For from his look shall a man be known,' Scripture says, 'and from meeting a man, a man shall be known. The attire of the man, and the gait of his feet, and the laugh of his teeth shew what he is.'[15]

Nevertheless, these men who so relentlessly get rid of the hair on the rest of their bodies, take great pains with the hair of their heads, all but wearing hairnets like the women. (24) The lion's glory is his shagginess; he is equipped with so much hair to protect himself. Boars are formidable for their bristles; they put fear in the hearts of huntsmen by making their bristles stand on end. 'And the fleecy sheep are laden down with their wool';[16] however, the loving Father of men has given this animal such an abundance of hair only to benefit you, O man, for He taught you to shear it. On the other hand, among the various nations, the Celts and the Scythians wear their hair long, but wear no other ornament.[17] The flowing hair of these barbarians strikes terror in our hearts and their fair hair suggests war, for it is a color akin to blood. Both of these peoples have always eschewed comforts. The German can point to the Rhine as evidence of this, and the Scythian to his war chariot. Sometimes the Scythian scorns even his chariot (for to his uncultivated mind, its size seems too close to luxury); rejecting its convenience, he turns to simple ways of frugality. That is to say, the man of Scythia may perfer a conveyance that moves itself and is less

---
15 Eccli. 19.29.
16 Hesiod, *Op.* 234.
17 A play on words: *komdō is* 'wearing the hair long'; *kommdō* is 'to wear an ornament.'

unwieldy than the chariot, his horse, mount it and ride where he will. When he suffers from hunger, he seeks nourishment from his horse, which offers him the only thing it has, blood from its open veins. This makes the horse both chariot and food for the nomad.

(25) Among the Arabs, other nomads, the young warrior rides on a she-camel that is pregnant. The camel grazes while it runs and carries its master, bringing its own larder with it. If drink fails, he can milk his camel, and if food runs short, the Arab does not spare even their blood, as they say of wolves on the prowl. The camel, gentler than the barbarian, does not think it is being wronged, but runs through the desert carrying its master trustingly, supplying him at the same time with his food. If only wild beasts were destroyed who wait to prey upon blood! Yet, it is not right for man to touch blood, either, for his own body is nothing less than flesh quickened by blood. Human blood has its portion of reason, and its share in grace, along with the spirit. If anyone injures it, he will not escape punishment.

A man can speak to the Lord, even if he is stripped of all clothing. I favor the plain simplicity of the barbarians. They respected a less cumbersome way of life and therefore avoided luxuriousness. The Lord calls us to be like them, stripped of all excessive love of finery, of all gaudy appearances, freed from sin, wearing only the wood of life[18] and intent only upon salvation.

Chapter 4

(26) But I forget myself, and have sailed in spirit right past the due progression of my thought. I must now retrace

---
18 That is, the Cross.

my steps and express my disapproval of the possession of too many slaves. Men resort to servants to escape work and waiting on themselves. They hire a great host of bakers and cooks and waiters and men who can carve meat skillfully into slices. They portion out this service into many different duties: some are engaged to minister to their gluttony, carvers and cooks of the rich dish called *caruce,* others to prepare and to make the pastries, others to make the honey cakes, and still others to prepare the porridges; then there are those whose duty it is to care for their innumerable garments; others keep watch over their gold like griffins, others guard their silver and keep their goblets clean and get the dishes ready for the banquets; then there are those who groom their beasts of burden; there are a host of wine-pourers in constant attendance upon them; and finally, there are a crowd of handsome youths from whom, like cattle, they draw milk: the milk of beauty.

The women employ beauticians and handmaids, some to take care of their mirrors; others, the hairnets; others, their combs.[1] Then there are scores of eunuchs, who are little more than panderers; because of the trust they inspire, since they are incapable of sexual pleasure, they can minister to those wanting to carry on some love affair and not incur suspicion. The true eunuch, however, is not he who is unable, but he who is unwilling to gratify his passions.

(27) The Word has given a complete description of these offenders when He promised through the Prophet Samuel that the people who were demanding a king would have, not a kind master, but one who would be an unfeeling tyrant, given over to immorality, 'who will take,' He said, 'your daughters to make him ointments, and to be his cooks

---
1 There is a lacuna in the text here.

and bakers,'[2] who will rule by law of war, and not be zealous for the administration of peace.

There are many Celts to lift and carry the litters for these women, but nowhere can one see any spinning or weaving or loom-working or, for that matter, any feminine occupations or household chores. Story-tellers spend the whole day with the women, idly spinning erotic legends, wearying body and soul by their false tales and deeds. 'Thou shalt not be with many,' Scripture says, 'for evil, nor join with a multitude,'[3] because wisdom is found only among the few, disorder in the multitude. These women hire carriers, not out of modesty, to keep from being gazed at (it would be praiseworthy if they hung up the draperies [of their litters] for such a purpose), but have themselves borne by their servants to attract attention and to play the coquet. At any rate, they betray their true character by keeping the curtain pulled back and staring intently at those who gaze; frequently, they lean far out, too, forgetting the most elementary rules of reserve in their eager curiosity. 'Look not round about thee,' Scripture says, 'in the ways of the city, nor wander up and down in its deserted places.'[4] A deserted place is that in which, even though there is a throng of boisterous men, no man is chaste.

These women are carried right up to the temples, there to offer sacrifices of atonement and to consult the oracles. Day after day, they mingle in the procession of the ordinary beggar-priests, and those of Cybele, and with the old beggar women who attend the altars and ruin homes. They prolong their whispered conversations over their cups like old women, sedulously learning from the sorcerers charms and incanta-

---

2 1 Kings 8.13.
3 Exod. 23.2.
4 Eccli. 9.7.

tions to destroy wedlock. They keep some men, and yearn for more, and the soothsayers promise them still others. They do not understand that they are deceiving themselves, and giving themselves over as vessels of pleasure to those who deliberately foster lewdness; while they are exchanging purity for the most shameful dishonor, they really believe such foul corruption is the doing of an oracle. The agents of demoralizing lechery are legion, each one joining the company in a different way. The sensual are as quickly disposed to lechery as swine rolling toward the lurching side of a ship. (29) That is why Scripture warns gravely: 'Bring not every man into thy house, for many are the snares of the deceitful.'[5] And in another place it says: 'Let just men be thy guests, and let thy glory be in the fear of God.'[6]

Away with all fornication! 'Know this well,' the Apostle says, 'that no fornicator or unclean person or covetous one (who is an idolater), has any inheritance in the kingdom of Christ and God.'[7] But these women who delight in the company of perverts are surrounded by a whole crowd of loose-tongued catamites, foul of body, foul of speech, grown into manhood only to satisfy their lusts, agents of adultery, guffawing and whispering, then indecently snorting out some suggestive sound from their nostrils, trying to entertain with obscene words and gestures, stimulating everyone to giddiness, the precursor of fornication. From time to time, either the fornicators themselves or the mob of panderers who are so zealous for other people's downfall, aroused by some passing fit of anger, make a noise in their nostrils as frogs do, for all the world as if they kept their wrath stored up in their noses.

(30) Women who are somewhat more genteel than these

---
5 Eccli. 11.29.
6 Eccli. 9.16.
7 Cf. Eph. 5.5.

others go in for raising Indian birds and Medean peacocks. They keep them on their couches when they lie down, and play with such peak-headed animals, amusing themselves with unsightly creatures that act like satyrs.[8] They laugh when they hear the story of Thersites, yet themselves buy many a Thersites at a high price, and take more pride in these things, burdens on the earth, than they do in their husbands. They will snub a prudent widow, though she is far more important than their Melitean puppy; they will ignore a good old man, better looking, as far as I can see, than any bought animal; they will not even come near an orphaned child, though they feed their parrots and bustards with their own hands. Even worse, they abandon to exposure the children born to them, yet lavish care on their brood of birds. They set a higher value on unreasoning animals than they do on rational men, despite their obligation to reverence those old men who cherish self-restraint and who are much handsomer, I think, than their monkeys, and able to speak much more eloquent pieces than their nightingales. 'Whatever you do to one of these least,' Scripture tells us, 'you do to Me.'[9]

Beyond all this, these women pay greater court to wilfulness than to self-control, for they turn their whole substance into stone: pearls and emeralds of India. Indeed, they throw their money away, and waste it on dyes that fade, and on slaves bought with silver, like glutted hens scratching in the dunghills of life. 'Poverty humbles a man,'[10] it is said; it means the poverty of the miserly which makes the rich poor in generosity, as if they possessed nothing to give away.

---

8 Literally, *sikinnon*, of obscure meaning here, but, since this was a dance performed by satyrs in the plays, this is probably its meaning.
9 Matt. 25.40.
10 Prov. 10.4.

Chapter 5

(31) What baths the women have! Buildings carefully constructed and joined together, yet easily moved about, covered with transparent muslin; the chairs gold-plated and of silver;[1] and a countless array of vessels made of gold or silver, some used for drinking the health of others, some for eating, and some for the bath itself. Why, there are even pans of charcoal! They have reached such a degree of unrestraint that they even wine and dine in the baths. With utter lack of taste they put their silver plates on display there, just to make an impression. Perhaps they are displaying their wealth with extravagant ostentation, but they are really displaying their culpable lack of self-discipline. In their lack of discipline, they prove that unmanly men have been surpassed by women, and show at the same time that they cannot live with their husbands, or even sweat without being surrounded with their dishes. Women who are poor share the same baths without indulging in such pomp. It must be that the uncleanness of the wealthy needs an abundant cloak of evildoing. Yet, by means of their uncleanness, as by a snare, they trap the wretches who cannot resist the glitter of gold. In fact, because they do dazzle the undiscriminating, they cleverly scheme to win the admiration of their lovers, who then insult them when they see them naked shortly afterwards. (32) It is odd that they will not undress before their husbands, insisting on some sort of pretended modesty, yet anyone else who likes may see her who was chastely veiled at home naked in the bath. They are not ashamed to undress there before the onlookers who are akin to traffikers in bodies.

Still, Hesiod advises: 'Do not wash your body in the

---
1 There is a lacuna in the text here.

woman's bath.'[2] The baths are open to men and women alike; there they strip for the sake of lust. 'For, from gazing, men go on to lusting,'[3] as if their modesty were washed away in the bath. Those whose sense of modesty keeps them from such an excess exclude men not of their own household, but they will bathe with their servants, and strip naked before their men-slaves. In fact, they even have themselves massaged by them, giving them full freedom of touch, when the slaves are already fearful of giving free reins to their lust. They who are admitted to the baths by mistresses who are naked are sure to strip to accomplish their desires the better, 'banishing fear by a perverse practise.'[4]

(33) The ancients, too modest to allow their athletes to be exposed naked, preserved modesty by engaging in the games in loincloths.[5] Yet, these women, stripping off modesty with their garments,[6] mean to reveal their beauty, but only give unwitting evidence of their moral ugliness. Truly, the lewdness of their desire is made manifest in the body itself, just as dropsy becomes evident in the moisture on the whole surface of the skin; in both cases, the disease is known by its visible effects.

Men, then, should give good example of truth to the women, and be loathe to undress before them. They ought, too, to be on their guard against dangerous glances. 'He who gazes without restraint,' it is said, 'has already committed sin.'[7] At home, we should respect our parents and servants; in

---
2 Hesiod, *Op.* 753.
3 Agathon, *Frag.* 29 *TGF* 768.
4 Cf. F. Blass, *Hermes* 35 (1900) S. 342.
5 Cf. Thucydides, 1.6.5.
6 Cf. Herodotus, 1.8.
7 Cf. Matt. 5.28.

the streets, those we meet; in the baths, women; in solitary places, ourselves; and, everywhere, the Word who is in all places and 'without whom nothing came into being.'[8] It is only in this way that a person will persevere without falling, if he considers God as everywhere present with him.

Chapter 6

(34) We should possess wealth in a becoming manner, sharing it generously, but not mechanically nor with affectation. We should be careful, too, not to turn love of the beautiful into love of self, and into poor taste, lest someone say of us: 'His horse is worth fifteen talents, or his estate or servant or gold plate, but he himself would be expensive at three cents.' To begin with, take ornaments away from a woman, and servants from the master, and you will discover that the master differs in no way from the slaves he has bought, neither in bearing, nor in appearance, nor in voice. In fact, he is very similar to his slave in these respects. He differs from his slave in one way only, in that he is more delicate and, because of his upbringing, more susceptible to sickness.

At any rate, we should repeat on every occasion that most inspiring of all our doctrines, that the good man, in his prudence and uprightness, 'lays up treasure in heaven.'[1] He who sells his earthly possessions and gives them to the poor will find an imperishable treasure where there is neither moth nor robber.[2] Such a man is truly fortunate, even if he is

---

8 John 1.3.

---

1 Cf. Matt. 6.20.
2 Cf. Matt. 19.21.

small and weak and unimportant, and is rich indeed in the most important sort of riches. On the other hand, if a man becomes wealthier than Midas and Cinyra,[3] but is unjust and arrogant—like the man who lived elegantly in purple and fine linen, yet despised Lazarus[4]—he is miserable, lives wretchedly, and will never find true life. (35) Wealth, in fact, seems to me like a snake; unless a person knows how to grasp it properly, dangling it without harm from just above the tip of the tail, the snake will twist about to the hand and strike. Weath, too, twisting in the grasp, whether experienced or not, can cling to the hand and bite unless a man rises superior to it and uses it with discretion; that is, to say, he may train the beast by the invocation of the Word and remain unharmed.

However, in my opinion, he who possesses things of higher value is the one, and the only one, who is truly wealthy, without passing for such. A gem is not worth much, nor is silver, nor clothes, nor beauty of body; but virtue is, because it is reason translated into deeds under the guidance of the Educator. This is reason forbidding luxuriousness, stimulating independence in service of self, and singing the praises of frugality, offspring of self-control. 'Receive instruction,' Scripture says, 'and not money, and choose knowledge rather than gold. For wisdom is better than precious stones, and all that is priceless cannot be compared to it.' And, again: 'My fruit is better than gold and precious stone and silver; and my blossoms than choice silver.'[5] If we must make distinctions, let the man with a fortune be considered the wealthy one, loaded down as he is with gold like a dingy purse; but the

---
3 Cf. Plato, *Laws* II 660E.
4 Cf. Luke 16.19-24.
5 Prov. 9.10,11,19.

holy man is the discreet one, for discretion is the quality that maintains a properly balanced moderation between spending and giving. 'Some distribute their own goods,' it is written, 'and become richer.'[6] Of such men, Scripture says: 'He hath distributed, he hath given to the poor; his justice remains forever.'[7] Therefore, it is not he who possesses and retains his wealth who is wealthy, but he who gives; it is giving, not receiving that reveals the happy man. Generosity is a product of the soul; so, true wealth is in the soul.

(36) Again, good things should be considered the possession only of the good. But the good are Christians; a man without understanding or self-control can neither perceive nor truly possess the good. Therefore, the Christian alone possesses good things; but nothing brings greater wealth than good things, so only they are wealthy. Holiness and that reason which is more precious than any treasure are the true wealth, and are not increased by cattle or lands but are given by God. It cannot be taken away (for the soul alone is the treasure of such a man), and is a possession that is supreme for him who owns it, making him blessed in possessing the truth. If a man is able to keep from desiring the things that are beyond his power of attaining but does possess the things he really desires, and then receives from God for the asking the things he craves in a holy way, is not such a man abundantly wealthy indeed, and possessed of all things, owning an eternal treasure in God? 'To him who asks,' Scripture says, 'shall be given, and to him who knocks, it shall be opened.'[8] If God refuses nothing, then all things belong to those who serve God.

---

6 Prov. 11.24.
7 Ps. 111.9.
8 Matt. 7.7.

Chapter 7

(37) When self-indulgence wanders off into sense-pleasures, then it makes serious shipwreck out of a man. Such an easy and dishonorable way of life, although pursued by many, is foreign to true love of the beautiful and to the higher pleasures. By nature, man is a noble and majestic animal who seeks the beautiful, simply because he is a creature made by the only true Beauty. But a way of life that thinks only of the stomach is without nobility, and is blameworthy and ugly and even ridiculous. Utterly alien to a nature that is divine is concentration upon pleasures of the senses: feeding like sparrows and mating like swine and goats.

To consider sense-pleasure a good is very poor judgment as to what is beautiful; attachment to wealth disorientates a man from a right way of living, robbing him of all shame in the presence of base things, 'if only he have the opportunity like a beast, of eating and drinking all sort of things, and of providing himself with ample opportunity for the pleasures of sex.'[1] That is why it is very rare that a rich man inherits the kingdom of God. What are all these dishes prepared for, except to gorge one single stomach? Privies are silent witnesses to the uncleanness of gluttony, for they are the depositories of the remains of the stomach's feasting. Why should men assemble all these many cup-bearers when they can satisfy their thirst with one single cup? Why a chest of garments? Why all the gold plate? And why all the ornamentation? These men are simply catering to thieves and greedy eyes. 'Let not alms and pledges leave thee,'[2] says Scripture.

(38) See how Elias the Thesbite offers us an excellent

---
1 Cf. Plato, *Laws* VIII 831DE.
2 Prov. 3.3.

example of frugality when he sat down beneath the juniper tree and the angel brought him food. 'There was a hearth cake and a vessel of water.'[3] The Lord sent that sort of meal as the best sort for him. It seems, then, that we should travel light on our road toward truth. 'Carry neither a purse nor wallet nor sandals,'[4] the Lord said, meaning that we should not hold any wealth stored away in our purse; that we should not fill up our storehouses as though we were laying away in a barn, but share it with the needy; that we should not trouble ourselves about cattle and domestics—which is what the sandals symbolize, for it is the sandals that bear the burden when the rich go on a journey.

We must, then, get rid of our multiplicity of vessels, our silver and gold drinking cups, our band of servants; we have received from our Educator those beautiful and holy mates, self-service and frugality. In fact, we must walk according to reason even if we have a wife and children in our home. A household is not a burden if it has but learned to follow in the lead of the wayfarer who knows self-control. (39) Invariably the wife who loves her husband will be his faithful reflection, both of them wayfarers carrying provisions best suited for a journey toward heaven: frugality, together with a united and determined practise of self-restraint.

Just as the foot is the measure of the sandal, so the physical needs of each man are the measure of what he should possess. Whatever is excessive—the things they call adornments—and the trappings of the rich are not adornments, but a burden for the body. If one is to use violence to ascend to heaven,[5] it is necessary to carry the good staff of holy deeds

---
3 Cf. 3 Kings 19.4.6.
4 Luke 10.4.
5 Cf. Matt. 11.12.

and first to share our goods with the oppressed before laying hold of the true rest. Scripture declares that really 'his own riches is the redemption of the soul of man,'[6] that is, if a man is rich, he will obtain salvation by sharing his wealth. Like the spring that remains full naturally, returning to its original measure after water has been drawn off, or like milk that flows back to breasts that have been suckled or milked, so too, generosity, which is the wellspring of love for men, increases and becomes full again when it gives drink to the thirsty. He who possesses the Word, who is Almighty God, needs nothing and never lacks any of the things he desires, for the Word is an infinite possession and the source of all our wealth.

(40) However, someone may object and insist that he has often seen the just in need of food. This is rare and happens only where no one else is just. Besides, let him read the beautiful sentence: 'It is not by bread alone that the just man lives, but by the Word of the Lord,'[7] who is the true bread, the bread of heaven.[8] The good man is never really in want, as long as he keeps intact his adherence to faith in God. For he can ask for and receive whatever He needs from the Father of all, and he can enjoy whatever belongs to Him, if only he obey His Son. Then, too, he has this advantage, that he can be free from feeling any want. The Word, who acts as our Educator, gives us riches; there is no need to envy the wealth of others with those who have gained freedom from want through Him. He who possesses this sort of wealth will inherit the kingdom of God.

---

6 Prov. 13.8.
7 Cf. Matt. 4.4; Deut. 8.3; Cf. above, p. 98 n. 22.
8 Cf. John 6.33,41.

Chapter 8

(41) If any of you will completely avoid self-indulgence by the careful cultivation of frugality, he will be developing a habit of enduring involuntary hardships readily. If he makes a further practise of looking on voluntary sufferings as a training for persecution, then when he is confronted with labors and fears and pains he cannot evade, he will not be unpractised in steadfastness. We have no fatherland on earth, that we may learn to despise earthly possessions. Therefore, frugality is exceedingly rich, for it is a quality that is not at all reluctant to spend money on things it requires and that need to be paid for, for as long a time as the need exists. The word payment implies the notion of expenses.

Now how the husband and wife should live together, the nature of self-service and management of the home, the use of servants, and in addition, the time for marriage and the things becoming to wives, all these we will explain in a treatise on married life.[1] Now we are treating only of the things proper to our education, stressing the life Christians should live, in general outline. The greater part, indeed, has been said or taught already, but we shall discuss now what is still left.

No small influence upon salvation is exerted by examples. 'See,' the tragedian remarks, 'Telemachus did not kill the wife of Odysseus, because she did not wed another husband in addition to the one she had, but kept the marriage chamber in her house intact.'[2] He condemns adultery as immoral by presenting us with a beautiful image of chastity in love for a husband. Again, the Spartans used to compel the Helots (that is the name of their servants) to get drunk while they

---
1 Cf. above, p. 139 n. 12.
2 Euripides, *Orestes* 588-590.

themselves remained sober, then they would point to their drunken deeds as a cure and correction for themselves. (42) They disciplined themselves by watching the misconduct of these servants at close range, that they might not fall into similar misbehavior, and drew the useful moral of keeping themselves free of blame. Some men are saved by being taught; others, by teaching themselves. They must earnestly strive either to acquire virtue or, at least, to find instruction. 'He is best of all who understands all things by his own efforts.'[3] Such a man was Abraham, who ever sought after God. 'And noble, too, is he who listens carefully to one who speaks well.' Such are the disciples who listened to the Word; therefore, the first one heard himself called a friend, and the others, apostles, because the one concerned himself about the one and same God, and the others preached Him; yet, both were good. There are disciples, in turn, of both of these: those who gain profit in seeking and those who gain salvation in finding. But, 'he who neither understands by his own efforts, nor lays up to heart what he hears from another, is a man of no account.' This is the sort the pagans are, of no account. It is they who do not follow Christ.

(43) The benign Educator bestows aid on us in different ways, now offering advice, now rebuke; He holds up to us the dishonor reaped by those who have sinned, and reveals the punishment they have merited, both to attract our notice and to warn us. In this way does He devise a gentle means of restraining us from evil, by such a picture of those who have already suffered. He forcibly deters those who are bent on evil by these images, hinders some who are ready to dare similar crimes, strengthens others in their endurance, draws

---

[3] This and the following two quotations are from Hesiod, *Op.* 293, 295-297.

still others from evil, and heals many, converting them to a better life by letting them see such an image. For, who is there who, following someone down a path and seeing him fall into a ditch, would not be careful not to stumble over the same obstacle, and would not avoid the consequences of sin?[4] Again, what athlete intent upon the path of glory, who sees a contestant before him receive a prize, will not also desire the crown, and imitate his predecessor?[5]

The images of this sort that divine Wisdom proposes are many. I recall one example, and bring it to your attention in a few words. The suffering the Sodomites endured was a judgment passed on those who sinned, but for those who hear the story, it is education. (44) The Sodomites were people driven headlong upon the shoals of immorality through much self-indulgence, for they committed fornication without restraint, and were continually inflamed by their frenzied passion for the objects of their lust.[6] The all-seeing Word looked down on them—for they who do unholy things cannot escape His gaze—and as the ever-vigilant Guardian of mankind did not remain unmoved by their corruption. Rather, to hinder us from imitating them, and to educate us to the self-control He wished from us, He inflicted punishment upon these sinners, lest, going unpunished, their sin turn into a torrent of unbridled licentiousness. Therefore, He gave command that Sodom be struck down by fire, and poured out some part of the fire of prudence upon their immorality, that their lust might not remain uncorrected and thus clear the way for those being swept along into the ways of pleasure.

The just punishment of the Sodomites has become, then,

---
4 Cf. Luke 6.39.
5 Cf. 1 Cor. 9.24.
6 Cf. Gen. 18.20; 19.

an example to lead men to holy salvation. By avoiding the sin of those who have been chastized, men will never become subject to the punishment meted out to those others; they will keep themselves from punishment by keeping themselves from sin. 'I desire to remind you,' Jude says, 'that God, who saved the people once from the land of Egypt, the next time destroyed those who did not believe. And the angels also who did not preserve their original state, but forsook their abode, He has kept in everlasting chains under the darkness of the savage angels for the judgment of the great day.'[7] (45) And a little later on He presents the picture of those who are judged, significantly: 'Woe to them, for they have gone in the way of Cain, and have rushed on thoughtlessly into the error of Balaam for the sake of gain, and have perished in the rebellion of Core.'[8]

Those who cannot support the power of the adoption of sons fear will hinder from excessive sin. That is why there are punishments and threats, that we may be kept from sin out of fear of the penalty. I could describe for you the punishments, not only for immorality, but also for vanity, and for vainglory, and I could mention the strong maledictions upon the wealthy with which the Word prevents sin by using fear. But, to avoid verbosity, I simply recall in my treatise the commandments of the Educator, that you may beware of His threats.

---

7 Cf. Jude 5-7.
8 Jude 11.

Chapter 9

(46) There are four reasons prompting us to frequent the baths (it was at this point that I digressed a while back in my discussion): either for cleanliness, for warmth, for health, or for the satisfaction of pleasure. We must not think of bathing for pleasure, because we must ruthlessly expel all unworthy pleasure. Women may make use of the bath for the sake of cleanliness and of health; men, only for the sake of their health. The motive of seeking warmth is scarcely urgent, since we can find relief from cold in other ways.

The continued use of baths undermines a man's strength, weakening the muscles of his body and often inducing lassitude and even fainting spells. Bodies drink up water in a definite way in the baths, like trees, not only by mouth, but also, as they say, through the pores of the whole body. A proof of this is that, often, when a man has been thirsty, his thirst is quenched on entering the water. Therefore, if the bath has no real benefit to offer, it should be completely avoided. The ancients called it a fulling shop for men, since it wrinkles the body before time, and forces the body to become old early; in much the way that iron is tempered by heat, the flesh is made soft by heat. We need to be hardened, as it were, by being doused in cold.

(47) We ought not bathe on every occasion, either, but if at times we are too hungry, or too full, we should omit it. As a matter of fact, [it should be adjusted] to the age of the individual, and to the season of the year. It is not useful at all times, nor to everyone at all times, as those versed in these things agree. Due proportion is sufficient guide for us; we call upon it for help in every part of our life. Again, we should not linger in the bath so long that we will need some-

one to lead us out by the hand, nor should we loiter long or frequently in it, as we might in the public square. Finally, to have a score of servants pouring water over one is grievously to offend a neighbor; it is a sign of one far advanced in self-indulgence and unwilling to understand that the bath should be common, on an equal footing to all who bathe there.

It is our souls, above all, that we should wash in the purifying Word; only now and then, our bodies, to get rid of the dirt that adheres to them, and, sometimes, to refresh ourselves after hard labor. 'Woe to you, Scribes and Pharisees,' the Lord says, 'hypocrites! For you are like whitened tombs; outwardly the tomb appears beautiful, but within it is full of dead men's bones and of all uncleanness.'[1] (48) And again He said to them: 'Woe to you, because you clean the outside of the cup and of the plate, but within are full of uncleanness. Cleanse first the inside of the cup that the outside may also become clean.'[2]

The most excellent cleansing is that which removes the filth of the soul, and is a spiritual bath; the inspired word says about such a cleansing: 'The Lord shall wash away the filth of the sons and daughters of Israel and shall wash away the blood from their midst,'[3] that is, the blood of immorality, as well as the slaughtering of the prophets; that is the purification He meant, because He adds: 'by the spirit of judgment and by the spirit of burning.' But the washing of the body is something material and is accomplished only by water; in fact, it can be done even in fields away from the baths.

---
1 Matt. 23.27.
2 Matt. 23.25.
3 Isa. 4.4.

Chapter 10

(49) The gymnasium is sufficient for the needs of young boys, even if there is a bath at hand. This is all the more true when even men may legitimately make use of it in preference to the bath. It offers considerable benefit to the health of the young, and besides, instils in them a desire and ambition to develop not only a healthy constitution, but also a wholesome character. If physical exercise is engaged in without distracting them from more worthwhile deeds, it is entertaining and not without profit.

For that reason, even women should be allowed some sort of physical exercise, not on the wrestling-mat or the racecourse, but in spinning and weaving and supervising the cooking, if need arise. Again, the women should themselves bring whatever we need from the storeroom, and it is no disgrace for them to take their place at the mill. Then, too, for her to busy herself about the meals that they may be pleasing to her husband is a deed one who is housewife, spouse and helpmate will not be reproached for performing. If she should also make the beds herself, and bring her husband drink when he is thirsty, and prepare the food, she would be exercising herself in a very becoming way, and maintaining her health by self-restraint. The Educator approves of such a woman who 'stretches forth her hands to useful things, and who applies her fingers vigorously to the spindle, who opens her hands to the needy and stretches forth fruit to the poor,'[1] and who, in imitation of Sara, is not ashamed to serve wayfarers generously. Abraham said to Sara: 'Quick, three measures of fine flour! Knead it, and make loaves.'[2] Again, Scripture

1 Cf. Prov. 31.19,20.
2 Gen. 18.6.

says: 'Rachel, daughter of Jacob, arrived with her father's sheep,' and, as if this was not enough, it adds, to give a convincing lesson of lowliness: 'for it was her custom to tend them.'[3] (50) There are innumerable examples given in the Scriptures both of frugality and of self-service, as well as of physical exercise.

As for the men, let some of them engage in wrestling stripped; let others play the game called *phaenind* with a small ball, particularly out in the sun. A walk will be sufficient for others, either strolling out into the country or into town. If, besides all this, they lay hold of the mattock, such a money-saving way of taking exercise will not be beneath their dignity. But I am almost forgetting to mention Pittacus, king of the Mitylenians, who wandered about taking energetic exercise.[4] It is well if a person draws his own water for his needs, and himself cuts the wood that he uses. Jacob pastured the sheep that Laban had given him with a rod of storax (which is a sign of royalty), and he took care to influence their nature for the better with such a rod.[5] Sometimes, reading out loud will be a good exercise for many.

(51) But let them especially engage in wrestling, which we approve of, not for vain competition's sake, which serves no end, but to get rid of manly sweat. They should not cultivate the tricks meant only for display, but only the art of wrestling erect, keeping the neck and hands and sides free. Such movements are much more orderly and manly, are performed with controlled strength, and are clearly undertaken to benefit one's health—a very desirable thing. The other exercises

---

3 Gen. 29.9.
4 Cf. Diogenes Laert. 1.81. He tells us this exercise was milling the grain.
5 Cf. Gen. 30.37-43.

of the gymnasium demand the practise of postures beneath our dignity. We must aim for moderation in all things. For, just as it is better for labor to precede meals, so, too, to labor beyond measure is both harmful and tiring, and leads to sickness. We should not be idle, yet we should not become completely exhausted by our labor, either. We were just discussing the proper conduct to be observed in taking food; similarly, in every thing and every place we should not live for pleasure nor for immorality; neither should we go to the other extreme. We should, instead, choose a course of life in between, well-balanced, temperate, and free from either evil: extravagance or parsimony.

(52) As we have already said, self-service is an exercise without any trace of pride: for example, to put on one's own sandals, wash one's own feet, and also to rub off the oil that has been put on. To rub down someone who has done the same for us is both a physical exercise and an act of communal justice, as is also sleeping by a sick friend, waiting on someone who cannot wait on himself, and providing for someone in need. 'And Abraham set before the three men a lunch under the tree and he stood by while they ate.'[6] So is fishing, as it was for Peter,[7] if we have leisure left over from the instruction we need in the word. But the best catch is the one the Lord entrusted to His disciples, when He taught them to catch men, as though fish from a sea.[8]

---
6 Cf. Gen. 18.8.
7 Cf. Matt 4.18; John 21.3.
8 Cf. Matt. 4.19.

Chapter 11

(53) We may conclude, then, that the wearing of gold and the use of soft garments need not be absolutely avoided. But desires that are unreasonable must be kept in check lest they drive us into an effeminate way of life and, by excessive indulgence, sweep us up and carry us away. Luxuriousness, grounding us on the shoals of repletion, is quite capable of becoming unruly and, rearing up, of throwing both the charioteer and the Educator. It is the Educator who, when the unreasoning part of the soul becomes uncontrolled in its pleasures and immoderate impulses and [desires] for jewels and gold and precious garments and other luxuries, tightens the reins of the steed that man is, and, urging him on, leads him to salvation.

We keep in mind these holy words particularly: 'Keep your conduct excellent among the heathens, so that, whereas they slander you as evil-doers, they may, by observing the nobility of your actions, glorify God.'[1] That is why the Educator teaches us to wear plain garments, of a white color, as we have already remarked, so that, accommodating ourselves not to art that embellishes, but to nature which gave us birth, we may reject every sort of deception and distortion of the truth. Sophocles rebuked the young men who lived daintily with the remark that they were 'conspicuous for their womanish clothes.'[2]

As with the soldier and sailor and ruler, the proper dress for a self-restrained man is plain yet becoming and clean. (54) In a similar way, the law set up in the Law of Moses concerning leprosy forbade as unholy all many-hued and striped

---
[1] 1 Pet. 2.12.
[2] Sophocles, *Frag.* 702.

clothing resembling the mottled skin of a serpent.³ It desires us not to be adorned with a variety of colors, but to be clothed in white from the top of our heads to the sole of our feet. We shall stay clean in that way, and put away all fickle and wicked dispositions of mind, symbolized by our changed bodily appearance, and love the unadorned and direct simple color of truth. The man who in his teaching followed Moses, Plato, excellent in every way, approved of that sort of woven garment, for there is no deed more indicative of a good woman than [wearing such a garment]. 'White is a color that would be suitable in dignity and in other ways,' he says, 'but dyes should be used only for the adornments of war.'⁴ White, then, is the color that bespeaks men of peace and of light. (55) Just as the presence of a sign intimately connected with its cause signifies, or rather proves the presence of the object that causes it, as smoke indicates fire, a good complexion and pulse good health, so also, with us, such a garment makes evident the bent of our character.

Self-restraint is pure and simple, for purity is a quality that keeps a man's life innocent and free of shameful deeds, while simplicity is a quality that will have no truck with superfluities. A rough and, even more, a new, as yet unwashed, garment retains the heat of the body; not that it has any heat in itself, but it holds in the heat of the body by not providing any means for it to escape. And if any heat is applied to it, such a garment absorbs and retains it, and, once warmed, it in turn warms the body. Therefore, this sort of clothing should be worn especially during winter. [Self-restraint] is also easily satisfied, for it works for a sufficiency that will avoid need, without pomposity, and for a life lived ac-

---
3 Cf. Lev. 13.47,59.
4 Plato, *Laws* XII 956.

cording to reason, healthy and happy. (56) Let the wife, then, always make use of a plain dress, dignified, softer than that allowed her husband, but not one that offends grossly against modesty nor one made with a view only to softness. Let the clothes be in keeping with the person's age, with the individual himself, the place, his character, and occupation. The Apostle well advises us: 'Put on Christ Jesus, and as for the flesh, take no thought of its lusts.'[5]

Reason also forbids us to do violence to nature by piercing the lobes of the ear. Why not pierce the nostrils also? The Scriptures would then be accomplished indeed: 'As a ring in the nose of the swine, so is beauty in a foolish woman.'[6] In fine, if anyone thinks he is decorated when he wears gold, then he is less than his gold, and he who is less than gold is not its master. Is it not the height of the absurd to advertise oneself as less comely and less valuable than Lydian scrapings? Just as gold is defiled by the filthiness of swine rooting about among garbage with its snout, so too, the sensual, incited by their violent passions to deeds of impurity, insult true beauty with the defilements of their sexual pleasures.

(57) He permits women the use of rings made of gold, not as ornaments, but as signet rings to seal their valuables at home worth guarding, in the management of their homes. If all were under the influence of the Educator, nothing would need to be sealed, for both master and servant would be honest. But, since lack of education exposes men to a strong inclination to dishonesty, we always stand in need of these seals.

In some circumstances, it is best to relax this stricture. We must be sympathetic with women who sometimes do not

---
5 Rom. 13.14.
6 Prov. 11.22.

succeed in finding restraint in their married lives and who therefore adorn themselves to keep themselves attractive to their husbands. But, let the attempt to win their husbands' admiration be their sole motive. For my part, I would not want them to cultivate bodily comeliness, but, instead, to offer their husbands a self-controlled love, a remedy that is powerful and honest. However, when they are tempted to be unhappy in mind, let them recall this thought, that, if they wish to continue self-controlled, they will gently appease the unreasonable desires and cravings of their husbands. They must lead them back to simplicity quietly, by accustoming them little by little to what is more restrained.

Dignity in dress comes not from adding to what is worn, but from eliminating all that is superfluous. (58) The unncessary luxuries that women wear, in fact, like tail-feathers, must be clipped off, because they give rise only to shifting vanity and senseless pleasure. Because of such vanity and pleasure, women become flighty and vain as peacocks, and even desert their husbands. Therefore, we should take care that the women are attired properly, and clothed abundantly in the modesty of self-restraint, so that they will not break away from the truth through vanity.

It is but right that husbands trust their wives and confide the care of their homes to them. It is for this purpose that wives have been given as helpmates. But if, while we are engaged in public affairs, or are attending to other businesses, as those of our fields, and need be away from our wives frequently,[7] we find it necessary to seal anything for safety's sake, then He allows us a signet ring for this purpose. But we should not wear any other rings, because, according to

---

[7] R. B. Tollinton (*op. cit.* I 270-272) sees in this passage a proof that Clement was himself married.

the Scriptures, it is only learning that is 'an ornament of gold to the prudent.'[8]

Women who wear gold seem to me afraid that, if anyone take their gold from them, unadorned they will be thought slaves. But the nobility of truth, appearing in a nature that is noble of soul, always recognizes a slave not from the fact that he has been bought or sold, but from his ill-bred disposition. We should prefer to be free rather than to only appear to be free, for we are under the guidance of our Educator who is God, and we have become the adopted sons of God. (59) Therefore, we must conduct ourselves, in the way we stand, and move about, in our gait, or simply, in the whole course of our life, in a way that indicates the highest degree of dignity.

Men should not wear a ring upon the knuckle of their finger (for this is the way women wear it), but at the base of their little finger. In this way, their hand will be free for action in whatever they need it for, and the signet ring will not easily fall off, kept in place as it is by the large knuckle of the finger. Let the seals be of a dove or fish or ship in full sail or of a musical lyre, such as Polycrates used, or of a ship's anchor, like the one Seleucus had engraved in an intaglio; or, if anyone be a fisherman, let him make an image of the Apostles and of the children drawn out of the water. No representation of an idol may be impressed on the ring, for we are forbidden to possess such an image, nor may a sword or bow, for we cultivate peace, nor a drinking cup, for we practise temperance. (60) Many of the more sensual have their loves or their mistresses engraved on their seal, as if, by this indelible memorial of their passion, they wish to be made unable to forget their erotic passion.

As for the hair, my opinion is this. A man's head should be

---

8 Eccli. 21.24.

bald, unless he has crisp, curly hair, but his chin should be covered with a beard. His hair should not be braided, nor should it hang down, flowing luxuriantly like a woman's. Being 'well-bearded'[9] is sufficient for a man. If anyone cuts off any of his beard, he should not at least shave all of it off, for that would be to his shame. Cropping off the beard from the chin is forbidden, because that is too much like plucking it out and making the skin smooth. The Psalmist takes delight, indeed, in the hair of his chin, saying: 'As oil falling down on the beard, the beard of Aaron.'[10] By repeating the word, he means to sing of the nobility of a beard, and he goes on to brighten the countenance with the myrrh of the Lord. (61) But when the hair must be cut for some particular reason, but not on the pretext of cleanliness—the hair of the head, lest it grow so long as to obstruct the vision, or the hair on the upper lip because it gets stained with food—then it should be cut with a pair of scissors, and not with a razor, for that is indecent. The hair on the chin should not be disturbed, because it does not interfere with anything, but imparts dignity to the appearance and inspires reverence.[11] Such an appearance may deter many from sinning, lest they the more easily be detected. If anyone wishes to sin openly, he will welcome an appearance that is inconspicuous and quickly forgotten, for, by making himself look like the many who can sin, he gains the opportunity to sin freely without being recognized. (62) In fact, a close-cropped head not only indicates a man who is austere, but it also keeps the head fairly immune to suffering; it accustoms it to being exposed to cold or heat, and so to be impervious to the injury either

---

9 *Odysseus* 4.456
10 Ps. 132.2.
11 There is a lacuna in the text here.

can inflict. Hair absorbs cold or heat like a sponge and so occasions permanent injury to the brain from moisture.

As for women, it is enough for them to soften their tresses and bind their hair neatly with a plain brooch at the neck. Such a simple treatment will at the same time set off the natural beauty of their hair. Coquettish braiding of the hair, however, and a courtesanlike hair-do disfigure their tresses to the point of making them ugly. They have thinned out their hair for these garish braidings so that they will not even touch their heads for fear of disarranging the locks; even when sleep comes, they are terrified that they will unconsciously undo the style of their hair-dress. (63) Again, it is absolutely forbidden them to add artificial hair, for it is unholy for them to add someone else's hair to their own, putting dead locks in with their own. In such a case, on whom does the priest lay his hands? Whom does he bless? Not the woman who is so dressed up, but the artificial hair that belongs to someone else, and through it the other head. If 'the head of the woman is the man, and of the man, Christ,'[12] is it not impious, then, for them to fall into a twofold sin? They deceive their husbands by all this extra hair, and at the same time offend the Lord, as far as they can, by dressing themselves up like harlots to distort the truth, and by tampering with their heads which are beautiful by nature.

By no means may they dye their hair, or stain gray locks. We are not permitted to color our clothes with a variety of hue; much less, then, may we conceal advanced years so worthy of respect. Venerability should be clearly evident by God's light, so that it may inspire reverence from the young. In fact, the appearance of gray hairs at times arrests the attention of those behaving shamelessly, and brings them

---
12 1 Cor. 11.3.

back to self-control, because its distinguished appearance abashes the desires of immaturity.

(64) Moreover, they should not rub their faces with cheap and showy articles of senseless devising. Let me sketch a picture of the embellishment inspired by self-restraint. First of all, spiritual beauty is the most excellent; by it, the soul is made beautiful with the presence of the Holy Spirit and the adornments He confers: justice, prudence, fortitude, temperance, love of the good, and modesty. No color has ever been seen as beautiful as these. Afterwards they may cultivate bodily beauty: 'symmetry of limbs and members, and a good complexion.'[13] The adornment of good health also deserves mention in this category, for it is by health that an artificially produced image is transformed into reality according to the design planned by God. Self-control in drinking and moderation in eating are natural means of producing beauty, for they not only preserve the body's health, but also heighten beauty. A fiery substance generates a gleam and sparkle; moisture, brightness, and pleasantness; a dry substance begets courage and steadfastness; and a substance formed of air gives freshness and poise. It is with all these that harmonious and beautiful image of the Word is adorned. Beauty is the noble flower of health. The one is caused within the body; the other, beauty, blossoming exteriorly, produces the good complexion that may be seen.

(65) Courses of action that exercise the body are the most effective in maintaining beauty and health, and produce a beauty that is lasting and true, because heat draws out all moisture and coldness of breath. In the process of drawing, the heat slowly turns the substance of food into vapor, because it warms it, and so carries the food throughout the

---

13 Cf. Plotinus, *De pulchritudine* 1.

body; the more the moisture, the more the heat. Food is used up in this way; if the body remains inactive, what is eaten is not absorbed into it, but is only passed off, like bread from a cold oven that is drawn out either entire, or with scrapings left in the bottom. No wonder, then, that for those who are excessive in their voidings, urine and offal are abundant, and other excrements, also; this applies to perspiration, too, because here, too, the food has not been digested by the body, but is passed off as a secretion. (66) Lusts are aroused when the excrement gathers about the organ of generation, and therefore the excess must be dissolved and absorbed by digestion. This is the way beauty will come to blossom.

It is absurd for those who have been made to the image and likeness of God to adopt some unnatural means of ornamentation, disfiguring the pattern by which they have been created, and preferring the cleverness of men to that of their divine Creator. The Educator bids women approach 'in decent dress, adorning themselves with modesty and dignity,'[14] 'being subject to their husbands, so that even if any husband does not believe the word, they may without word be won through the behavior of their wives, observing reverently your chaste behavior. Let not theirs be the outward adornment of braiding the hair or of wearing gold, or of putting on robes, but let it be the inner life of the heart, in the imperishableness of a quiet and gentle spirit, which is of great price in the sight of God.'[15]

(67) It is the work a woman performs with her own hands that creates true beauty. It exercises her body and at the same time adorns her, not with some ornament made by others, inelegant, undignified, and gaudy, but something

---
14 1 Tim. 2.9.
15 1 Pet. 3.1-4.

labored over and woven by the modest woman herself with her own hands at the time she needed it. In fact, it is never right for women who live in obedience to God to go about attired with articles bought at the market, but only with the products of her own hands in her house. It is a heart-warming sight to see a woman clothe herself and her husband with the garments she herself has made; everyone takes pleasure in such a sight: her children, in their mother; the husband, in his wife; herself, in her handiwork; and everyone, in God. In a word, 'a treasury of virtue is the brave woman,'[16] who 'hath not eaten her bread hesitatingly, and the laws of mercy are on her tongue,' who 'hath opened her mouth wisely and justly,' whose 'children rising up have called her blessed,' as the Holy Spirit says through Solomon, 'and her husband has praised her. For a pious woman is praised, let her praise the fear of the Lord,'[17] and again, 'a courageous wife is the crown of her husband.'[18]

(68) The posture and look and gait and speech must also be reformed, as far as possible. Not as some do, however, who imitate the actions of the comedy, copying the swaying motions of the dancers, and in company act as if they were on the stage, looking about languidly, with the same sort of dainty gestures, supple bearing, and artificial inflections, assumed as an inducement to pleasure. 'The lips of a harlot drip with honey, who, speaking to please, puts oil on thy throat, but later, you will find her more bitter than gall and more sharp than a two-edged sword. The feet of a foolish woman lead those who use her with death into hell.'[19]

---

16 Alexandros, *Frag.* 5, *CAF* III 373.
17 Cf. Prov. 31.27,26,28 (In Septuagint, Prov. 29.45,43,46).
18 Prov. 12.4 (Septuagint).
19 Prov. 5.3-5 (Septuagint).

A harlot overcame the noble Sampson, and another woman, become his wife, cut off his hair.[20] Joseph, however, was not deceived by any woman, but overcame the Egyptian; then chastity put into chains showed itself more admirable than licentiousness in all its freedom.[21] (69) The verse may express it very well: 'I do not understand at all how to whisper, nor how to walk about effeminately with my head to one side, as I see many others do, panderers there in the city and smooth-skinned fellows.'[22] We must entirely avoid all effeminate motions and all softness and daintiness. Daintiness of bearing in a man as he walks and, in the words of Anacreon, 'walking with a sway,'[23] are positively indecent; at least it seems that way to me. The comedy speaks of the 'time to abandon all traces of harlotry and lust.'[24] 'The steps of harlotry do not bear directly toward the truth, for it does not walk by the path of life, and its steps are dangerous and unaccountable.'[25]

We should also be particularly careful of our eyes, for it is better to slip with the feet than with the eyes. (70) The Lord offers a remedy for this weakness, indeed, with curt words: 'If thy eye scandalize thee, cut in out,'[26] thereby tearing lust up by the roots. Melting glances, and sly looks out of the corner of the eye, which is what is also called winking, are nothing more than adultery with the eyes, since lust operates at a distance through them. The sight sins before the rest of the body does. 'The eye, seeing beautiful things, gladdens the heart,' that is, when it knows how to

---

20 Cf. Judges 16.1; 19.
21 Cf. Gen. 39.12.
22 *Adesp.* 339, *CAF* III 470.
23 Anacreon, *Frag.* 168.
24 *Adesp.* 622, *CAF* III 520.
25 Cf. Prov. 5.5,6 (Septuagint).
26 Matt. 5.29.

see what is right it gives joy, 'but he that winketh with the eye deceitfully, shall cause men sorrow.'[27] The effeminate Sardanapalus, king of the Assyrians, is pictured to us as such a man, lolling on his couch, smoothing down his purple dress, and showing the whites of his eyes.[28]

Women who practise such things put themselves in danger of falling into prostitution, just by their appearances. 'The eye is the lamp of the body,'[29] Scripture says, because what is inside is illuminated and made visible by the light that shines in through it. 'But the fornication of a woman [is] in the haughtiness of her eyes.'[30] (71) 'Put to death your members that are on the earth. Fornication, uncleanness, passion, evil lust, and avarice, which is the worship of idols, through which comes the anger of God,'[31] cries out the Apostle. Yet we excite our passions and are not ashamed. Some women amble along nibbling on mastich, and grin in a silly way at everyone they pass. Others, scratching their heads with their brooches as if they had no fingers, play the coquet, taking care, incidentally, that the brooches be made of tortoise-shell, or ivory, or part of some other dead animal. Still others smear their faces over, as if the skin were broken out, daubing it with various tints of preparations to create a pleasing effect upon those who see them. Scripture declares by the lips of Solomon that she is a 'foolish and bold woman who does not know shame. She sat at the door of her house upon a seat, loudly calling'—that is, saying by her mode of dress and whole manner of living—'to the passers-by on the road, who continue straight on their road: Who of you is

---
27 Prov. 15.30.
28 Cf. Plutarch, *Moralia* 336C.
29 Matt. 6.22.
30 Eccli. 26.12.
31 Cf. Col. 3.5.6.

the most foolish? Turn to me. To those lacking understanding, she calls out saying: Taste the pleasantness of hidden bread, and sweet stolen waters.'[32] 'By 'stolen waters' it means the pleasures of sex. (72) Even the Boeotian Pindar bears us out in this interpretation with his remark: 'The delight of love is a sweet thing that is stolen.'[33] 'But,' the Educator continues, 'the wretched man does not realize that the earth-born are destroyed with her, and go down with her to the pit of Hades. But turn away quickly, do not delay in the place. Do not set your eyes upon her. For thus shall you walk on the water belonging to someone else and pass by Acheron.'[34] It is for this reason that the Lord tells us through Isaias: 'Instead of which, the daughters of Sion walk with proud carriage of their head, and with winkings of their eyes, and as they walk, trail their cloaks and do a kind of dance; the Lord also will humble the daughters of Sion, and strip their comeliness from them,'[35] that unattractive attractiveness of theirs.

(73) As for me, I do not think it right that serving maids who wait at the left hand of their mistresses[36] or those who belong to their retinue speak or act immodestly with them; rather, they should practise real restraint in their presence. The comic poet Philemon expresses it quite artistically: 'As I am going out, I see the pretty maid of a noble freewoman following her alone, glancing sideways at any of the people of Platea who walk alongside of her.'[37] Lack of restraint in a maid reflects upon the mistress, for to those who attempt liberties of minor consequence it affords the occasion of be-

---

32 Cf. Prov. 9.13-17 (Septuagint).
33 Pindar, *Frag.* 217 (Schröder).
34 Cf. Prov. 9.18 (Septuagint).
35 Isa. 3.16,17 (Septuagint).
36 Or, according to the reading of Schwartz, 'who wait on noble women.'
37 Philemon, *Frag.* 124 *CAF* II 517.

coming reckless in things of greater moment; the mistress, indeed, though conscious of the immodesty of her maid, evidently does not condemn it. When one shows no indignation at those who are dissolute, she gives proof that her own mind is sinfully attracted to the same thing. 'As the mistress, so the whelp,' the proverb-makers say.[38]

There is something else we must carefully guard against: walking like a man in a frenzy; rather, we should cultivate a gait that is dignified and leisurely, yet not dilly-dallying. We should not sway from side to side, either, as we walk, or roll our eyes about, staring at everyone we meet to see if they turn to look at us, for all the world as if we were on the stage parading about grandiosely and pointing with our finger. Neither should we have our servants push us uphill and then down again, as we see the more delicate do, who, although seemingly robust, lose their manliness through such physical softness. No traces of softness should be visible in the face of a good man, or for that matter, in any other part of his his body, (74) so that there will be no unbecoming effeminacy either in his movements or in his posture. A man who enjoys good health should never make use of his servants as though they were beasts of burden. Certainly it was to the servants of such a master that the command is given: 'Be subject to your masters in all fear, not only to the good and moderate, but also to the severe,'[39] as St. Peter says. Impartiality and patience and kindness are very appropriate qualities for a master to possess. 'Finally, be all like-minded, compassionate, lovers of the brethren, merciful, humble,' and so on, 'that you might inherit a blessing.'[40]

---
38 Cf. Plato. *Republic* VIII 563C.
39 1 Pet. 2.18.
40 1 Pet. 3.8,9.

Zeno of Citium has left a beautiful and admirable description, I believe, of a young man, chiseling it out in this fashion: 'Let him be clean of face, without heavy eyebrows, with eyes neither wide open nor tightly shut, his chin not thrust forward, the limbs of his body not too relaxed, yet alert like sinews, quick-witted in his reasonings, ready with a store of pertinent remarks, his appearance and gestures not a stimulant for the lustful; let modesty and manliness be his glory; let the languor associated with the perfume shop and the goldsmithy and wool shop have no place in him, nor that derived from any other shop, where men pass the day, decked out garishly like women who sit waiting in a brothel.'[41] (75) The men should not while away their time in barber shops or taverns, either, gossiping and indulging in small talk, and they must positively stop chasing the women who pass by. Some never leave off slander just to get a laugh. Even more, they must refrain from dice-playing, and from habitual gambling with dice, a thing they love to engage in. Such pastimes indicate an unbridled tendency to self-indulgence in those who so waste their time. Idleness is responsible; one is then excessively fond of frivolities beyond the bounds of truth. Besides, it is not possible to indulge in such light-heartedness without harm. The way a man chooses to live is a good indication of the disposition of his mind. Furthermore, it seems to me that only association with good men is of any benefit. For that reason, the all-wise Educator, by the lips of Moses, compared association with corrupt men to living with swine, when He forbade the ancient people to partake of swine.[42] He made it plain in those words that they who invoke God should not seek the company of the unclean who,

---

41 Zeno, *Frag.* 174 (Pearson).
42 Cf. Lev. 11.7; *Ep. of Barn.* 10.3.

like swine, revel in bodily pleasures and filthy habits of life and impure delights, itching for evil-minded pleasures of sex. He adds, too, that they are not to eat 'kite nor mastophage nor eagle,'[43] meaning: 'Thou shalt not go near those who make their livelihood by plundering others.' He says other similar things under some sort of allegory.

(76) With whom, then, should we live? With the just, He replies, again under a metaphor: everything 'of split hoof and chewing the cud'[44] is clean, because the split hoof obviously is a sign of evenly balanced justice, which chews the cud of its own food of justice, the word, which enters from without through instruction, and, once within, is recalled as if from the stomach of the mind for the musings of reason. The just man chews the cud of spiritual nourishment, because he holds the Word in his mouth; and justice undoubtedly divides the hoof, in that it both sanctifies in this life and prepares us as well for the life to come.[45]

As for the theater, the Educator, guide of little ones, certainly does not lead us there; one could—not unreasonably—call the stadium and theater 'seats of pestilence.' The gathering in such a place is indeed wicked, and, as it were, set up against the just; therefore, attendance at it is cursed. Those assemblies are filled with much disorder and sin; in fact, the very excuse for the gathering together occasions disorderly behavior, in that men and women meet promiscuously just to look at one another. (77) In that fact the gathering already proves the falseness of its pretenses. Desires are enkindled by the licence of the eyes, and, when the eyes grow accustomed to gazing on the neighbor without inhibition at

---
43 Cf. Lev. 11.13,14; *Ep. of Barn.* 10.4.
44 Cf. Lev. 11.3; *Ep. of Barn.* 10.11.
45 Cf. *Ep. of Barn.* 10.11.

such a time of idleness, the passion of lust is quickly aroused. Leave the theater alone, then, and recitals, full of coarse jokes and of gossip. What disgusting deed is not depicted in the theater? What shameless talk do the comedians not speak out? Those who enjoy the lewdness represented on the stage will surely reproduce such images of lewdness in their homes; on the other hand, those who are impervious to and unaffected by them would never be attracted by such wild pleasures. Even if people say they attend the theater only for entertainment and amusement, I should still say the cities in which such pastimes are so much sought after are not chaste. Vying for a reputation with an intensity even to the point of death, is no longer a pastime, any more than aimless bustling or unreasoning love of honor; neither are foolish lavishness of money or attendance at these games entertainment. Lightheartedness must never be bought by a feverish searching for frivolities. (78) No one in his right senses would even prefer what is more entertaining to what is worth while.

But, someone may say, we are not all philosophers.

But do not all of us desire life?

What do you mean?

Where is your faith? How do you love God and neighbor, if you do not love wisdom? How can you love yourself, if you do not love life?

I have not learned letters, he may answer.

But, even if you have not learned to read, hearing is inexcusable, as if it, too, needed to be taught.[46] Faith is not the possession of the wise according to this world, but of the wise according to God. That is taught without letters, and its textbook both for the unlearned and the divine is called charity, a book that is spiritual. Because it is possible

---
46 Cf. Rom. 10.17; John 6.45.

to hear divine wisdom, because it is possible to live, it is not impossible to conduct the affairs of the world in a fitting way in keeping with the laws of God.

Then, when buying or selling, let no one name two prices for the things he is purchasing or selling, but speak plainly and honestly. If he lose on something, he will at least gain in truth, and be the richer by an upright disposition. (79) There should not be any intensive advertising of, or any oath about what is being sold (nor should there be any oaths about other things). Let the merchants and hucksters reason in this way: 'Thou shalt not take the name of the Lord in vain; for the Lord will not cleanse him who takes His name in vain.'[47] Those who offend in this matter, the lovers of silver, liars, pretenders, those who haggle with truth, are excluded by the Lord from His Father's house, for He did not want the holy house of God to be a home of dishonest barter or words or of goods on sale.[48]

Further, the man and woman each must come to the church dressed becomingly, with an unaffected walk, respecting silence, possessing 'charity unfeigned,'[49] pure of body and pure in heart, prepared to offer worship to God. Let the woman observe this further practise: except when she is home, she should be completely veiled, for her appearance will be dignified only when she cannot be seen. She will never fall into sin if she always keeps modesty before her eyes, and retain her veil, nor will she lure others into an occasion of sin by baring her face. This is what the Word demands, since it is proper for her to pray covered. They say that the wife of Aeneas, in an outburst of propriety, did not remove

---
47 Exod. 20.7
48 Cf. Matt. 21.12.
49 Cf. Rom. 12.9.

her veil even when Troy was captured, although she was greatly afraid, but remained covered as she fled from the conflagration.[50] (80) They who have been consecrated to Christ ought to have such an appearance and behavior throughout their whole lives that they will conduct themselves in a dignified way when in church, and really be, not just seem to be, meek, devout and charitable. As it is, I do not see them adapting themselves to the place either in their bearing or in their manners, like the octopus which is said to change its color according to the rocks in which it dwells. They do this, I know: they shed the inspiration gathered from their attendance [at church] on their departure from it and adapt themselves to the people with whom they live. Rather, in doffing what was only an assumed pretense of gravity, they prove the sort they have been all along, but secretly. After paying homage to the word of God, they leave inside what they have heard; once outside, they roam about with the ungodly, taking their fill of erotic pieces played on or sung to the accompaniment of the lyre, dancing and drinking and trifling in every way. Those who now sing and join in the refrains of such pieces are the same men who but a while before were chanting the praises of immortality; now they impiously intone that monotonous refrain to the end: 'Let us eat and drink, for tomorrow we die.'[51] (81) But they are, in fact, dead, not tomorrow, but already, dead to God, themselves burying their own dead,[52] that is, burying themselves in the earth, for their own death.

The Apostle rebukes them very sternly: 'Do not err; neither fornicators nor effeminates nor sodomites nor thieves

---

50 Reference unknown.
51 Cf. 1 Cor. 15.32.
52 Cf. Matt. 8.22.

nor the covetous, nor drunkards, nor the evil-tongued,' and all the others he includes with them, 'shall inherit the kingdom of God.'[53] But, if we have been called to the kingdom of God, let us live worthy of that kingdom by loving God and our neighbor. Love is judged not by a kiss, but by good will. There are some who make the assembly resound with nothing but their kisses while there is no love in their hearts. We should realize that the unrestrained use of the kiss has brought it under grave suspicion and slander. It should be thought of in a mystical sense (the Apostle speaks of it as holy[54]). Let us, instead, taste the kingdom with a mouth that is chaste and self-controlled, and practise good will in heart, for this is the way a chaste character is developed.

There is another kiss that is unholy and full of poison, under the guise of holiness. Do you not realize that just as a poisonous spider touches a man only with its mouth, yet inflicts pain, so the kiss often injects the poison of lust? (82) It is clear to us that the kiss is not charity, 'for charity is of God.'[55] 'This is the love of God,' St. John tells us, 'that we keep the commandments,' not that we fondle one another with a kiss. 'And the commandments are not heavy.'[56] Caresses, indeed, expressing the foolish passion of lovers out on a street, indifferent to the gazing of strangers, manifest not the least sign of charity. For, if it is right to 'pray to God' secretly, 'in the chamber,'[57] it would follow that we should also show our love for our neighbor, whom we are commanded to love after God,[58] secretly, as if to God, interiorly

---
53 1 Cor. 15.32.
54 Cf. Rom. 16.16; 1 Cor. 16.20.
55 1 John 4.7.
56 1 John 5.3.
57 Cf. Matt. 6.6.
58 Cf. Matt. 22.39.

redeeming the time.[59] In the light of the saying that we are 'the salt of the earth,'[60] it is said: 'He who blesses his friend with a loud voice in the morning, shall be like to him that curseth.'[61]

Above everything else, it is necessary to avoid staring at women. It is possible to sin, not only by touching them, but even by looking at them, and one under the guidance of the Educator should flee from sin promptly. (83) 'Let thy eyes look straight on, and let thy eyelids nod at just things.'[62] Is is not impossible for one who keeps staring to continue steadfast? No, we must guard ourselves against a fall. One who indulges in looks can fall, but there is no way for one who does not look to become aroused. It is not enough for one who is self-controlled to keep free of guilt; we must also try to keep far from blame, and eliminate every cause for suspicion in any part of holiness, that we may be not only faithful, but also show ourselves trustworthy. We must be careful in this matter, as the Apostle says, 'lest anyone should slander us. For we take forethought for what is honorable, not only before God, but also in the sight of men.'[63] 'Turn away thy eye from a beautiful woman, and gaze not upon another's beauty,' Scripture says.[64] And if you want to know the reason, look for it in yourself: 'For many have perished by the beauty of a woman, and hereby lust is enkindled as a fire.'[65] A friendship that starts in fire— what is called passion—is unquenchable in its sinfulness, because it leads back to fire.

---

59 Cf. Eph. 5.16; Col. 4.5.
60 Matt. 5.13.
61 Prov. 27.14.
62 Cf. Prov. 4.25 (Septuagint).
63 2 Cor. 8.20,21.
64 Eccli. 9.8.
65 Eccli. 9.9.

Chapter 12

(84) For my part, I would advise husbands never to manifest their affection for their wives at home when slaves are present. Aristotle does not permit them ever to laugh with slaves,[1] and certainly much less to openly show love for their wives in their presence. It is better to practise reserve at home beginning with the first day of marriage. A chaste union redolent of pure delight is a wonderful thing. Indeed, the tragedian says, in his striking way: 'How strange, indeed, O woman, that among men, not gold, not tyranny, not greed for wealth holds pleasures so excellent as the wholesome mind of a good man and of a pious woman, when they are filled with upright thoughts.'[2] These are the suggestions of justice, and must not be rejected, for they are expressed even by those skilled in worldly wisdom.

(85) Therefore, realizing 'the work of each, behave yourselves with fear in the time of your sojourning, knowing that you were redeemed from the vain manner of life handed down from your fathers, not with perishable things, with silver or gold, but with the precious blood of Christ, as of a lamb without blemish and without spot.'[3] 'For sufficient is the time past,' Peter continues, 'for those to have accomplished the desire of the pagans, walking as they did, in dissipation, lusts, drunkenness, revellings, carousings and unlawful worship of idols.'[4] We have the Cross of the Lord as our boundary line, and by it we are fenced around and shut off from our former sins. Let us be born again, then, and be nailed to the Cross

---
1 *Frag* 138, in V. Rose, *Aristotelis Fragmenta* (Leipzig 1886).
2 Apollonides, *Frag.* 1 *TGF* II 825.
3 1 Pet. 1.17-19.
4 1 Pet. 4.3.

in truth;[5] let us return to our senses and be sanctified, 'for the eyes of the Lord are upon the just, and His ears unto their prayers; but the face of the Lord is against those who do evil. And who is there to harm you, if you are zealous for what is good?'[6] Good order is the perfect way of life, for it is entirely well behaved, is a quality that establishes constancy, fulfills virtuously in deed the things imposed on it, one after the other, and is unsurpassed in virtue.

(86) Now, the Educator says, if I have proposed these things harshly when I administered healing correction, consider them said by Me, since 'he who corrects freely makes peace,'[7] and as for you, if you listen to them, you will be saved, but if you do not attend to what has been said, I have no further interest. Yet I am interested inasmuch as 'He prefers the conversion of sinners rather than their death.'[8] 'If you hearken to Me, you shall eat the good things of the land,'[9] the Educator says at another time, meaning by 'the good things of the land' things that are dear to men: beauty, wealth, health, strength, and food. The good things, however, are really the things 'which ear has not heard nor has it ever entered into the heart,'[10] the things that are really good and laid up in store for us, in our relation with Him who is truly King. It is He who is the Giver and Preserver of good things. He names the things of this life, however, by that same common name, because, as the Educator and Guide of little ones, the Word leads man from things seen to the spiritual, in His own divine way.

---

5 Cf. Rom. 6.6.
6 1 Pet. 3.12; Ps. 33.16.
7 Prov. 10.10 (Septuagint).
8 Cf. Ezech. 18.23.
9 Isa. 1.19.
10 1 Cor. 2.9.

(87) The things we should be on our guard against at home, and how we are to preserve our lives upright, the Educator has shown us in abundant detail. The things that are dear to Him to discourse about along the way until He lead us to the Teacher, these, too, He has suggested and proposed by way of a general summary right in the Scriptures; He gives His commands plainly, adapting them to the time of guidance, but entrusting the interpretation of them to the Teacher. The purpose of His rule is to eliminate fear and free the will for its act of faith. Hear, He says, O child so well trained by the Educator, the articles of salvation: I will reveal to you the way of life I want from you, and I will impose the precious commands by which you will gain salvation. Turn away from the paths of error, 'for the Lord knows the way of the just, and the way of the impious shall perish.'[11] Follow, then, the good road which I shall lead you by, O little one! Lend an attentive ear to Me and hear: 'And I will give you hidden treasures, concealed, unseen'[12] by the Gentiles, but visible to you, 'never-failing treasures,'[13] which the Apostle marveled at when he said: 'O the depth of the riches and of the wisdom!'[14] The treasures offered by the one God are manifold, some revealed in the Law, others through the Prophets, and others directly by God Himself. There is still another in tune with the sevenfold gift of the Spirit.[15] The Lord is one, and in all these things is therefore one and the same Educator.

(88) There is also the counsel that sums up everything,

11 Ps. 1.6.
12 Isa. 45.3 (Septuagint).
13 Cf. Luke 12.33.
14 Rom. 11.33.
15 Literally *tē heptádi*. The Scholion understands it, however, of the seven gifts of the Spirit. Cf. A. de Barre, 'Clément d'Alexandrie,' *DTC* cols. 159-160.

advice that leads to life and embraces everything: 'As you wish that men do to you, do you to them.'[16] All the commandments may be summed up in these two, as the Lord Himself said: 'Thou shalt love the Lord Thy God with thy whole heart and with the whole soul and with thy whole strength; and thy neighbor as thyself.'[17] Then He adds: 'On these two the whole Law and the Prophets depends.' In fact, even to the man who asked Him: 'What shall I do to obtain eternal life?' He replied: 'You know the commandments,' and when the man assented, He continued: 'Do this and you will be saved.'[18] Still, we must offer the Educator's loving kindness as inspiring separate and saving commandments, that through such a generously bestowed dispensation we might have an easier grasp of the Scriptures and of salvation.

(89) We have the Decalogue of Moses, proposed in a simple and unified elementary form, outlining a healing denunciation of sins: 'Thou shalt not commit adultery; thou shalt not worship idols; thou shalt not corrupt boys; thou shalt not steal; thou shalt not bear false witness; honor thy father and mother,'[19] and so on. We must be careful in these matters, and in whatever impiety the other commandments proscribe in the Bible. He directs, through Isaias: 'Wash yourselves, be clean, take away the evil from your souls from before My eyes. Learn to do well, seek judgment, relieve the oppressed, judge for the fatherless, defend the widow. And then come, and accuse Me, says the Lord.'[20]

---

16 Luke 6.31.
17 Matt. 22.40.
18 Cf. Matt. 19.16-19.
19 Cf. Exod. 20.12-15; *Ep. of Barn.* 19.4.
20 Isa. 1.16-18.

We can discover many counsels about other things, also, as about prayer, for example: 'Good works are a prayer acceptable to the Lord,'[21] Scripture says. The way to pray is prescribed: 'If you see one naked, cover him, and do not look away from the members of thy seed. Then shall thy light break forth as the morning, and thy garments shall speedily rise, and thy justice shall go before thy face, and the glory of God shall encircle thee.'[22] What is the fruit of this sort of prayer? 'Then shalt thou call, and the Lord shall hear thee; while you are yet speaking, He will say: Behold, here I am.'[23]

(90) He speaks of fasting: 'Why do you fast to Me? says the Lord. I have not chosen such a fast, for a man to humble his soul even for a day. Do not wind your neck about like a circle, and spread sack-cloth and ashes, nor call this an acceptable fast.'[24] What does fasting mean, then? It is said: 'Behold, this is the fast that I have chosen, says the Lord. Loose the whole band of wickedness, loose the knots of enduring contracts, release those that are broken with forgiveness, and break asunder every unjust bond. Deal thy bread to the hungry, and bring the harborless needy into thy house; if thou see one naked, cover him.'[25]

Then of sacrifice: 'Why [do you offer] Me the multitude of your victims? saith the Lord. I am full of the holocausts of rams, and the fat of sheep, and blood of bulls and goats I do not desire, not even if you come to appear before Me. For who required these things at your hands? If you bear the finest flour, it is in vain. Sacrifices are an abomination to

---
21 Cf. Prov. 15.8.
22 Cf. Isa. 58.7,8 (Septuagint).
23 Isa. 58.9; cf. *Ep. of Barn.* 3.3-5.
24 Cf. Isa. 58.4,5 (Septuagint).
25 Isa. 58.6,7.

Me. Your new moons and sabbaths I will not abide.'[26] How shall I make sacrifice to the Lord, then? 'A sacrifice to the Lord,' it answers, 'is a contrite spirit.'[27] How shall I pay homage with libations, or anoint with myrrh? Or what shall I sacrifice to the Lord? 'An odor of sweet-fragance to God is a heart honoring Him who made it.'[28] This is garlands and sacrifices and aroma and flowers in God's sight.

(91) Again, about patience with the evil: 'If thy brother sin, rebuke him; and if he repent, forgive him. And if seven times in the day he sin against thee, and seven times in the day turn back to thee saying: I repent, forgive him.'[29] He commands soldiers, through John, to be satisfied with their pay and nothing besides; publicans, to exact nothing more than had been imposed by tax;[30] to the judge, He says: 'Do not accept persons in judgment; for gifts blind the eyes of those who see, and change just words,'[31] 'Relieve the oppressed';[32] and to those who do housekeeping: 'Substance got in haste illegally shall be diminished.'[33]

About love, He says: 'Charity covereth a multitude of sins.'[34] Of the state: 'Render to Caesar the things that are Caesar's, and unto God, the things that are God's.'[35] Concerning oaths and revenge: 'I did not command your fathers as they journeyed out of the land of Egypt to offer to Me holocausts and sacrifices. But this thing I commanded them: Let none of you imagine evil in your hearts against his friend,

---

26 Isa. 1.11-13 (Septuagint); cf. *Ep. of Barn.* 2.4.
27 Ps. 50.19.
28 Cf. *Ep. of Barn.* 2.10.
29 Luke 17.3,4.
30 Luke 3.12-14.
31 Cf. Deut. 16.19.
32 Isa. 1.17.
33 Cf. Prov. 13.11 (Septuagint).
34 1 Pet. 4.8.
35 Matt. 22.21.

and love not a false oath.'³⁶ (92) He threatens liars and the proud, saying somewhere to the one: 'Woe to those who say sweet is bitter and bitter is sweet,'³⁷ and to the other: 'Woe to you who are wise in your own eyes and prudent before them,'³⁸ 'he who humbles himself shall be exalted and he who exalts himself shall be humbled.'³⁹ He calls the merciful blessed: 'because they shall obtain mercy,'⁴⁰ while Wisdom calls anger miserable, 'because indeed it will destroy even the prudent.'⁴¹ He had already ordered us to love our enemies and to bless those who curse us, and to pray for those who calumniate us,⁴² 'To him who strikes thee on one cheek,' He says, 'offer the other also, and if anyone take away thy cloak, do not forbid him also thy robe.'⁴³ Of faith, He says: 'All things whatever you ask for in prayer, believing, you shall receive';⁴⁴ 'to the unbelieving, nothing is worth believing in,' adds Pindar.⁴⁵

We must treat servants as we do ourselves, for they are men even as we are. 'God is the same to all, free or slave, if you consider.'⁴⁶ (93) We ought not to inflict torture on servants who do wrong, but only chastise them: 'He who spares his rod hates his son.'⁴⁷ Again, He excoriates vainglory: 'Woe to you, Pharisees, because you love the front seats in the synagogues and greetings in the market-place.'⁴⁸ He

36 Jer. 7.22; Zach. 8.17.
37 Isa. 5.20.
38 Cf. Isa. 5.21.
39 Luke 14.11.
40 Matt. 5.7.
41 Cf. Prov. 15.1 (Septuagint).
42 Cf. Luke 6.27,28.
43 Cf. Luke 6.29.
44 Matt. 21.22.
45 Pindar, *Frag.* 233 (Schröder).
46 Possibly Menander; cf. Bywater, *Journal of Philology* 10 (1881) 68.
47 Cf. Prov. 13.24.
48 Luke 11.43.

takes delight in the conversion of sinners,[49] for He desires the conversion which follows their sins. Surely, He Himself is the only sinless one. 'To sin is natural and common to all, but to repent of sin is not the deed of an ordinary man, but of one who is unusual.'[50] Concerning almsgiving, He says: 'Come to Me, all ye blessed, take possession of the kingdom prepared for you from the foundation of the world; for I was hungry, and you gave Me to eat; I was thirsty, and you gave Me to drink; I was a stranger, and you gave Me shelter; naked, and you covered Me; sick, and you visited Me, in prison, and you came to Me.'[51] And when did we do any of these things for the Lord? The Educator says it is a good deed, and in His charity considers the good deed done to a brother as done to Himself: 'As long as you did it to these little ones, you did it for Me.'[52] Such as they shall come into eternal life.

(94) These are the laws of reason, words that impart inspiration, written by the hand of the Lord, not on tablets of stone, but inscribed in the hearts of men,[53] provided only that those hearts are not attached to corruption. Therefore, the tablets of the hard of heart have been broken, that the faith of little ones might be formed in impressionable minds. Both laws served the Word as means of educating mankind, the one through Moses, the other through the Apostles. But, what a means of education is the one given through the Apostles!

It seems necessary to me that this sort of education be thoroughly described; rather, the Educator Himself says so, as far as I recall. It is His counsels that I am explaining in

---
49 Cf. Ezech. 18.23.
50 Menander, *Frag.* 993 *CAF* III 251.
51 Cf. Matt. 25.37-46.
52 Cf. Matt. 25.40.
53 Cf. 2 Cor. 3.3.

their implications: 'Putting away all lying, speak truth, each one with his neighbor, because we are members of one another. . . . Do not let the sun go down upon your anger, do not give place to the devil. He who was wont to steal, let him steal no longer; but rather let him labor, working with his hands at what is good, that he may have something to share with him who suffers need. . . . Let all bitterness, and wrath and indignation and clamor, and reviling, be removed from you, along with all malice. Be kind to one another, merciful, generously forgiving one another, as God in Christ has generously forgiven you. Be you therefore prudent and imitators of God, as very dear children, and walk in love as Christ also loved us.'[54]

'Let wives be subject to their own husbands, as to the Lord . . . and let husbands love their wives, just as Christ loved the Church.'[55] (95) Let them, then, love one another, they who are joined together, 'as they love their own bodies.'[56] 'Children, obey your parents. . . . And you, fathers, do not provoke your children to anger, but rear them in the discipline and admonition of the Lord. Slaves, obey your masters according to the flesh with fear and trembling, in the sincerity of your heart, as you would Christ . . . giving your service from your heart with good will. And you, masters, act well toward your servants, and give up threatening, knowing that their Lord who is also your Lord is in heaven, and that [with Him] there is no respect of persons.'[57]

'If we live by the Spirit, by the Spirit let us also walk. Let us not become desirous of vainglory, provoking one another,

---
54 Eph. 4.25-5.2.
55 Eph. 5.22,25.
56 Eph. 5.28.
57 Eph. 6.1,4,5,7,9.

envying one another. Bear one another's burdens, and so you will fulfill the law of Christ. . . . Be not deceived, God is not mocked. . . . And in doing good let us not grow tired; for in due time we shall reap, if we do not relax.'[58] 'Be at peace among yourselves. And we exhort you, brethren, reprove the irregular, comfort the fainthearted, support the weak, be patient toward all men. See that no one renders evil for evil to any man. . . . Do not extinguish the Spirit, do not despise prophecies, but test all things, hold fast that which is good. Keep yourselves from every kind of evil.'[59]

'Be assiduous in prayer, being wakeful therein with thanksgiving. Walk in wisdom as regards outsiders, making the most of your time. Let your speech, while always attractive, be seasoned with salt, that you may know how you ought to answer each one.'[60] (96) 'Be nourished by the words of faith. . . . Train thyself in godliness. For bodily training is profitable for little, but godliness is profitable in all respects, since it has the promise of the present life as well as of that which is to come.'[61]

'When they have masters who are believers, let them not despise them, because they are brethren, but let them serve them all the more, because they are believers.'[62] 'Let him who gives, be in simplicity, he who presides, with carefulness, he who shows mercy, with cheerfulness. Let love be without pretense. Hate what is evil, hold to what is good. Love one another with fraternal charity, anticipating one another with honor. Be not slothful in zeal, but be fervent in spirit, serving the Lord, rejoicing in hope. Be patient in tribulation, per-

---

58 Gal. 5.25,26-6.2,7,9.
59 1 Thess. 5.13-15,20-22.
60 Col. 4.2,5,6.
61 1 Tim. 4.6-8.
62 1 Tim. 6.2.

severing in prayer . . . practising hospitality, share the needs of the saints.'⁶³

(97) These few precepts the Educator has selected by way of illustration from the Scriptures out of many, and proposed to His children. By them He uproots evil completely and imposes a limit upon injustice. Innumerable counsels relating to particular individuals have been written in these holy books, some to priests, some to bishops and deacons, others to widows (about whom there should be occasion to speak in another place). There are many things, too, spoken in enigma, and many things by way of parables that benefit those who chance upon them. But, the Educator insists, My function is no longer to teach these things; now we need the Teacher to explain these holy words, to whom we should go. Therefore, it is time for Me to lay aside leading you as Educator, and for you to hearken to the Teacher. (98) After we have been trained by a sound education, He will take us and teach us the word of God.⁶⁴ The Church is the school, and the Bridegroom is the one only Teacher; His noble desire, as of a noble father, is excellent wisdom, the holiness of knowledge.

'And He Himself,' as John says, 'is a propitiation for our sins,' He who heals both our souls and our bodies, the eternal Man, Jesus, 'and not for our sins only, but also for those of the whole world. And by this we can be sure that we know Him, if we keep His commandments. He who says: I know Him, and does not keep His commandments, is a liar, and the truth is not in him. But he who keeps His word, in him the love of God is truly perfected. By this we know that we are in Him. He who says that he abides in Him, ought himself also to walk just as He walked.'⁶⁵

---

63 Rom. 12.8-13.
64 *lógia*, which is used of the commands and teachings of God in both Testaments.
65 1 John 2.2-6.

(99) Oh, the nourishment supplied by this blessed education! Let us fill up the beautiful appearance of the Church, running to that good mother as little ones. Let us become hearers indeed of the Word, esteem the blessed dispensation by which man is educated, by which he is consecrated as the son of God, dwells in heaven although educated upon earth, and looks up to his Father there while learning from Him upon earth. The Word does all these things, and teaches all things, and uses all things to educate us. A horse is led by a bit, an ox by a yoke, a wild beast is snared by a trap, but man is reformed by the Word by whom He is tamed as though he were a wild beast, caught as though he were a fish, and restrained as if he were a bird. It is in fact He who fashions the bit for the horse, the yoke for the ox, the trap for the wild beast, the rod for the fish, the net for the bird. He dwells in the city and tills the soil; He rules and He ministers to, and engineers the whole thing. 'Therein He wrought the earth, therein the heavens, therein the sea, and therein all the constellations wherewith heaven is crowned.'[66]

(100) Oh, the workings of God! Oh, the commands of God! This is water: let the waves toss upon it; this is fire: let it continue to rage; this is air: let it expand into the atmosphere; let the earth, too, become solid and be borne wherever I will. I desire yet to fashion man; I have the primary substance: I will dwell in this creature of Mine, and, if you recognize Me, fire will be your servant. So great is the Word, this Educator, the Creator of the world and of man, become the Educator of the world, also, in His own person. By His command both of us are united together, awaiting His judgment. 'Wisdom does not offer to mortals a spoken

---

66 *Iliad* 18.483,485.

word that is hidden; it will be the word,'[67] as Bacchylides says. But, 'shine,' as Paul says, 'as blameless and guileless children of God without blemish in the midst of a depraved and perverse generation as stars in the world.'[68]

(101) Let us, then, make our prayer to the Word, the last thing remaining in our panegyric of the Word:

O Educator, be gracious to Thy children, O Educator, Father, Guide of Israel, Son and Father, both one, Lord. Give to us, who follow Thy command, to fulfill the likeness of Thy image, and to see, according to our strength, the God who is both a good God and a Judge who is not harsh. Do Thou Thyself bestow all things on us who dwell in Thy peace, who have been placed in Thy city, who sail the sea of sin unruffled, that we may be made tranquil and supported by the Holy Spirit, the unutterable Wisdom, by night and day, unto the perfect day, to sing eternal thanksgiving to the one only Father and Son, Son and Father, Educator and Teacher with the Holy Spirit. All things are for the One, in whom are all things, through whom, being the One, are all things,[69] through whom eternity is, of whom all men are members, to whom is glory, and the ages, whose are all things in their goodness; all things, in their beauty; all things, in their wisdom; all things, in their justice. To Him be glory now and forever. Amen.

Since the Master Himself, in establishing us as His Church, has taken charge of us as Teacher and all-governing Word, it would be well for us, having reached this point, to offer to the Lord, in return for His wise education, the eternal offering of holy thanksgiving.

---

67 Bacchylides, *Frag.* 29.
68 Cf. Phil. 2.15.
69 Cf. Col. 1.16.

Hymn to the Educator[70]

Bridle-bit of colts untamed,
Thou Wing of birds not straying,
Firm rudder of our ships at sea,
Thou shepherd of God's regal sheep.

Thy simple children
Gather round Thee;
They would sing holily,
They would hymn truthfully,
With lips ne'er stained,
To Thee, O Christ, their Guide.

O Thou King of saints,
Word of Father on high,
Thou Governor of all things,
Ruling e'er wisely,
Balm for all labors,
Source of endless joy,
Jesus, holy Saviour
Of men who cry to Thee;
Thou Shepherd, Thou Husbandman,
Thou Rudder, Thou Bridle-bit,
O Wing, heaven leading
The flock of innocence;
Fisher of men

---

[70] This is one of the earliest recorded Greek Christian hymns. Possibly it was not composed by Clement himself, but it is added to the manuscript and certainly is Clementine in thought, if not in origin. Only a free-verse rendition has been attempted here.

*Drawn safely in
From ocean of sin;
Snaring to spotless life
Fish unstained by
Sea of hostile foe;
O all-hallowed Shepherd,
Guide us, Thy children,
Guide Thy sheep safely, O King!*

*The footsteps of Christ
Are pathway to heaven,
Of ages unbounded,
Everlasting Word,
Light of eternity,
Well-spring of Mercy,
Who virtue instills
In hearts offering God
The gift of their reverence,
O Jesus, our Christ!
Milk of the bride,
Given of heaven,
Pressed from sweet breasts—
Gifts of Thy wisdom—
These Thy little ones
Draw for their nourishment;
With infancy's lips
Filling their souls
With spiritual savor
From breasts of the Word.*

*Let us all sing
To Christ, our King,
Songs of sweet innocence,
Hymns of bright purity,
Hallowed gratefulness
For teachings of life;
Let us praise gladsomely
So mighty a Child.*

*Let us, born of Christ,
Chant out in unison,
Loud chorus of peace,
We, undefiled, pure flock,
To God, Lord of peace.*

INDEX

INDEX

Aaron, 218, 247
Abel, 44, 45
Abimelec, king, 22
abortion, 174
Abraham, 209, 234, 239, 241
Achilles, 50
actors, lewdness of, 251, 258
Adam, 186; law born of, 119; sin of, 90
admonition, defined, 68; like diet for sick, 69
adoption, of sons, conferred by God, 22, 26, 87, 236, 246
Adrastus, 50
adultery, 138, 141; condemned by Plato, 170; condemned under figure of hyena, 165; encouraged by paganism, 223; symbolized by golden ornaments, 195
advertising excessive, condemned, 259
advice, 4; defined, 79, 80; Educator's, 83, 84
Aeneas, wife of, 252

affability, weakness of, indicated, 67
Agathon, 226 n.
Agape, 96-99, 108, 123, 261
age, may jest with youth, 143; needs wine as stimulant, 113, 114; speech proper for, 144; venerable, 213
alabaster, sign of ostentation, 123, 128
Alcibiades, 50
alertness, weakened by sleep, 163
Alexander, 50
Alexandria, catechetical school at, ix; Church of, xiv; Clement and, vii; corruption of, xv; cultural atmosphere of, viii, x; medicine at, 30 n.; spirituality of, xv
Alexandrios, 251 n.
Alexis, 151 n.; 205, 206
allegory, viii, x, 37, 46, 146, 147, 154; *see* symbolism
almsgiving, 270

281

amethysts, 190
Anacreon, 252
anchor, figure of, permitted on rings, 246
angels, 161, 164, 211, 231
anger, 199, 269
animals, examples for men: in lack of vanity, 207; in restraint, 173; kinds forbidden Jews, 108, 109
anointing, of Christ, as allegory, 146, 147
Antiphanes, poet, 204
Antiphanes of Delos, physician, 94
apathes, xvi, xvii, 5 n.
Apelles, 196
aphrodisia, etymology of, 45 n.
Aphrodite, 195
Apollonides, 263 n.
Apostles, 142, 146-148, 234, 246
apothecary, 152
appearances, as opposed to truth, 189, 190, 201, 202, 208, 209, 213
Arabs, 131, 220
Arcadians, 131
archons, 181
areté, 193 n.
Aristippus, 149, 152
Aristophanes, 184 n., 195, 203 n., 204 n.
Aristotle, 107 n., 110, 135 n., 166 n., 263
Artemis, 155
Artorius, 114

atheists, Plato says sinners are, 177
Athena, 120
Athenians, 181, 190, 194
athletes, 190; figure for Christians, 235; modesty of ancient, 226
autarkeia, 87 n.
avarice, 197

bacchanals, 183
Bacchus, 156
Bacchylides, 83 n., 275
bakers, 221
ball game, 240
banquets, blessing before, 132, 133; Christian behavior at, 102-105, 121, 129, 130, 140; contrasted with Agape, 96-98; occasions of sin, 101
baptism, effects of, 25-28, 30, 161; by John, of Christ, 25, 26; rites of, 32 n., 42 n., 46 n.; water of, 47
barbers, 212, 256
baths, dangers and luxury of, 225-227, 237, 238; reasons for using, 238; spiritual, 238
beards, hairs of, numbered, 215; natural adornment of men, 214, 218; not to be shaved off, 247
beauticians, 221
beauty, artificial, evils of, 150, 181, 194, 204, 208, 209, 216; Esther's, mystic significance

282

of, 209; is flower of health, 249; natural, and artificial, contrasted, 127, 181, 187, 197, 202, 203, 207, 208, 211, 212; natural, desired, 207, 208, 230, 249, 264; spiritual, 186, 193; true, in God, 198, 200

beds, should be simple, 159-161

bees, harmed by oil, 150

beets, 95

behavior, at banquets, 101-105, 140-145; in drinking, 120-123; in general, 246, 251

belching, 123, 145, 162

belly-madness, 104

Bergh, T., 149 n.

Bigg, C., v

Biotus, 46 n.

birds, 15, 165, 166, 207, 224

bishops, 273

blackbird, 165

blame, arouses sluggish, 59, 83

Blass, F., 83 n., 226 n.

blessing, before meals, 132; for education through Christ, 81, 82

blood, allegorical use of, 16, 44; comes from food, 41; first substance of man, 38, 46; of grapes, symbol of, 111; should not be eaten, 220; turns into flesh, 45; turns into milk, 38, 42, 46

Blood, of Christ, allegorized: by blood of Abel, 44, 45; by blood of grape, 111; by milk, 39, 44; by wine, 119; allegory of Passion and teaching, 46; allegory for promise, 37; anoints, 111; begets a new people, 40; corporeal and spiritual, 111; food of little ones, 40; forgives sins, 121, 122; garment of Word, 44; redeems mankind, 46, 263; redeems from incorruption, 111; saves souls, 16, 23; symbolizes Word, 41; is true drink, 35; is wine blessed by Redeemer, 121

boars, 219

body, attitude toward, 93; companion of soul, 90, 91; equipped with beauty and harmony, 8; garment of soul, 184; governed by soul, 178

boorishness, 103, 104, 140-142, 145

bow, condemned in rings, 246

boys, beauty of, misused, 221; exercise for, 239; laughter among, causes quarrels, 136; not allowed wine, 112; older, may tease, 143; should keep silent among elders, 144; of slave dealers, 216, 217; to be excluded from banquets, 141; to be respected as sons, 169

bread, oversifted, 95

Bread of Heaven, 44

breast, of God, in the Word, 41;

of women in pregnancy, 38, 39, 41, 232
brooch, 181
buffoonery, condemned, 134
bush, burning, 158
bustards, 224
butter, symbol of Word, 48
buying and selling, 259
Bywater, I., 269 n.

calf, golden, 196, 197
calves, figures for children, 15
camels, 220; hair of, 186
Cana, miracle at, 118, 119
caresses, 261
Carian melodies, 130
carnal, described, 36; those not fully purified, 35
Casey, R., xvii
cat, Egyptian god, 202
catch, best, is men, 241
catechumens, 30 n.
cattle, 229, 231
caution, 71
Cayré, F., vi, x
Celts, 219, 222
ceraunites, 190
censure, 69
chamber-pots, 128
change, accidental, 165, 166
character, marks of poor, 141, 182
charcoal, as cosmetic, 205; for heat, 225
charity, acts of, 241; at banquets, 97, 140; covers sins, 268; inner love of neighbor, 261; textbook of faith, 258; true beauty for men, 201
chastisement, beneficial, 55, 56, 73
chastity, 150, 176, 184, 187, 188, 252, 263; of Penelope, 233
cheese, 107
chewing cud, metaphor of, 257
child, duties of, 271; gives name to education and culture, 17; goal and flower of marriage, 154, 164
childishness, bad sense, 32, 33; in attachment to gems, 190; to be avoided, 17, 19
childhood, of Christians, 3, 12-14, 21, 22, 34; explained, 17, 18; objected to, 20, 24
Christ, Alpha and Omega, 35; anointed, 146, 147; baptism of, 25, 26; birth of, 40, 148, 149; Bread of Heaven, 43; breast of Father's love, 41, 43; at Cana, 118, 119; and Church, 11, 19, 23, 154, 156, 185, 275; Educator, xiv, 4-7, 9-11, 13, 16, 21, 30-32, 46, 50-55, 59-61, 66-68, 73-82, 85-89, 105, 107, 111, 122, 127, 132, 135, 155, 158, 169, 174, 178, 184, 196, 197, 234, 235, 242, 246, 252, 264; footwear of, 190; forgives, 9, 61; God and, 9, 23, 25, 50, 57, 64-66, 86, 158; Good Shepherd, 12, 17,

36, 50, 74, 75, 86; greatness in childhood, 23, 24; Healer and Physician, 4, 7, 8, 74, 85, 273; High Priest, 151; image of Father, 5, 86, 87; image for us, 5, 26; Incarnation of, 23, 53, 191, 200, 201; Judge, 61, 76; and justice, 64-66, 78; King, 157; love of man, 11, 27, 40, 41, 46, 56, 57, 76, 87, 112, 200; manner of drinking wine, 121, 122; Mediator, 200; one, 40; Only-begotten, 10; Passion of, 23, 40, 43, 45, 46, 56, 59, 76, 84, 111, 146-148, 156-158; perfect, 18, 25, 33; persecuted by St. Paul, 32; prayer to, 75; prefigured by Isaac, 23; resurrection of, 23; Saviour, 88, 121; sinless, 270; Spirit, 41; spiritual nourishment, 34, 37, 40, 42-44; symbolized by: Abel, 45; by blood, 41, 46; by colt, 16; by grapes, 111; Tamer, 16; Teacher, xiv, 4, 10, 18, 31, 265, 273, 275; vine, 16, 60; washed feet of Apostles, 146, 147; Wisdom, 7, 129; Word, xvi, 4, 6, 7, 9, 11, 20, 27, 35, 40, 41, 44, 54, 57, 64, 89, 111, 129, 147, 191, 196, 238, 249

Christian, becomes like God in practice of virtue, 88; good man is, 229; man of gentleness, 146; names for, 16; way of life, xv, 84, 86, 88, 91, 93, 94, 106, 127, 128, 233

christoi, 148 n.

choir, 133

Chrysippus, 169 n.

Church, assembly of Christ's children, 23; awaits resurrection, 131; behavior in, 259, 260; choir, 133; crown of, is Christ, 154; garment of, is faith, 185; good mother, 274; head of, is Christ, 156, 185, 275; holy mountain of Good Shepherd, 75; nourished by Eucharist, 37; one, 11; prefigured by Rebecca, 22, 23; salvation for men, 27; school, 273; Virgin Mother, 40; we are, 19

Cilicia, 188

Cinyra, 228

Clement of Alexandria, birth of, vi; character of, vi, ix-xiii; conversion of, vi, vii; death of, viii; erudition of, xv; as educator, v, vii-ix; humanism of, v, vi, viii; influences on, vii, viii, xv, xvii; marriage of, 245 n.; orthodoxy of, xiii; a priest, 36 n.; and Scriptures, x-xii; style of, xii, xiii, xvi; unorthodoxy of, vi, ix, xiii; writings of, ix xi-xvii, 31 n., 139 n., 170 n., 172 n., 180 n., 233 n.

clothes, color of, 183; of cour-

285

tesans, 181; expensive, forbidden, 178, 188; of first man, 186; immodesty in, 187, 188; should be plain, 125, 182-185, 188, 224, 242-244; should be same for both sexes, 181; for women, 185, 186, 251
clowns, to be barred, 134
cold, wine remedy against, 119
color, of garments, 183
colt, figure for Christ, 16
commands, of God, and Educator, 236, 265; evil effects of disobedience of, 210; expressed in way they can be fulfilled, 86; for our good, 91; give life, 84; love of, 10, 11, 261; summed up in two, 266
community, of possessions, 192, 193
companions, should be just, 256, 257
complaint, defined, 69
conception, biology of, 172, 173
conscience, 176
consolation, in Christ, 4
constancy, 264
contemplation, in divine food, 101; of human and divine natures, 89; preparation for, 198; of light, 162
continence, 172
conversion, of Clement, vi, vii; of sinner, 62; symbolized by unloved hair, 147, 269, 270
cooks, 101, 221

coquetry, 222, 253, 254
correction, compared to reflection in mirror or medical diagnosis, 78; defined, 70; etymology of, 83; given by Word, 79; good effects of, 74, 76; to restore self-control, 73
corruption, 75, 111, 177, 178
cosmetics, condemned, 180, 203, 204, 206, 249, 253
couch, unadorned, 161
counsel, of Educator, 270-273; truth as goal of, 90; of Word, 4
courtesans, clothing for, 181
Covenant, New, 21, 53, 54
covering, of head, 188
covetousness, 128, 129
conviviality, not condemned, 101
Crates, 172
Cretans, 131
crobulus, 181
crocodile, droppings of, as cosmetic, 205; Egyptian god, 202
crocus, 154, 155
Cross, the, extended hands suggest, 24 n.; our boundary line, 263; wood of life, 220 n.; wood of, prefigured by Isaac, 23
crown, allegorical sense of, 154; image of Lord's incorruptibility, 149; of thorns, 156-158; symbol of Christ, 148

cups, ostentatiousness of, 124, 125, 225
cup-bearers, 230
Cybele, 222
Cynics, 82 n., 160
cypress, 155

dancing, 187; indecency of, 130
darkness, opposed to enlightenment, 161; as veil for passion, 175
David, 109, 110, 132, 150, 208
deacons, 142, 273
decorations, of soldiers, 194
de la Barre, A., 36 n., 111 n., 265 n.
delicacies, condemned, 101
Democritus, 7, 172
denunciation, raises up sluggish, 59
depression, after drinking, 143
derision, defined, 72
desire, limited by self-sufficiency, 108; of money is destruction, 192; must be plucked out or restrained, 123, 216, 242; symbolized by Proteus, 200; third part of soul, 199, 200
detachment, in clothing, 181; in food, 100-103; in furnishings, 125, 126; makes men like God, 199; from ornaments, 197; of possessions, 192, 193, 231, 232
Devil, consummate in evil, 18; inspires superfluity, 179; rendered ineffective by Cross, 157; as serpent tempting Eve, 195
dicing, 256
diet, for frugality, 107
digestion, 249, 250
Diogenes Apolloniates, 45
Diogenes the Cynic, 212
Diogenes Laertes, 144 n., 149 n., 240
Diomedes, 160
disciples, of Christ, 234, 241; we on earth are, 18
discipline, begets alertness, 162
discourse, Stoic division of, xv, 3 n.
discretion, 229
discrimination, against persons, 224
dignity, 245, 246
dishonesty, 244, 259
dissipation, 171
Dives, 180, 228
divinity, man must contemplate, 89
dove, 15, 246
dreams, 162-164
drinking, Christ is congenial companion of our, 132; dangers of, 141; excesses of, 115-119, 124, 129, 130, 234; proper behavior while, 120-123; source of quarreling, 140, 154, 171
dropsy, 226
drowsiness, 163
duty, defined, 90; to conform to will of Christ, 91

dyes, for garments, deplored, 125, 182-185, 188, 224, 243; for hair, condemned, 152, 203, 204, 212, 213, 248

eagle, 257
earrings, forbidden, 198, 244
eating, act of, indifferent, 100; is animal act to be temperate, 102, 103; only a necessity, 179; purpose of, 94
Echle, H. A., 25 n., 30 n., 32 n., 42 n.
education, defined, 12, 17; different senses of, 50, 51; by Christ: demands duties, 91; disposition imparted by, 88, 265, 274; does not mix with ornaments, 196; goal of, 106; in harmony with men's deeds, 88; is eternal possession, 50; is imparting of truth and holy deeds, 51; makes a man sin rarely, 6; not for war, but peace, 87, 88; severity of, 68-78
Educator, *see* Christ
eels, as food, 95
effeminacy, 211, 212, 214, 218, 219, 252, 255
Egypt, 131, 188, 202, 252
electrum, 202
Elias, 186, 230, 231
Elpenor, 123
emeralds, 190, 224
encouragement, by Educator, 80

engastrimythos, 107
Encratites, 122
Epicharmis, 110
Epictetus, 194 n.
Epicurus, 83 n., 124 n.
encomium, defined, 79
enlightenment, of baptism, 25 n., 26, 27, 30, 161
Epistle of Barnabas, xv, 7 n., 165 n., 168 n., 256 n., 257 n., 266-268 nn.
Eratosthenes, 118 n.
Eriphyle, 184
Ethiopia, 202, 207
Etruscans, 131
Eucharist, Holy, 37, 102 n., 111, 132
eunuchs, 221
Euripides, 115 n., 153 n., 209 n., 210 n., 233 n.
Eusebius, vi n.
Eve, 195, 214, 215
evil, love of money, root of, 129; takes root if overlooked, 63
examples, given for our instruction, 4, 10, 53, 80, 177, 211, 233, 234
excoriation, defined, 71
exercise, benefits of, 239, 240, 249
expense, not goal in useful things, 126, 127; of wardrobe condemned, 178, 188
exposure, of infants, 217
external things, material, 178; reason draws man from, 93

extravagance, in amusements, 258; in clothing, 181; generosity is the true, 192; of gluttony, 179; of vain women, 203
extremes, dangerous, 108
eyes, custody of, 252, 253, 257, 258, 262

faith, beginning of perfection, 28, 29; in Christ is goodness, 63; Christ's words on, 269; comes by Holy Spirit and baptism, 30; contrasted to hope, 37; Educator frees will for act of, 265; garment of Christ, 185; and Gnostics, x; looses bonds of ignorance, 29, 30; incorruptible possession, 126; increased by Spirit, 111; love of money harms, 129; obedience to Word, 89; possession of wise of God, 258; salvation for all men, 30; substance of duty, 89; symbolized by crown of thorns, 156-158; symbolized by food, 37
fasting, 267
Faye, E. de, 31 n.
fatherland, of Christian, 233
fear, bitter herb conferring health, 74; childishness, 32, 33; defined, by Stoics, 89; Educator's instruction in, 50; good effect of, 61; restrains old from sin, 85; turned into love through Christ, 53, 54; two kinds, reverence and hate, 77; whets appetite for salvation, 70
fidelity, 185, 198
figs, 95
finery, of dress, condemned, 180-184
fire, of prudence, 235; reward of wantonness, 169
fish, figure of frugality in eating, 105; figure for man, 274; image of, permitted on rings, 246
fishing, permitted, 241
flax, 188
flesh, a slave, 200, 201; of Christ: figure of Holy Spirit, 41; food of little ones, 40; symbol of faith, 37
flowers, beauty of, 179; beneficial, 158, 159; effects of, on men, 154; may be enjoyed, but not worn, 153, 154; uses of, 155, 156
flute, banned, 130
food, changes into blood, 41, 42; excess of, hinders growth, 109; given by God, 108, 180, 264; heavenly, 39, 40; idol-offered, forbidden, 99, 100, 109; is indifferent, 108; kinds of, in relation to salvation, 100, 108, 109; pleasures of, 98; qualities of, permitted, 94, 95; simple, more beneficial, 97, 107; solicitude about, condemned, 180;

solid, 34-37, 41; stimulating, to be avoided, 180
footwear, permitted, 189, 190
fornication, condemned by Plato, 170, 175; harms self, 176, 177, 217, 223
fortitude, 249
fowl, as food, 95
francolins, as food, 95
freedom, in Christ, 246; love of, taught by Christ, 88
friendship, good, lessens danger of obscenity, 138
frivolities, 146, 147, 258
frugality, benefits of, 233; of Christ, 105, 127; in eating, 101, 105-107; of feast given by David, 110; Jews commanded to practice, 108; moderate, to be practiced, 87, 160, 161; of pagan Scythians, 219; reason sings praises of, 228; of St. John the Baptist, 186; Scriptural examples of, 239, 240; self-indulgent criticize, 127; Stoic virtue of, adopted by Clement, xvi
fruits, in frugal diet, 107

Galen, 30 n.
garishness, 211
garrulousness, 136, 144, 145
gems, of Egyptian temples, 202; of heavenly Jerusalem, 191; kinds of, 193; purpose of, 193; symbolize Christ, 148

generosity, manner of, 227; never empties itself, 232; quality of soul, 229; true ornament, 198
Germans, 219
giggle, condemned, 135
glass-workers, 125
gloominess, caution against, 135
gluttony, Christ forbids, 179; contrary to reason, 101; description of, 95, 96, 103, 104; devil of, 107; effect of wantonness, 171; evils of, 98, 99; insatiable, 106; profanes Agape, 96; twofold offense in wealthy, 104, 106; uncleanness of, 230
gnosis, 82 n.
Gnostics, ix, 24, 31, 37, 48
God, above all needs, 199; anger of, 58, 59; artificial beauty insults, 204; as Beauty, 200; and Christ, 21, 50, 88, 246; as Creator, 9, 27, 57, 65, 78; as eternal Old Man, 213; as Father, 18, 39; feared, 77; goodness of, 56, 58, 63-66, 78, 229; hostility of, to evil, 63; justice of, 57, 58, 62-66, 77, 78; love of, 18, 27, 39, 56-58, 61, 62, 68, 74, 78, 192, 232; in man, 200; mercy of, 64, 65, 73, 77, 78, 147 n.; oneness of, 40, 63, 64; only Good, 78; possession of, true wealth, 232; presence of, 227, 235, 274; providence of, 8, 57, 58, 106,

131, 232, 235, 264; and punishment, 61, 62; rules reason, 199; seen only through baptism, 28; sinless, 6, 50; and sinners, 27, 62, 74; as Teacher, 18; will of, 27; wisdom of, 83; and Word, 58, 192
godliness, 272
gold, corrupting effects of, 124, 125, 129, 194, 196, 202, 214, 244; of Magi, symbolizes kingship of Christ, 149; symbolizes incorruptibility of Word, 147
gold-plate, 230
good, deeds, 198, 199; and evil, images of, 185; health, 249; men, 194, 229; things of the land, 264; will, 86, 261
goodness, arouses hatred for evil, 63; Christ consummate in, 18, 19; renders benefits, 57
gossip, 256, 258
gourmandizing, 95, 103, 179
grace, common to men and women, 12; concept of, xvi n.; given through Christ, 54, 55; unlooses bonds of ignorance, 30; waters world, 180
grapes, symbol of Word, 111
grass, symbolizes multitude, 180
gratitude, due Educator, 89
greed, 128
Greeks, x, xi, xv, 155, 226
grief, defined by Stoics, 89
griffins, 192, 221

grooms, 221
guffaw, condemned, 135
gymnasium, 239, 241

habits, under influence of persuasion, 3
hair, artificial, forbidden, 248; biological effects of, 247, 248; foppishness of, 213; gray, 212-214, 248, 249; not to be dyed, 152, 203, 204, 212, 213, 248; plucking, condemned, 212; proper treatment of, 246-249; proves manhood, 214, 215
hair-do, elaborate, condemned, 208, 248; of effeminate men, 211, 219
hairlessness, immoral, 215, 216
hair-nets, 208
handmaids, modesty of, 254, 255
happiness, not found in luxuries, 160; in practice of virtues, 107, 198; true meaning of, 83
hare, symbol of licentiousness, 165, 168
harlotry, 252
headache, relieved by drug, 154
heat, of body, restored by wine, 113, 114
healing, art of human wisdom, 7; of passions, by Christ, 7
health, gift of Christ, 85, 264; spiritual, 16 n.; wine confers, 16

heathen, without discipline, 179
heaven, place of reward, 156, 180
heavenly food, in contemplation, 101
hedonists, fail to enter heaven, 172
Helen of Troy, 196, 209, 210
hell, 180
helots, 233
hems, 214
Hephaestus, 123
Hera, 155
Heraclitus, 22, 119 n., 176, 200
heresy, avoided by accepting Christ, 19
Herodotus, xv, 177 n., 192 n., 194 n., 226 n.
Hesiod, 219 n., 225, 226, 234 n.
hierophant, 202
hissing, condemned, 145
holiness, is light, 28; only true wealth, 229; promoted by plainness, 197
Homer, x, xv, 38 n., 41 n., 46 n., 47 n., 99 n., 100 n., 123 n., 125 n., 135 n., 136 n., 144 n., 155 n., 160 n., 163 n., 174 n., 181, 184 n., 185, 188 n., 194 n., 195 n., 200 n., 210, 218 n., 247 n., 274 n.
homosexuality, 166, 167, 169, 217; condemned by Roman law, 218
honesty, in trade, 259
honey, 47, 85, 107, 186

hoof, split, symbol, 257
hope, is soul of Church, 37
horse, 207, 214, 219, 220
hosanna, meaning of, 13
household, chores for wife, 239, 268; must reflect Christian life, 128, 233; not a burden, 231
hucksters, 259
human nature, insight into, 93; must be contemplated by man, 89; serviceable in perception of God, 94
humility, taught by Christ, 88
husband, crowned by marriage, 154; duties of, 271; how to live with wife, 233; restraint of, toward wife, 263
hyena, symbol of licentiousness, 165-167
hylikoi, 31 n.
Hymn to Educator, 276-278
hypocrite, 148

idleness, 256
idols, images of, condemned on rings, 246
Ignatius, St., 102 n.
ignorance, is darkness, 29; symbolized by night, 162
ill-will, shown in speech, 143
immorality, contemporary, 217, 218; forbidden, 138; frequency of, at banquets, 130; with eyes, 253, 254, 262; not to be confused with prudery, 139;

present in consent to pleasure, 177; of Sodomites, punished, 235; of tempter, how to avert, 136; of women, 225, 226, 253, 254
immortality, Christ guides to, 46; cloak of, saving the body, 75; nourished by Bread of Heaven, 44; true beauty of body, 201
impartiality, 255
impiety, of some church-goers, 260
impurity, names animal of man, 175
incorruptibility, eternal shares, 21; Eucharist is participation in, 111; garment for body, 184, 201; makes man like angels, 177
indecency, of jests, 135; of look, 145, 146; of talk, 137-139, 175
India, 202, 207
indignation, righteous, defined, 72, 73
indifference, in use of drinking cups, 123; to wealth, 129
industry, 198
inexpensiveness, criterion of, what we should use, 128
insanity, 189
insects, harmed by oil, 150
insolence, accompanies drunkenness, 140; discordant with reason, 143
instruction, contrasted to contemplation, 36; engenders faith, 30; symbolized by milk, 35
intaglio, 246
intemperance, 116, 117, 123, 124, 171
intelligence, first part of soul, 199
intercourse, 164-178; evil effects of, 176-178; lawful, 169-171; a minor epilepsy, 172; restrictions of, 170, 174; to engage in, without intending children, outrage to nature, 173; unlawful, 167-169, 171, 172
iota, in name of Jesus, 76, 132
Isaac, figure of little one, 22; type of Christ, 23
Israel, meaning of name, 69, 157
Italy, 186
ivy, 154

Jacob, 52, 160, 240
jasper, 190
Jerusalem, heavenly, 42, 191
Jesus, son of Naim, as figure of Christ, 55
jewelry, 180
Jews, commanded to be frugal, 108; and Christ, 156, 157; idolatry of, 196; king of, immoral, 220, 221
John, St., 261, 273
John the Baptist, St., 24, 72, 108, 186, 190, 268
jokes, discouraged, 134

Joseph, 252
Judas, 147
judge, advice for, 268
Jülicher, G., xiii
justice, adornment of Holy Spirit, 249; came down among men in flesh and Scriptures, 78 n.; Christ is scale of, 64, 78; defined, 58; expression of, in pagan dramatists, 263; of God, originates in love, 78; is mother of simple, 198; parts of, balanced by correction and praise, 79; split hoof, symbol of, 257

katéchesis, 30 n.
kids, as food, 95
kindness, not appreciated unless it recalls justice, 77; recommended to a master, 255
kiss, at Agape, 261
kite, 257
knowledge, and Christ, 5, 88; end of life, 106; enlightenment, tending to enjoyment, 29; and God, 25, 82, 199; symbolized by milk, 35

Laban, 240
Lacedemonians, 181
Laconia, maidens, of, 187; sea of, 188
lamb, Christ called, 24; Christians are, 16; figurative name for children, 15

lamentation, defined, 72
lampreys, as food, 95
lands, not true wealth, 229
last day, meaning of, 28, 29
laughter, must be moderate, 134-136, 142, 143
law, natural, 270
Law, New, better than Old, 270
Law, Old, accompanied by fear, 30; childishness, 32; on clothing, 242; disposed Jews to accept the Educator, 85; a gift through Moses, 54; incarnation of God's justice, 78 n.; as means of education, 270; prohibitions of, 108, 109; revealed treasures of God, 265
Lazarus, beggar, 180
lectures, 113
Leonides, 50
leprosy, 242
lewdness, disoriented, 171
liars, 269
life, already possessed in faith, 29; dependent on commandments, 84; is in obeying Educator, 89; material, commands for, 91; physical, depends on health and strength only, 94; spiritual, makes us divine, 87
light, and baptism, 27, 28; in mind, cannot be ignored, 176; name for, same as old name for man, 28; possession of, gives wakefulness, 161, 162; and repentance, 31

lily, 155, 158, 159
linen, 186, 188
lion, 192, 214
liquids, effects of excessive drinking of, 113
litters, 222
little ones, Christ revealed to, 32, 35; Church, mother of, 274; faith of, 270; given milk to drink, 34-49; meaning of name, 19, 20; nourished by Eucharist, 40; qualities of, 20; ready for salvation, 31; are sheep, figuratively, 50; we are, sharing Christ's forgiveness, 8, 54
locusts, 186
logia, 273 n.
logos, xvi, 6 n., 89 n., 107 n., 111 n.
Lot, 163, 209
love, desires to do good, 57; of God, 132, 266; of the good, 249; grows, in marriage act, 174; messages, on soles of shoes, 189; of neighbor, 132, 192, 261, 266; not fear, in New Testament, 53, 54; not judged by kiss, 261; self-controlled, to be given by wives, 245; songs, at banquets, condemned, 133
lukewarmness, 13
lust, aroused by improper digestion, 250; corrupt deeds, 138; defined, by Stoics, 89; enkindled at a gathering, 257, 258; of eyes, 252, 253; sinful to be inflamed by, 178
luxuries, 180, 181, 193, 245
Lydian, river, 202 n.; scrapings, as cosmetic, 244
lyre, 132, 246, 260

Magi, gifts of, 149
male, characteristics of, 215
man, animal made for true Beauty, 230; animal that can laugh, 135; becomes like God by knowing Him, 199; Christ is only one Scripture calls, 18, 33; created with loveableness, 9; defiled by sin, 216; desirable in himself, 9, 10; distorted by artificial beauty, 250; duties of, contemplation and action, 89; equal before God, 31; erroneously considered bad, 83; is in God, 200; inner, 162, 199; instrument for peace, 131; made free by Educator, 246; name means consummate, 18; needs a guide in darkness, 11; noblest creature, 37; once called by same name as light, 28 n.; outer, 202; and reason, 199; reformed by Word, 274; rejuvenated in Christ, 16; resembles God, 9, 86, 87, 156, 164, 170, 200; should be united to Spirit and Word, 111; should fulfill

commandments, 10; should imitate Educator, 10, 11
mankind, love of, 88
manna, 39
Marcionites, 56 n.
marriage, Clement's treatise on, xii, 139 n.; to be esteemed, 173; turned into fornication by excess, 176; what is permissible in, 164, 169; whether permitted, 172
masters, 255, 271
mastich, 211 n., 253
mastophage, 257
materialists, unlightened, 31 n.
mattock, 240
maturity, in Christ, 33, 35
mean, observed in: beautification, 244, 245; dress, 185, 242; eating, 108; exercise, 241; Paradise, 154; relaxation, 134-136; sleeping, 162; use of luxuries, 159, 160; use of perfumes, 151
meat, carvers, 221; in frugal diet, 107; spiritual, contrasted to milk, 34-47
medicine, Alexandria's interest in, 30 n.; use of myrrh in, 150, 151; of flowers in, 152-155, 158
men, effeminacy of dress of, 182; may go without shoes, 189, 190; modesty to be observed in baths, 226, 227; reasons for use of baths, 237; should not idle time, 256; way to wear rings, 246
Menander, 12, 113 n., 138 n., 204, 269 n., 270 n.
menstruation, 170
merchants, 259
Midas, 207, 228
milk, allegorical use of, 47, 48; biological relationship to blood, 38, 39, 46; in frugal diet, 107; is knowledge, 35; nourishes man, 45, 46; produced less copiously in summer, 48; qualities of, 39; symbol of childhood of Christ, 34-39
Miletus, 186
mines, 192
mirror, 78, 208
modesty, adornment given by Holy Spirit, 249; of dress, 244, 250; in gymnasium, 241; in marriage, 174; true ornament, 198; with oneself, 169, 177; of women, at feasts, 122, 123, 141; of women, in church, 259, 260
Mondésert, C., vii n., ix, x n., xi, 78 n.
Molland, E., xiii, 119 n., 218 n.
monkeys, 224
Moses, 6, 51-55, 85, 158, 165, 168, 170, 208, 242, 270; and Plato, 169, 243
mullets, 95
Musonius, xvii, 127 n.

mussels, as food, 95
mustard seed, allegory of, 85
music, chaste, may be used, 133; inflames passions, at banquets, 130
musical instruments, 130-132, 246, 260
muslin, 225
myrrh, emasculates, 150, 151; of the Lord, 247; medicinal effects of, 151, 152, 158, 159; symbol of Holy Spirit, 147, 150
myrtle, 155
mysteries, of Bacchus, 156; pagan, vi; initiation into Christian, 10, 119; rites of, 183

name, new, given Christians, 16
Narcissus, 208
narcissus, 154, 155, 159
Nausithoon, 50
necklaces, 190, 194
necessities, always available, 106; avoidance of, a mean, 108; division of, 91; God's will, in giving, 191, 192; of the just, 232; of man, measure of possessions, 231; proper use of, 193; satisfaction with, 94
népios, 19 n., 20
net, for birds, 274
nightingale, 165, 224
Nikostratos, 195
nobility, true, in poverty of heart, 129

Noe, 124
nomads, 219, 220
nouthetein, etymology of, 83

oaths, 268, 269
obedience, founded on commands, 90; to Word, 89
obligations, distinguished, 91
obscenity, 137-139
octopus, 260
Odysseus, 144, 160, 233
oil, effects of, on man and insects, 150; of gladness, 87; kinds of, 149; proper use of, 151; symbolizes Judas and Peter, 148; symbolizes mercy, 147 n.
olives, in diet, 107
oracles, immorality of, 222, 223; Sibylline, 175 n., 212
organ, 131
Origen, vii, x
ornaments, disapproved, 193, 195, 230, 250; worn by Jewish kings, 146
orphans, 224
ostentatiousness, 124-126, 160, 161, 179, 180, 183, 184, 187, 188, 194-196, 225
Overbeck, J., v
overindulgence, in eating, 109, 162, 163
oyster, biology of, 191; as food, 95
ox, 274

Paean, healer, 30 n.
pagans, vi, x, 156, 234
paidagogia, 12 n., 17 n.
paidagogos, xiv, 12 n.
paideia, 17 n.
Palestine, 188
Pantaeus, St., vii
parables, 273
parents, duties of, 271
Paris, lover of Helen, 209, 210
parrots, 224
passions, affected by wine, 112; aroused by music, 130, 131; defile reason, 177; defined, by Stoics, 89; healed by consolation, 3; healed by teaching, 58; removed by new life, 40, 41, 67; surrender to, is sinful, 178; symbolized by Proteus, 200; unquenchable, 262; water allays, 112
pastophore, 202
pastries, 221
patience, 255, 268
Patrick, J., v, xi n., xiii, xvi n., 9 n., 16 n., 139 n.
Paul, St., 32, 33, 36, 48, 66, 74, 110, 133, 148, 167, 175, 177, 178, 200, 201, 244, 260, 261, 275
peace, of Christian banquets, 121; has no need of abundance, 88; of those upon whom God looks, 63; we cultivate, 246
peacocks, 95, 224

pearls, 191, 192, 224
pedagogues, 50, 51
pederasty, 165-169, 217, 218
Penelope, 135 n., 174, 233
people, Christians are new, 21, 40; old, hard of heart, 20; old, needed Law, 85
perfection, in baptism, 26-29; is childhood in Christ, 34; man's, in virtues, 193, 194; odor of, 150; is repentance and rebirth, 48, 49; under symbol of milk, 35-46
perfume, symbolizes good deeds, 148; use and misuse of, 146-152
Persia, 50
persuasion, and Christ, 4, 11, 79, 80; cornerstone of knowledge, 3; we are amenable to, as children, 20
perspiration, 250
Peter, St., 105, 108, 196, 197, 241, 255, 263
phaenind, ball game, 240
Phenix, 50
Philemon, 183 n., 194, 254
Philip of Macedon, 50
Philo the Jew, viii, x, xv, 22 n., 158 n.
philosophers, on blame and praise, 82, 83; self-control of, 97
philosophy, defined, 90; Greek, vii n.
photizo, 25 n.

physician, diagnosis of, 78; only sick need, 74; to be honored, 152
Pindar, xv, 83 n., 155 n., 254, 269 n.
pipe, musical instrument, 130
pitch, for removing hair, 212, 215-217
Pittacus, 240
plainness, 197
Plato, vii n., x, xv, 12 n., 60, 62 n., 67 n., 73, 74 n., 93 n., 109, 114 n., 121 n., 124 n., 126, 133-135 nn., 143 n., 150 n., 160-170, 173 n., 177, 199 n., 228 n., 230 n., 243, 255 n.
play on words, 20, 43, 83, 89, 90, 98, 99, 107, 129, 133, 147, 148, 169, 218, 219
playing, mystical, 22, 23
pleasure, defined, by Stoics, 89; deteriorates mind, 210, 211; for its own sake, a sin, 170; must have some use, 151, 152; not our chief ambition, 94; not truth, 197; search for, waste of time, 180
Plotinus, 249 n.
Plutarch, 154 n., 253 n.
Plutus, 207
pneuma, 111 n.
poets, pagan, x, 96 n., 97 n., 106 n., 118, 153 n., 190 n., 193 n., 203 n., 211 n., 252 n.
Polycrates, 246
porridge, 221

possessions, detachment from, 18; not to be boasted about, 129; should be in common, 192
Potter, J., xvii
poverty, of heart, is true wealth, 129; of miserly, 224; reproach to wealthy, 193; taught by Christ, 88
praise, form of advice used by Educator, 79; remedy for man, 83
prayer, during night, 161; to God, 261; to Lord, 220; manner of, for women, 259, 260; not in much talk, 145; for putting on sandals, 190; Scripture on, 267, 272; to Word, 275
preaching, 37, 147
pregnancy, effects on woman, 38, 39, 170
priests, 273
privies, 128, 129, 230
procreation, co-operates with God in creation, 171
Prodicus, 185 n.
promiscuity, encouraged by banquets, 130
prophets, call us children, 14; Word educated through, 85, 265
proportion, sense of, as guide, 237
Proteus, 199, 200
proud, the, 269

prudence, adornment of Holy Spirit, 249; given by God, 8; is knowledge, 81; of the old, 214
prudery, 139
psalms, defined by St. Paul, 133; at Eucharistic feasts, 132
punishment, aims at salvation of sinner, 60; corrects, 63; educative, 236; heals passions, 58, 59; of others, an example, 234, 235; our own doing, 62; reconciled with God's goodness, 58
purification, in baptism, 32; of body and soul, 93, 94, 238
purity, 174, 177, 243
purple, vanity of, 188
Pythagoras, 31 n., 83, 102

quarreling, discordant, 140, 144

Rachel, 240
raillery, occasion of quarreling, 140
Rand, E. K., x n.
razor, 247
reading aloud, as exercise, 240
reason, avoids base pleasure. 185; is deed of Christian soul, 90, 91; directs diet, 107; draws man from material, 93; dulled by wearing of wreaths, 155; is god dwelling within, 177; gluttony is sacrifice of, 99, 123; makes man steady, 200;
meaning of, xvi, 89-91; neglected by drunkards, 117, 123; only true good, 229; passions and virtue, in relation to, 89, 90; should control drinking, 116; we must walk according to, 231
Rebecca, 22, 23
rebirth, effect of, 5; given to us as children, by Educator, 21, 22, 32; makes members of Christ, 46; spiritual food given after, 39; through water, 86, 87; through Word, 191, 263; way of life demanded by, 163
rebuke, dissolves hardness of heart, 58, 59; signifies interest in person, 67, 68
recitals, 258
redemption, Christ gave life for our, 76
relaxation, in moderation, 134-136
remedies, of Christ, 74
remorse, wearing wreaths arouses, 154
repentance, God's call to, 82; is of lower things in relation to higher, 31; like recovery from illness, 73; opportunity of, proof of God's love, 68; is perfection, 48, 49; step to salvation, 6; symbolized by tears of sinful woman, 147
reprimand, defined, 70

reproach, art of rebuke in good will, 59
reprobation, defined, 72
reproof, like surgery on passions, 58; reconciled to divine love, 66
reserve, with wives, recommended, 263
resurrection, Church awaits, 131; faith anticipates, 29, 82
rest, eternal, 90
retribution, defined, 71
revenge, 63, 268
ridicule, dangerous, 143
rings, 244, 246
robe, symbolism of Christ's, 187; flowing, condemned, 185, 187
rod, symbolic of power of Educator, 55, 56
roosters, 214
roots, as food, 107
roses, 154, 155, 159
Ruben, 53 n.
ruler, proper dress of, 242

sackcloth, 186
sacrifice, to God, 267, 268
sailor, proper dress of, 242
salvation, articles of, 265; cause of joy, 22; Christ's concern with our, 87, 88, 242; is Church, 27; common to men and women, 12, 28; first principle for gaining, 128; following of Christ, 27; life to be made conformable to, 87;

most noble of God's actions, 88; of sinner, God's object in punishing, 58-67; spiritual health, 16 n.; under figure of mustard seed, 85
salves, 152
Samaritan woman, 127
Samson, 252
Samuel, 208, 221
sandals, 189, 231
Sappho, 155
Sara, 239
Sardanapalus, 253
satiety, arouses passions, 178; implies more than necessity, 179; luxuriousness grounds on shoals of, 242
scallops, as food, 95
scarab, 150
Scholia, on *Paidagogos*, 14 n., 53 n., 83 n., 107 n., 112 n., 115 n., 116 n., 124 n., 131 n., 153 n., 187 n., 203 n., 265 n.
scissors, 247
Scripture, Holy, cautions against vanity, 206; Clement and, vii n., xi; describes Christian life, 93, 94, 265, 266; exists for obedience, 7; praises temperance, 124; repudiates drunkenness, 124; teaches way to eternal life, 91; value of, 187

Quotations from or references to:
Acts, 99, 108, 109, 142, 157

Aggeus, 128
Amos, 15, 62, 120
Apocalypse, 35, 42, 183, 191
Baruch, 81, 82, 126
Colossians, 5, 86, 132, 133, 253, 262, 272, 275
1 Corinthians, 17, 31, 32, 34-36, 56, 88, 96, 97, 100-102, 104, 105, 123, 125, 156, 157, 177, 184, 192, 198, 201, 235, 248, 260, 261, 264
2 Corinthians, 5, 18, 36, 65, 148, 208, 209, 215, 262, 270
Daniel, 81, 183, 213
Deuteronomy, 18, 42, 48, 51, 54, 55, 61, 62, 73, 81, 82, 109, 138, 165, 208, 216, 232, 268
Ecclesiasticus, 56, 60-62, 64, 65, 67, 73, 77, 86, 90, 99, 111, 114-116, 121, 122, 124, 133, 135, 139-142, 144-147, 152, 159, 172, 176, 178, 184, 213, 219, 222, 223, 246, 253, 262
Ephesians, 19, 26, 28, 37, 118, 133, 137, 140, 151, 175, 213, 223, 262, 271
Esther, 209
Exodus, 34, 42, 51, 53, 64, 68, 80, 85, 111, 138, 143, 158, 168, 196, 208, 210, 222, 259, 266
Ezechiel, 7, 53, 60, 68, 75, 81, 84, 157, 173, 264, 270
Galatians, 26, 30, 31, 33, 74, 85, 272
Genesis, 9, 11, 16, 22, 23, 44, 51-53, 69, 87, 108, 111, 121, 124, 125, 138, 154, 157, 160, 163, 164, 169, 173, 186, 205, 209, 211, 235, 238, 240, 241, 252
Habacuc, 98
Hebrews, 26, 44
Isaias, 7, 14, 16, 17, 20, 21, 24, 48, 54, 55, 61, 68-71, 73, 75, 81, 84, 88, 99, 111, 148, 158, 176, 186, 201, 238, 254, 264-269
James, 26
Jeremias, 7, 16, 36, 54, 68-72, 82, 88, 167, 186, 207, 269
Job, 106
John, 8, 10, 13, 14, 24, 27-29, 35-37, 40, 43, 44, 49, 54, 55, 57, 60, 63, 64, 76, 86, 105, 111, 112, 118, 127, 144, 146, 160, 176, 200, 227, 232, 241, 258
1 John, 199, 261, 273
3 John, 144
Jude, 236
Judges, 252
1 Kings, 186, 208, 222
2 Kings, 15, 110, 146, 147
3 Kings, 231
Lamentations, 70, 72
Leviticus, 15, 109, 169, 170, 218, 243, 256, 257
Luke, 8, 12, 15, 24, 31, 40, 63, 65, 74, 78, 96, 97, 100, 107, 128, 134, 146, 160, 179, 180, 184, 196, 228, 231, 235, 265, 266, 268, 269
Mark, 66, 97, 121

Matthew, 8, 11, 13-15, 17, 18, 21, 25, 29, 41, 43, 54, 63-66, 68, 71, 72, 75, 76, 80, 81, 85-88, 97, 98, 100, 105-108, 121, 122, 125, 127-129, 132, 137, 138, 140, 147, 149, 157, 164, 177, 183, 186, 191, 192, 213, 215, 224, 226, 227, 229, 231, 232, 238, 241, 252, 253, 259-262, 266, 268-270

Nahum, 72

Numbers, 6, 7, 80, 111, 177

Osee, 49, 69, 197

1 Peter, 41, 111, 156, 185, 242, 250, 255, 263, 264, 268

Philippians, 48, 94, 110, 129, 157, 200, 201, 275

Proverbs, 69, 71, 73, 76, 79, 81, 84, 95, 106, 108, 117-119, 139, 140, 143, 154, 160, 171, 198, 206, 224, 228-230, 232, 238, 244, 251-254, 262, 264, 267-269

Psalms, 3, 7, 14, 18, 26, 47, 54-56, 65, 72, 75-77, 80, 82, 90, 131-133, 146, 147, 150, 185, 187, 200, 218, 229, 247, 264, 265, 268

Romans, 20, 24, 26, 27, 35, 62, 63, 66, 74, 98, 101-103, 130, 138, 146, 167, 200, 216, 244, 258, 259, 261, 264, 265

1 Thessalonians, 19, 27, 36, 76, 146, 162, 272

1 Timothy, 110, 129, 197, 250, 272

Titus, 26

Wisdom, 57, 81, 98, 176

Zacharias, 16, 269

———

Scythians, 219, 220

seals, on signet rings, 246

seed, as figure for intercourse, 164, 165, 170

Seleucus, 246

self-control, blessing before meals, act of, 133; forestalls passions, 100; frugality, offspring of, 228; garment for body, 199, 202; of a household, 231, 245; makes us like God, 106; produces beauty, 249; qualities of, 243; in sexual pleasure, 169, 170, 174, 177; swept away at banquets, 103

self-indulgence, basis for prohibition, in Old Law, 109; in baths, 225; in desire for wealth, 128; in dress, 182; in drinking wine, 115, 117, 120; in eating, 94, 179; evils of, 230; in furnishings, 227; idleness, cause of, 256; opposed to Christian way of life, 105, 106; in ornamentation, 194, 224, 225; practicers of, criticize frugality, 127; reason, remedy of, 178; in sleeping, 159, 160; Trojan War, result of, 210; in use of oils, 151; in use of per-

fumes, 149, 150; in utensils, 125
self-service, as virtue, 233, 240, 241
self-sufficiency, and Clement, xvi; Educator trains in, 87; nurse of Christians, 198; regulates eating, 98; restricts desires, 108; universe made for, 128
semen, is foam of blood, 45; must find proper resting place, 164, 165
Seneca, xvi, xvii, 3 n., 94 n., 106 n., 108 n.
sense pleasure, 150, 151, 230
sensuality, 153, 177, 223, 244, 246
seriousness, keeps sinful away, 136; proper limits of, 135
serpent, 195, 203
servants, 269
service, of God, 90; willing, 77
severity, of Educator, 76
sexual excesses, against nature, 169; condemned even within marriage, 173; condemned under figures of hare and hyena, 165, 166; destroy love, 174, 175; effects of, 171; reason best remedy for, 178; under figure of stolen waters, 254
shaving, censured, 213, 247
sheep, 186, 219
shepherds, rulers of Church are, 36

Sicels, 131
Sichemites, 211
Sicinnos, 50
Sidon, 188
sign, indicates presence of cause, 243
silence, a virtue, 143, 144
silks, 182
silk-worm, 182
silver, 124-126, 202
simplicity, avoids superfluities, 243; of barbarians, praised, 220; of children, to be imitated, 13; in food, praised, 94-97; of husband and wife, 245
Simonides of Amorgos, 149
sin, of Adam, made him like beasts, 90; aided by inconspicuousness, 247; carried by Christ, 157; contrary to reason, 6, 89, 90; effects of, 27, 82; encouragement alleviates, 80, 81; forgiven by baptism, 30; is ignorance, 29; kinds and degrees of, 6
sincerity, 193
singing, at Eucharistic feasts, 132
sinless, need not fear God, 74
sinners, die to God, 177, 260; Educator desires conversion of, 264, 270; like beasts, 90; lose right to respect, 176, 177
skolion, drinking song, 133
slaves, in baths, 226, 238; boy, 216, 217; compared with mas-

ters, 227; conduct before, 263; duties of, 271, 272; lavishness, in buying, 224; not beasts of burden, 255; number of, permitted, 221, 231; true, of the soul, 246
sleeping, bad effects of, 162; for body not soul, 163; proper manner of, 159-163; is time for digestion, 160; we should not waste time of, 161
slippers, 189, 190
smile, expression of joy, 135
snake, Egyptian god, 202; figure of wealth, 228
sneeze, at table, 145
snapping fingers, boorishness, 145
sociability, in drinking, 132
Sodom, 168, 169, 235
sodomy, 167
soldiers, 194, 242, 268
Solomon, 179
songs, types forbidden, 133
Sophocles, 115 n., 155 n., 173 n., 196 n.; rebukes effeminacy, 242
sorcerers, 222, 223
soteria, 16 n.
soul, accomplishes Christian duty, with body, 90, 91; clothed by body, 184; disfigured by sin, 203; eye of, to be purified, 93; image of Word, 249; must be washed in Word, 238; needs Educator, 5; only treasure of man, 22; operates in sleep, 163, 164; should govern body, 178; three parts of, 199; virtue, the ornament of, 202
Spartans, 233
speech, indicates disposition of the man, 137; must be controlled, 143, 144; Scripture on, 272
spider, 261
spinning, 222
Spirit, Holy, adornment of soul, 249; aids us to see God through baptism, 28; calls us children, 13; declares drunkards wretched, 120; described greatness of Lord as Child, 23, 24; exults in His children, 22; and faith, 30, 111; lambs, 17; nourishment of hungerers for Word, 44; is One, 40; purifies music of liturgy, 131; rebukes gluttons, 99; sevenfold gift of, 265; strength of Word, 111; symbolized by anointing of Christ's feet, 147, 150; symbolized by flesh of Christ, 41; union of, with man, 111, 112
spiritual, the, believe in Holy Spirit, 35; are less perfect, according to Gnostics, 31
sprats, as food, 95
springs, 232
Stählin, O., xviii, 40 n.
stage, lewdness of, 187

staring, forbidden, 262
stater, allegory of, 105
steadfastness, 198, 233
Stobaeus, 127 n.
Stoicism, xi n., xv-xviii, 26 n., 87 n., 89 n., 90 n., 93 n., 156 n.
Stoics, x, xv, 82 n.; on control of impulse, 169; on passions, 89 n.; on virtue as fitting and dutiful, 90
story-tellers, 222
strength, physical, 94, 264
substances, kinds and qualities of, 249
suffering, trains in steadfastness, 233
Sulpicius Severus, viii
superfluities, artificial beauty presents appearance of, 201; come from Devil, 179; dignity of dress comes from eliminating, 245
suspicion, avoiding, 262
sweetmeats, 107
Swete, H. B., v, vi
swine, 244, 256
sword, image of, condemned for rings, 246
symbolism, 15, 16, 18, 24, 34-41, 46-48, 50, 55, 56, 58, 73, 74, 76, 85, 105, 111, 119, 121, 131, 132, 147-150, 156-158, 162, 164-167, 170, 180, 184, 187, 191, 195, 200, 201, 220, 228, 242, 243, 254, 257, 274

Syracuse, 109

taverns, 256
teachings, divine, perfection and salvation, 27; under symbol of blood and milk, of Christ, 46; under symbol of anointing of Christ's feet, 146, 147
teasing, permissible only for old, 143
Telemachus, 233
temperance, admirable, 112, 124, 193, 198, 249; description of a man of, 141, 142; given by God, 8; in sleeping, 159, 160; we practice, 246
temperament, 134
temples, pagan, 222, 223
thanksgiving, after meals, 133, 159, 174; true food, 102
theater, 207; condemned, 257, 258
Themistocles, 50
Theocritus, 160 n.
Thersites, 144, 224
thirst, 113, 120
Thracians, 131
threats, Educator's, reasons for, 76, 77, 236
thrift, 127
thrushes, as food, 95
Thucydides, 226 n.
Titus, E. Lane, 14 n., 25 n., 57 n., 98 n.
Tollinton, R. B., vii n., x, xvii, 245 n.

tongue, is harp of Lord, 131
topaz, 190
trap, 274
treasures, offered by Lord, 265
Trojan War, 210
truth, adornment for ears, 198; artificial distorts, 242; end of our effforts, 180; excessive comforts, false imitation of, 179; mixture of Old and New Law, 119; nobility of, in character, 246; possession of, a blessing, 229; vanity offends, 245
turgots, as food, 95
turnips, as food, 95
Tyre, 188

ugliness, in soul, 193
unicorn, figure of strength of God, 18 n.
uprightness, of Christ, 76; given by God, 8
utensils, materials for, 125-127

vainglory, 269
vanity, degenerates into immorality, 200; of dress, 185-187, 194, 245; opposes God and reason and charity, 201; punishment for, 236; stronger passion than others, 206
vegetables, in frugal diet, 107
veil, proper for women, 188, 259, 260
vigils, 163

vine, prophetic of Christ's sufferings, 111
violets, 154
Virgin Mother, 40
virtue, cardinal, 193, 194; defined by Clement, xvi; defined by Stoics, 90; not developed by ornamentation, 194; only true good, 228; is true beauty, 193, 202
voice, proper modulation of, 144
vultures, 150

waiters, 221
walking, as exercise, 240
walnut tree, 154
wantonness, 108, 168, 171
water, drink for thirsty, 110, 112; effects of, on milk, 46; imported, foolishness of, 120; symbolism of, 111, 119
wealth, difficult to handle, 228; gift of Educator, 264; maledictions on man of, 236; must be shared, 128, 231, 232; not true nobility, 129, 194; true, only Christians possess, 229
weaving, 222
weeping, to be avoided, 143
Wendland, P., xvii
whistling, condemned, 145
white, color of peace, 242, 243
widows, 224, 273
wigs, 180

will, of God, food of Christ, 43; fulfillment of, exhorted, 87; ignorance of, 192

Wilson, W., xviii

wine, abstinence from, praiseworthy, 112, 121, 162; amount that may be taken with impunity, 114; of Cana, meaning of, 118, 119; cultivation of God, 120; effects of, 113-115, 136; expensive kinds, condemned, 119, 120; figure of Blood of Christ, 16, 121; how Christ drank, 121, 122; mixed with milk, symbolism of, 47, 48, 111; native, 120; pourers, 221; recommended by St. Paul, 110; time to be taken, 113-116, 119; used in mystical sense by Scripture, 119

winking, 252

wisdom, absence of, is sleep, 117; better than wealth, 228; bought not by wealth but by Word, 129; Christ's desire for us, 273; cultivated by Christians, 17; definition of, always present, 116; destroyed by wine, 113; of Educator, 75; faith and, 258; fear of Lord, 62; found only among few, 222; human, not crown of knowledge, 36; never sins deliberately, 6; not found among multitude, 222; qualities of, 21; source of, is God, 83; symbolized by robe of Christ, 187; true ornament, 198

wittiness, in moderation, approved, 134

wives, duties of, 271; on living with husbands, 233, 244, 245; not completely detached, 184; of others, to be respected, 169; plain dress, should be used by, 244; reflect husbands' qualities, 231; should make own clothes, 251

wolves, 220

womb, biology of, 170

women, in catechetical school at Alexandria, ix; characteristics of, 215; created as helpmate for man, 205; crown of, is husband, 154; educated, as well as men, by Christ, 12; love of: for gems, 190; for perfume, 149, 150; for ornamentation, 194, 202-206; manner of drinking wine, 122; modesty proper to, at banquets, 140; not to be stared at, 262; painted, are ridiculous, 125; proper dress of, 181-188, 193, 243; quickly drawn to immorality, 123, 188; reasons permitted baths, 237; rich, silliness of, 128, 129; smooth-skinned, so intended by God, 214; treatment of hair, 248; unmarried, free for God, 184; wearing gold, 246

wood, decayed, as cosmetic, 205
wool, forbidden, 186
Word, twofold sense of, 89 n.; see Christ, as Word
work, makes woman beautiful, 250, 251; at night, 163
worldliness, despises little ones, 18; lack of readiness for salvation, 31; of ordinary people, 128; revelation hidden from, 32
wreaths, condemned, 146, 147, 153; symbol of freedom from care, 156

wrestling, recommended, 239-241

Xenophon, 133 n., 185 n.

youth, description of good, 256; grow better when nourishment is less, 109; of mankind in Christ, 16; should avoid banquets, 141; should avoid wine, 112

Zeno, 256
Zeus, 22, 123, 210
Zoporus, 50

www.ingramcontent.com/pod-product-compliance
Lightning Source LLC
Chambersburg PA
CBHW032027290426
44110CB00012B/700